Jesus in an Age of Neoliberalism

BibleWorld

Series Editors: Philip R. Davies and James G. Crossley, University of Sheffield

BibleWorld shares the fruits of modern (and postmodern) biblical scholarship not only among practitioners and students, but also with anyone interested in what academic study of the Bible means in the twenty-first century. It explores our ever-increasing knowledge and understanding of the social world that produced the biblical texts, but also analyses aspects of the Bible's role in the history of our civilization and the many perspectives—not just religious and theological, but also cultural, political and aesthetic—which drive modern biblical scholarship.

Jesus in an Age of Neoliberalism

Quests, Scholarship and Ideology

James G. Crossley

equinox

Published by Equinox Publishing Ltd.
UK: Unit S3, Kelham House, 3, Lancaster Street, Sheffield S3 8AF
USA: ISD, 70 Enterprise Drive, Bristol, CT 06010

www.equinoxpub.com

First published 2012

ISBN 978-1-908049-70-4 (hardback)

British Library Cataloguing-in-Publication Data

A catalogue record for this book is available from the British Library.

Library of Congress Cataloging-in-Publication Data

Crossley, James G.
Jesus in an age of neoliberalism: quests, scholarship, and ideology / James G. Crossley.
p. cm.—(BibleWorld)
Includes bibliographical references (p.) and index.
ISBN 978-1-908049-70-4 (hb)
1. Jesus Christ—Biography—History and criticism. 2. Neoliberalism—
Religious aspects—Christianity—History. 3. Jesus Christ—Historicity. I. Title.
BT301.9.C76 2012
232.9'08—dc23

2011026250

Typeset by S.J.I. Services, New Delhi
Printed and bound by CPI Group (UK) Ltd, Croydon

For Serena and Dominique

Contents

Preface

This book is effectively a non-comprehensive cultural history of contemporary scholarship mostly relating in some way to the historical Jesus. In a previous book, *Jesus in an Age of Terror* (Equinox, 2008), which this present book complements, I argued for the importance of contemporary Anglo-American foreign policies and geopolitics concerning the Middle East to be seen as a significant driving force behind major cultural trends and the ways in which academic ideas have been framed, not least those which involve historical research into the Middle East in some form, such as New Testament and Christian origins scholarship. In this present book, I want to look at the related economic and cultural trends in which such geopolitics are embedded and which in some way influence almost everything we do, whether in academic roles or outside work in leisure time or, indeed, whatever and wherever.

Put simply, a major aim of this book is to show how some presentations of the historical Jesus, from learned academics to amateur bloggers, have been, over the past forty years, embedded in the context of neoliberalism. This inevitably means a dominant focus on North American-led scholarship because, as might be expected and as we will see throughout this book, this is where the power currently lies in scholarship and the past forty years has marked the shift away from the dominance of German scholarship. Hence, German scholarship, so influential up to the mid-twentieth century, will have to be put largely to one side as it would have to be properly analysed in light of its own historical and cultural peculiarities, much admired though it still is in some parts of the English-speaking scholarly world.

While this book remains a history of contemporary scholarship, it is emphatically not comprehensive. Instead, it is hoped that the book will establish the general case for the importance of the context of neoliberalism for understanding contemporary scholarship and for others to provide new case studies. This book is merely about certain examples of the impact of neoliberalism in understanding Jesus and contemporary scholarship.

Chapter 1 looks at the problematic nature of the periodization of the quests for the historical Jesus and suggests alternative ways of analysing this intellectual history, particularly in terms of ideology and cultural contexts. There is also some discussion of the nature of intentionality, definitions of liberalism and the significance of the construction of extremes.

Part I attempts to establish an increasingly focused neoliberal context for historical Jesus scholarship. Chapter 2 introduces and outlines the rise and importance of neoliberalism over the past forty years and its links with the cultural phenomenon usually called postmodernism. Chapter 3 develops previous work on the role of 'biblioblogging' in highlighting the connections between scholarship and broader cultural contexts, particularly in this instance with neoliberalism, with two notable instances in recent biblioblogging history: responses to the Haiti earthquake and the handling of the pseudonymous blogger N. T. Wrong. Chapter 4 looks at the general historic connections between historical Jesus scholarship and the cult of the individual, which makes historical Jesus studies particularly suited to a key tenant of neoliberal thought. In chapter 5 attention turns to why Jesus might be significant in all this. This chapter provides some general examples of the ways in which neoliberalism and postmodernity have had an impact on historical Jesus studies over the past forty years, including the influence of related historical trends such as multiculturalism and the cultural absorption of liberal thinking.

Part II provides two case studies of the impact of neoliberalism and postmodernism on Jesus studies. Chapter 6 further develops recent work done on the 'Jewishness' of Jesus, showing how this construct is partly dependent on an often patronizing multiculturalism of the Other without the Otherness which has influenced scholarship of a wide variety of political and religious stripes, from E. P Sanders and N. T. Wright to Joseph Ratzinger and Terry Eagleton. The longer-term impact of neoliberalism, its symptoms and reactions generated, are analysed in chapter 7, which focuses on the contemporary 'secular' versus 'religious' discussions of the historical Jesus that have become particularly heated since September 11, including the recent relatively prominent reemergence of a non-existent Jesus.

Part III explores the role of contradictions between personal beliefs and dominant ideological trends by looking at how personal politics seemingly at odds with major ideological trends can be absorbed and transformed to become (unintentionally) some of the most vigorous defences of dominant ideological positions. Chapter 8 takes the apparent contradictions in beliefs to extremes by looking at vocal opponents of American imperialism and of the state of Israel and Zionism and seeing how they still manage to reproduce ideologically convenient scholarship supporting the things they oppose. Chapter 9 interacts with one of the more peculiar recent developments in historical Jesus studies, namely the Pope's intervention in 2007 and how he has been received by the latest academic defenders of both the present Catholic and British political establishments, especially by those figures in or around Radical Orthodoxy. Part III shows how those apparently hostile to neoliberalism and liberalism can end up providing a potential shield for, as well as being a symptom of, neoliberalism and liberalism. The Conclusion briefly looks at the extent of neoliberal influence on contemporary scholarship, how long this may or may not last and what sort of challenges we are seeing to such a dominant ideological position.

Acknowledgements and Pre(r)amble

These acknowledgements are being written in the aftermath of an apparently monumental event: the royal wedding of William and Catherine. As this book regularly covers the liberal, cynical and ironic ways in which power and privilege are perpetuated, there can be few better spectacles than the kitsch media presentation of that union and the apparent non-stop celebrations a united country enjoyed. I seemed to have met none of these excited members of the public, not even the ironic ones, and not even the apparent hordes my local newspaper told me were celebrating (perhaps most had gone camping for days outside the palace to join 'the million' – including tourists – lining the London streets or were at parties I wasn't invited to), though numerous people I know watched the wedding with curious indifference. It is little surprise that pundits from the right were overflowing with enthusiasm but perhaps a little surprising that pundits from the left (such as the Fearne Cotton of the left, irony's Dan Hodges) were joining in with talk of the shared heritage, how 'we' as a country 'need' such a symbolic event (symbolic of what...? what happens if we don't have one...?), how 'we'should just enjoy it and how the service may have been sexist (or maybe others were being sexist towards Kate?), but – hey! – wasn't the pomp and ceremony wonderful! Little surprise that we were endlessly being told of the common touch of a very contemporary monarchy, and all this as the incredibly privileged 'down-to-earth' couple drove away in a vintage Aston Martin Volante covered with common balloons and a 'JU5T WED' registration plate. Even Simon Schama, author of the brilliant *Landscape and Memory*, is now spinning out of control, writing as he now does about foolproof recipes for cheese soufflés and joyfully telling the television audience that the celebrations around Buckingham Palace show what 'Britishness' is really all about.

Happily, the rest of this book is not about the British royal family but (usually) about how more 'normative' aspects of ideology underpinning historical Jesus studies more specifically, and contemporary 'Western' culture more generally, are perpetuated, often in places we might least expect.

Alas, a section of a chapter in this book has been removed for quasi-legal reasons (and *not*, I hasten to add, at Equinox's prompting – they have not been involved in this issue). For good or ill, I have followed advice with which I do and do not agree and have not published it. I think the point remains clear in the chapter but it would have been stronger if the relevant material was included.

I would like to thank the following for helpful discussions on issues relating to the main themes of this book: Alex Andrews, Bill Arnal, Ward Blanton, Roland Boer, Maurice Casey, Zeb Crook, Steph Fisher, Will Lamb, John Lyons, Halvor Moxnes, Robert Myles, Todd Penner, Hugh Pyper, Alison Robinson, Yvonne Sherwood, Francesca Stavrakopoulou and Keith Whitelam. I owe much to Deane Galbraith, who read a draft of the manuscript, for help in framing and developing specific arguments at key points in this book. Jim West has read everything I have thrown at him, including the draft manuscript of this book. Presumably as part of his *imitatio Christi*(/Zwingli?), Jim has reclined and cavorted with the most depraved of sinners in biblical studies and lucky for them that he did and does. Many ideas were also probably discussed at the various board meetings in certain establishments close to the University of Sheffield and particularly with refreshed hosts Philip Davies, Jackie Harrison and Neil Sellors. I have also appreciated the constant support of John Barrett who, as a leading pre-historian and archaeologist, must still be wondering what hit him after (very effectively) running a department of Biblical Studies for two years.

I am again grateful to Janet Joyce at Equinox not only for accepting this book for publication but, more generally, for being prepared to promote some of the more interesting scholarship in biblical studies, religious studies and beyond.

I should thank Craig Murray for permission to republish a revised form of 'Biblioblogging, "Religion", and the Manufacturing of Catastrophe', *Bulletin for the Study of Religion* 39 (2010), pp. 23-29, and Roland Boer and Julie Kelso for permission to republish a revised form of 'N.T. Wrong and the Bibliobloggers', *Bible and Critical Theory* 6.1 (2010), pp. 1-15. Both of these revised articles appear in chapter 3. Likewise, thanks to Bob Webb for permission to republish parts of 'Writing about the

Historical Jesus: Historical Explanation and "the Big Why Questions", or Antiquarian Empiricism and Victorian Tomes?', *Journal for the Study of the Historical Jesus* 7 (2009), pp. 63-90, in chapter 4.

I would, as ever, like to thank Caroline Watt, if not for finally giving me the luxury of sleeping at night without being forced to perform.

I should thank Pamela Crossley, Glennis Watt and Mike Watt, and not simply for nursery duties. And if I forgot to mention Francis Crossley, Richard Crossley or Gill Turner, my life would barely be worth living.

Finally, I dedicate this book to Serena and Dominique, a pretty poor return for everything they give me.

Chapter 1

Introduction: Jesus Quests and Contexts

> Historical-Jesus research, if it aims to be scientific, must always engage not only in ideological construction but also in ideological criticism... I understand ideology first in the broader sense as a practice and politics of meaning-making.
>
> – Elisabeth Schüssler Fiorenza[1]

Introduction

An outsider to the discipline of biblical studies might be forgiven for thinking that locating scholarship in cultural contexts ought to be a relatively commonplace enterprise. Not so in historical Jesus scholarship at least, certainly not to any serious extent. As Ward Blanton rightly claimed, 'most contemporary accounts of biblical scholarship seem to me to be oblivious to the peculiar cultural logics of our own time'.[2] That said, the recent work of Blanton, along with, among others, the work of William Arnal, Shawn Kelley, Halvor Moxnes, Elisabeth Schüssler Fiorenza, R. S. Sugirtharajah, and this writer on political, ideological and philosophical readings of the history of scholarship may suggest that things are beginning to change, though there is little sign that traditional New Testament scholarship has taken too much notice of scholarship of such direct relevance.[3] However, we may now be at a point where there is a genuine opportunity for different kinds of historical, political, ideological and philosophical readings of Jesus scholarship to make an impact beyond their niche audiences because it is becoming increasingly clear that the conventional analysis of the quests for the historical Jesus has failed in providing a coherent and convincing contextualization of scholarship, particularly in the numbering of distinct chronological quests. What I want to do first is to show why the standard numbering of quests ought to be abandoned before providing an outline of some ways analyses of the quests for the historical Jesus might be developed in future.

How Many Quests for the Historical Jesus?

Conventionally, the Quest for the Historical Jesus has been divided into three different sub-quests: 'Old Quest', 'New Quest' and 'Third Quest'. There is a related and relatively self-explanatory category of 'No Quest'. The 'Old Quest' is typically deemed to be eighteenth- and nineteenth-century historical Jesus scholarship, often characterized by the nineteenth-century so-called 'liberal lives' of Jesus. It is widely believed that Schweitzer's influential *Von Reimarus zu Wrede* at the turn of the twentieth century brought an end to this first quest. Schweitzer's apocalyptic prophet was so devastating that he is typically thought to have ushered in an era of 'No Quest', or at least minimal interest in the historical Jesus with Bultmann's seemingly anti-historical, form critical approach and theological existentialism dominating. The 'New Quest' is typically deemed to have been inaugurated by Käsemann in 1953, ushering in an era of largely Protestant historical Jesus studies, and a Jesus quite different from his Jewish context in particular, and carried out by Bultmann's students. The 'Third Quest', dated from the 1970s onwards, is typically deemed to be more 'historical' and less 'theological', or at least with a range of diverse scholars from religious and non-religious backgrounds, with Jesus seen more embedded in his cultural context, an emphasis on his 'Jewishness' and a use of a wider range of interdisciplinary methods.

While these categorizations are widely held in contemporary scholarship, they have been shown to be inadequate, rightly in my view, by scholars such as Stanley Porter, Maurice Casey, Clive Marsh, Dale Allison and Fernando Bermejo Rubio.[4] The pre-Schweitzer era – lasting a suspiciously long two centuries – did not ignore the Jewish context of Jesus (see Reimarus!), was not all Renan-style romanticizers, witnessed Weiss's fierce prophet of end times and so on. The era of No Quest was anything but, with plenty of historical Jesus books published, including the popular and notorious work of the Nazi scholar Grundmann and historical Jesus work by plenty of well-known writers (e.g. Dodd, Jeremias, Headlam, Goguel, Loisy, Klausner, Vincent Taylor, T. W. Manson, Montefiore and even Bultmann). The so-called New Quest did not lack scholars appreciative of Jewish contexts of Jesus, as might be expected from scholars like Sandmel, and Jeremias, for all his faults, was still at least interested in, and knowledgeable of, Jewish contextualization of Jesus' teaching. Quite how Brandon's study of Jesus and the zealots and Winter's analysis of the trial of Jesus, to name but two, fit into the New Quest category is not easy to establish. As to the so-called Third Quest scholars coming from diverse backgrounds, this has always been the case, from Strauss, Renan and Reimarus, through Klausner, Tyrell and Brandon to Casey, Vermes, Sanders and Meier. As for interdisciplinary approaches, for every Crossan, Herzog and Horsley there is still a Meier, Sanders and Vermes.[5]

There is much more to the counter arguments than this, but this summary should already show just how problematic the Received History really is. How else, then, can we analyse historical Jesus scholarship? Dale Allison suggests the following concerning categorizing the quest for the historical Jesus:

> it has not been very helpful to divide all the post-Schweitzerian activities into chronological segments or different quests. It is much more useful to lay aside the diachronic and take up the synchronic, to abandon periodization for a typology that allows us to classify a book, whether from the 1920s or the 1990s, with those akin to it.[6]

This seems fair enough, but I think there is a case to be made for an alternative chronological approach which does not resort to the periodization of the quest for the historical Jesus in the sense which Porter, Casey, Marsh, Allison, Bermejo Rubio and others have between them demolished. Alternatively, what I aim to do is something quite simple, though largely overlooked, and show how historical Jesus scholarship reflects the cultural, social, historical and so forth contexts of its time. This does not mean that there is necessarily a sharp difference between a Jesus book of the 1920s and the 1990s – there are, as noted, plenty of similarities between scholarly Jesuses past and present. However, all the scholarly Jesuses are obviously part of their own times and can be recognized as such.

That scholarship is as much embedded in contemporary culture as anything else is clear as major examples ought to show. People are increasingly aware of the Nazi quest for the historical Jesus and how the Aryan Jesus is so obviously part of that cultural context, while Shawn Kelley's important work has shown how related concepts became embedded even in the most liberal New Testament scholarship.[7] When Günther Bornkamm wrote about Bolsheviks in his discussion of Jesus and the kingdom of God, while also devoting more space to Marxist interpretations (which were not then taken seriously in New Testament scholarship) of the Sermon on the Mount than even Schweitzer or Bornkamm's favoured Lutheran tradition, scholarship was presented with an explicit example of the historical Jesus in the Cold War.[8] Of course, some examples of cultural influence are more subtle than others. One of the more notable features of scholarship since the 1970s is the massive emphasis on Jesus' Jewishness and how Geza Vermes' *Jesus the Jew* would become a scholarly cliché. As I argued in *Jesus in an Age of Terror*, one of the key reasons for this massive emphasis is (Anglo-) American cultural, religious and political support for Israel – and intensified interest in the Holocaust – post-1967 and the Six Day War. Scholarship has also followed the general pattern of a limited pro-Israeli, 'pro-Jewish' stance by consistently placing Jesus over against Judaism constructed in scholarship, even if there is a regular attitude of superficial positivity and sympathy in discussing Judaism. Bermejo Rubio, with justified bitterness, has since remarked in relation to historical Jesus scholarship that 'Unless we are to assume that supposedly learned and sensitive people need forty years to react to a hideous atrocity, the claim that the Holocaust has conditioned the progress in scholarship is nothing but wishful thinking.'[9]

The remainder of this book will focus mainly on Jesus scholarship over the past forty years, the period which has seen the rise of two major trends in 'the West' (as well as their numerous offshoots): neoliberalism and postmodernism. Before we turn to the impact of these trends on the historical Jesus in scholarship and culture, the rest of this chapter will now outline something which might loosely be called 'methodology', or better, the perspectives which will inform this study.

Contexts

While I have long had some (secret) sympathy with Adorno's critique of the 'culture industry', I always accepted it was not quite right for the standard reasons. The well-known criticisms of the culture industry – that it attributes too much influence to power imposed from above, that people can actually be coercive, that there are plenty of people who are indifferent or resist, that liberal capitalist contexts are more complex than the basic culture industry would suggest and that high culture is hardly immune from capitalist trends – are well taken. I have also had greater sympathy with Gramscian ideas about ideology, negotiations and tacit acceptance from different subordinated groups along with his analysis of 'common sense'. These may not be quite what Adorno, Horkheimer and others had in mind as qualifications, but necessary these qualifications were and are. Yet, along with a constant historicizing of our cultural contexts, the generalizing idea of the importance of dominant cultural trends affecting the ways in which we live and think retains its significance.

All this may well explain, in part, the use of specific thinkers and their ideas underlying the arguments in this book: David Harvey's detailed analyses of capitalism and neoliberalism and their links and overlaps with the emergence of postmodernism and postmodernity; Wendy Brown's analysis of the double-edged nature of 'tolerance' and its links with imperialism; Noam Chomsky and Edward Herman's work, inspired in part by Gramsci and having obvious affinities with Althusser on ideological state apparatuses, on the subtle (and not-so-subtle) influence of political ideology, framing and omitting of ideas, and the general manufacture of consent through the corporate media, intellectuals and education; and Slavoj Žižek's cultural analysis of the impact of these kinds of issues on contemporary thinking, the ways in which multiculturalism is framed and how dominant liberal ideas are perpetuated.

An aside on 'context' is required to try and avoid the seemingly inevitable misunderstandings. As with *Jesus in an Age of Terror*, this present book will locate scholarly, as well as not-so-scholarly, ideas concerning Jesus in a broad cultural context which will mean extended analyses of contemporary culture, politics and ideology. My guess is that this is both alien and yet familiar to the more conventional historical critic of the Bible. It may be alien because extended analyses of contemporary culture, politics and ideology are not commonplace in conventional reviews of historical Jesus scholarship, or biblical studies scholarship more generally. It may be familiar because contextualizing the historical Jesus in terms of (say) eschatology, purity or Cynic philosophy, regularly involves extended analyses of eschatology, purity or Cynic philosophy in the ancient world. In this sense, this book is no different. This analogy with conventional historical criticism can be pushed further because I am reading scholarly literature as historical or (some forms of) literary criticism would read the biblical texts in their ancient cultural contexts. Instead of lengthy exegesis of Gospel texts, here I will exegete scholarly texts *and* general scholarly positions in their modern contexts. Methodologically, the sort of historical study I am pursuing here is not necessarily dramatically removed from conventional biblical scholarship; if anything, it is simply the chronology and focus of study that is different. Though I would stretch fieldwork beyond conventional scholarship, the primary source material for this sort of study tallies with Russell McCutcheon's explanation of his fieldwork as a scholar of religion:

> Because I study the ways scholars construct religion, I do fieldwork in publications and at national and international conferences on religion, where the methodological and theoretical hegemony in the field is often most evident. So, to the question, 'Where do you get your hands dirty?' I can honestly answer that I do it as a participant-observer-analyst of the scholarly profession of constructing and studying religion in North America.[10]

By way of a different comparison we might also point to Stephen Prothero's book, *American Jesus*, which looks at different appropriations of Jesus in American culture (Jesus as rabbi, Jesus as enlightened sage, oriental Christs, the superstar, the fighter and so on).[11] The cultural context of the Jesuses collected by Prothero is, unsurprisingly, American, but an America which, for all its religious pluralism, retains a strongly Christian overlay and influence and also a context wherein religious pluralism, Christianity and secularism play their role in shaping the culture and portrayals of Christ. I will attempt to build on this sort of approach not because I intend simply to give more examples of American Jesuses (though I certainly do that). In fact, there are other Jesuses from different national contexts: the Pope (chapters 6 and 9), after all, is a German based in the Vatican. My approach certainly has a strong interest in what may broadly be called 'Western' intellectual and historical Jesuses, particularly Anglo-American historical Jesuses (as stressed above and as I stress again). But I see this partly as an extension of Prothero's project because the non-American Jesuses are invariably drawn to a centre of world power that is America and may even influence American Jesuses, particularly those from the British sidekick.

Where I also echo Prothero's work, as well as my own previous work, is viewing scholarship as much a part of contemporary culture as Mickey Mouse (no offense meant to either). Prothero weaves Robert Funk, Liberal Protestantism, manly redeemers and Jewish Jesuses with civil rights movements, counter-culture and immigration. As mentioned above, in *Jesus in an Age of Terror*, I read Jesus and New Testament scholarship, as well as the not-so-scholarly views, in the context of Anglo-American power and foreign policy and the ways in which scholarship can conform to dominant political tendencies of its time. This also involved an attempt to show how scholarly trends and broader cultural trends overlap and intertwine. To re-emphasize yet again, this is to say that intellectual thought is, as is implicitly recognized by many scholars (not least in that scholarly mantra, 'we all have presuppositions'), bound up in the culture and (Gramscian) 'common sense' of its day. This book will keep these sorts of emphases by attempting to show how Jesus scholarship buys into broader cultural trends, wittingly or unwittingly, in its various portrayals of Jesus and his context. To borrow Prothero's phrase, this present book is part of 'a quest for the cultural Christ'.[12]

Intentions

As everyone knows, thanks to George Tyrrell's ever-popular remark, scholars are all too liable to see their face reflected at the bottom of the deep well when engaging in historical Jesus studies. This adage is typically repeated in historical Jesus scholarship in order to critique opponents or wearily to survey the landscape of historical Jesus studies or to warn how careful we all must be. These scholarly receptions no doubt make reasonable points but what I also want to do here is to challenge the idea that we merely see ourselves as individuals at the bottom of the well. Dale Allison has offered his own qualifications:

> I am no millenarian prophet; and a Jesus without eschatological error would certainly make my life easier...if motives are somehow disharmonious, other times they are just not apparent... I am uncertain, for example, what makes Ed Sanders tick...motives need not be ideological. Some people, for instance, can take this or that position on an issue not because they care about the issue but because they enjoy playing devil's advocate. Furthermore, people often do things...simply out of habit... People can be, like cats, genuinely, greedily curious, and surely the desire to learn things of interest really does partly animate some of us... Everything we know about Weiss indicates that he reluctantly entered the grim portals of imminent eschatology while he was conscientiously working as a historian... I cannot see that what he took to be a discovery appeared from anything other than a desire to recover history... Jesus comes from another time and place; I accordingly do not expect his beliefs simply to match mine.[13]

Certainly, it is difficult to disagree with Allison's general points on individual motivation and reducing all scholars to reproducing a Jesus which simply reflects their theology would, of course, be unfair and inaccurate. I would, however, modify Allison's criticisms by shifting the focus away from the individual because his approach does not take into account some very real driving forces behind why people act the way they do. In many cases what is reflected is not the face of the individual historian, so to speak, but what lies behind the reflection of the face.

I am not a fan of the over-use of picturesque language so let me spell this out bluntly. What we see in historical studies of Jesus is also the broader social, cultural and political world of the interpreter and the replication of this world in describing Jesus' world can, at times, but certainly not always, stand in direct contrast to the personal beliefs of the interpreter. As ever, we can use an analogy from Herman and Chomsky's Propaganda Model, more specifically what the Propaganda Model does not do. It does not mean journalists or intellectuals are all slavishly following the party line because they have been told to (although this certainly happens), but that the systems of media and education, typically 'unconsciously', filter out the politically problematic, something we will all have encountered throughout our lifetimes. Moreover, journalists and intellectuals can believe all sorts of things personally but overall the mass media will, for instance, reflect the attitudes of corporate ownership and those who progress through the system will be the ones who do not make serious challenges to such power. As Chomsky put it slightly differently in an interview with the prominent British journalist of the establishment, Andrew Marr, in response to Marr's question about whether he, as a journalist, self-censors, 'I'm sure you believe everything you say...'[14]

In chapter 8 we will see a clear example of this tension between personal beliefs and broader dominant ideological trends in Bruce Malina's analyses of the key term 'Ἰουδαῖος and 'the land'. Despite his contrary personal politics, Malina still reproduces the ideologically convenient stereotypes of contemporary Arabs found in modern scholarship as well as some curiously Zionist tendencies. The above qualification, 'but certainly not always', is important because we will see that individuals do reconstruct a Jesus who so happens to cohere with personal beliefs, though at times this may well be because those personal beliefs cohere with broader cultural concerns. However, the main focus of this book will be to show how Jesus is a cultural icon in the sense that he is reconstructed by historians not simply as a figure for Galilee in the 20s and 30s CE but also, intentionally or not, as a figure for our 'postmodern' times. As Blanton claimed of an earlier generation of scholarship, but which can obviously be reapplied to our own, 'Far from more or less accurate repetitions of an ancient object, modernity's depictions of original Christianity must be read as a working through of its own identity.'[15]

There are further ramifications. All comments above also mean that my analysis of scholarship, polemical though it is in a number of places, is not necessarily reflective of what I think of the work in terms of historically accurate scholarship and the polemic is more reflective of what I think of the (often unconscious) ideology. I happen to think many of the people critiqued in this book have made some important and accurate contributions to our understanding of the historical Jesus and his world, but that does not mean that they are immune to historical, ideological and cultural trends any more than I am. The obvious cannot be stressed enough (though I will no longer be surprised if some people ignore the following): even if the ideological analysis carried out in this book is one-hundred per cent accurate, this does *not* mean a scholar is right or wrong in their historical analysis. In a similar way we might mention (to take one example among many) Lukásc's sustained attack on what he saw as an ideologically problematic bourgeois history. Such history may have been obsessed with facts at the expense of totalizing history, Lukásc argued, but he still accepted that details could, obviously, be factually accurate.[16]

This is also why, as in *Jesus in an Age of Terror*, there are extended analyses of cultural contexts and also the interweaving of the scholarly and not-so-scholarly views of Jesus: they are all part of an interconnected cultural context and removing scholarship from this context would only serve to imply that scholarship is somehow beyond the apparent trivialities of contemporary culture and protected from the dirtiness of the outside word. It is not. Again, this is obviously and emphatically *not* to say that an amateur blogger is on the same level of learning as an E. P. Sanders or a Richard Bauckham when it comes to critical historical analysis of Jesus, but we all share certain cultural contexts and that is why much space is not only devoted to critical historical scholarship in flagship publications but also to publications in lesser-known evangelical journals or online debates over the existence of Jesus. This is also why the emphasis could be placed on the greatest historic critic of our age, an obscure article in an evangelical journal or a rant on a blog: they all provide insight into our cultural contexts, irrespective of how good or bad they are. Generally my focus will be on historical Jesus scholarship, primarily because the ideological trends underpinning this scholarship are what provoked me to write this book, but this will not mean covering all the major scholarly positions and all the major scholars: the following analysis is designed to show how historical trends and ideology work with reference to the eclectic, an approach made conventional elsewhere in the humanities by prominent thinkers such as Slavoj Žižek and numerous scholars of cultural studies and anthropology. A primer on critical historical Jesus studies this book is not and readers will have to look at the countless publications for those kinds of summaries, reports and introductions. This book is at least as much about contemporary politics, ideology and culture as it is about Jesus, and in many ways, not least due to unfamiliar approaches in historical Jesus studies, this is almost inevitable.

Liberal Centre

The terms 'liberal', 'liberalism' and 'liberal centre' should also be briefly explained because they are common words used in this book and elsewhere. I use the terms in some fairly popular senses and each use ought to be obvious from its context, though they can be used interchangeably. In a general political sense I use the terms broadly. Given that the Anglo-American context is emphatically the most significant for this book, such a designation can be, for instance, the dominant Clinton–Blair, Bush–Blair, Bush–Brown, Obama–Brown and Obama–Cameron liberal democratic and capitalist consensus in the broadest possible terms: the common interests, in other words, of political, corporate and mainstream media power. After all, none of the previously mentioned presumably believes in the overthrow of capitalism and all accept variants of parliamentary democracy, even if ways of upholding the system differs from leader to leader. We cannot, of course, deny the constructed nature of such discourses and so what counts as broad assumptions of the debate will differ from context to context. And, as Herman and Chomsky's Propaganda Model emphasizes so strongly, there are a range of competing positions within the broad consensus. I do not typically use 'liberal' so much in the common American sense of anyone left of the Republican party (or should that now be anyone left of the Tea Party?), though I will touch upon this use occasionally, and I do use the not unrelated use of 'liberal' in terms of attitudes to homosexuality, gender and so on.

This is where the construction of extremes becomes significant, particularly in relation to liberalism, and we might point to some of the histories, genealogies and uses of extremes (though couched especially in the language of 'fanaticism') recently analysed by Alberto Toscano.[17] Typically such discussions of the constructions of extremes and fanaticism might focus on the role of the more palatable (at least for those with universalist egalitarian sympathies) utopian ideals, but we should not lose sight of the similar role of the construction of less palatable extremes which likewise form an important Other for liberalism. For instance, a decade ago, Jörg Haider was leader of Austria's far-right Freedom Party and his rise led to widespread international condemnation. In response to this situation, Slavoj Žižek wrote 'Why We All Love to Hate Haider'.[18] For Žižek, one function of the popularist right is to supply the 'negative common denominator of the entire established political spectrum' and 'furnish the proof of the benevolence of the official system'. This function legitimizes the international liberal consensus and hegemony while effectively strangling any radical alternative, particularly from the left, anti-capitalist movements and class-struggles, which become de-legitimized through association with similar concerns among the popularist right. We might add that, in more concrete terms, figures such as Clinton and Blair, epitomizing the international liberal consensus, could use a figure such as Haider to make themselves, and their ideological position, look thoroughly credible in contrast to someone tainted with Hitler and fascism, while at the same time perpetuating policies which attacked anything associated with class-conflict and criticisms of involvement in (say) the Balkans.

This angle of Žižek's argument can be developed with reference to any number of figures on the popularist right. In September 2009, for instance, the leader of the far-right British National Party, Nick Griffin, was controversially allowed a platform on the BBC's flagship political debating programme, *Question Time*. Inevitably, Griffin came across as an idiot, certainly in media terms, with his talk of a more moderate KKK member, his discomfort with the idea of men kissing men and true British genealogies belonging to the island since the Ice Age. The British press from right to left were unsurprisingly unanimous in their condemnation of Griffin. The *Daily Mail* columnist, Richard Littlejohn, himself usually placed firmly on the right, summed up the attitude of the British press when he called Griffin 'shifty and unsavoury'.[19] However, what was also significant was that, on a programme supposedly designed for a public grilling of politicians, it actually made leading politicians such as Jack Straw, who was on the *Question Time* panel with Griffin, look thoroughly credible. Yet Straw, it might be thought, has some questions to answer: he has been a public defender of Britain's involvement in Afghanistan and Iraq; he was the Foreign Secretary when the Foreign Office were discrediting Craig Murray (the former British Ambassador in Tashkent) when Murray spoke out against the brutal police state of Uzbekistan, a then British ally;[20] he has had some interesting things to say on his wish to have veiled Muslim women unveiled if they were speaking to him; and was representing the government on *Question Time* in the midst of the harsh recession. All the troubles were washed away by the presence of a 'shifty and unsavoury' figure who made Straw look like an honourable moderate fellow as he was applauded generously for his morally upright condemnation of the far right.

Such broad definitions of 'liberal', 'moderate' and 'centre' are easily transferable into scholarly issues of consensus and widely held assumptions. But first, this needs further qualification. I am not working with a basic module of centre versus margins, at least in terms of dissent. In a panel debate in an Ideological Criticism session at the SBL annual meeting in Atlanta in 2010, Roland Boer (via Negri) raised the following questions in relation to Herman and Chomsky's Propaganda Model about the nature of Power: 'why does Power constantly need to reassert itself, to repeat the same message in many different [ways], to adapt constantly to maintain power? Is it because resistance is in fact central, constitutive and that Power needs to create new ways to manage that resistance?' In answer to these related questions, clearly significant dissent from dominant discourses does indeed lead to P/power reasserting itself. Similar situations of overt resistance might range from the Chartists and the Suffragettes to 1968 and the British Poll Tax protests of 1990, all of which have led to compromises and modifications in dominant discourses and elite opinion. As Raymond Williams put it in his essay on Matthew Arnold, where the right of working-class men to vote and the right to demonstrate in Hyde Park were once deemed scandalous they would, within a century became part of our 'sacred and immemorial' democratic tradition.[21] Indeed, one of the key arguments of this book is precisely how power is maintained through the use of liberal credibility and an implicit theme in this book is precisely how dominant discourses and P/power assert, reassert and continue reasserting themselves, not least in the face of potential challenges. Power and dominant discourses are anything but static.

As this should imply, then, there is a great deal of complexity underlying dominant ideological positions and the arguments presented in this book (which, we should not forget, implicitly owe much to Gramsci) work with such an assumption of the complexity of ideology, even if generalizations are abstracted.[22] As this should also strongly suggest, I am also emphatically not reducing historical Jesus (or any other) scholarship to simple abstractions. As with ideology or dominant discourses, it is better to see the procedure as extracting certain abstractions from the complexity of scholarship.

So, it probably would not be a bad generalization to suggest that scholars such as E. P. Sanders, John Meier and Dale Allison represent the credible 'centre' of historical Jesus studies, with scholars, including those religiously conservative, using such work as a way of generating their own plausibility through agreements and (relatively) polite disagreements or more vigorous disagreements when the aforementioned really get things wrong. As Todd Penner often tells me, there can be no better example of the construction of the liberal or credible centre, or indeed of the links between academic centring and political centring, than the work of Bart Ehrman. Ehrman is open in his desire to provide the public with work on Jesus and Christian origins which reflects broad consensus views in scholarship:

> The perspectives that I present in the following chapters are not my own idiosyncratic views of the Bible. They are the views that have held sway for many, many years among the majority of serious critical scholars teaching in the universities and seminaries of North America and Europe, let alone among people of faith who revere the Bible... For all those who aspire to being well educated, knowledgeable, and informed about our civilization's most important book, that has to change.[23]

In addition to constructing the centre, we can also transfer the ideological function of the far right in contemporary political terms into the ideological function of the construction of the extremes in Jesus scholarship. Here we can turn again to Ehrman who does 'say a word about idiosyncrasy' by pointing out that 'some rather unusual views of Jesus sell well: "Jesus Was a Marxist!" "Jesus Was a Feminist!" "Jesus Was a Gay Magician!"'. Ehrman then contrasts this with the view 'shared probably by the majority of scholars over the course of this century, at least in Germany and America' and that these views need to be shown more popularly in the 'right *kind* of book'.[24] Ehrman is a classic case of constructing the centre with help from constructing extremes. And it is these constructed norms which have the potential to perpetuate credibly cultural trends without serious challenge,[25] an issue we will develop throughout this book.

On the subject of constructing norms, a final word on what might be deemed a notable omission from this book: gender. While issues of gender will be mentioned in passing, they will not be discussed in any detail here. This is because I think the ongoing discussion of ways in which politics and gender have been used in contemporary scholarship has been carried out in ways in which I do not feel I could add anything sufficiently useful or original. In terms of historical Jesus studies, an obvious place to begin would be Elisabeth Schüssler Fiorenza's *Jesus and the Politics of Interpretation* which, notably on social sciences and Orientalism, complements my critiques (in *Jesus in an Age of Terror*) of the uses of 'the Mediterranean' and 'the Arab world' in contemporary scholarship. While not technically concerned with historical Jesus scholarship, I should also add Caroline Vander Stichele and Todd Penner's *Contextualizing Gender in Early Christian Discourse* which also covers not dissimilar issues to the ones which have interested me, particularly issues of centrist scholarship, but have done so from, again, complementary postcolonial and gender-critical perspectives.

A final point on radicalism, opposition and difference in scholarship needs to be made. This book is not meant to function as a plague on all your houses. While I tie in a great deal of scholarship and postmodernism with neoliberal tendencies and trends, I do not deny the genuinely radical aspects of postmodernism or Jesus scholarship and, to repeat *ad nauseam*, I do not think that all historical Jesus scholarship is simply 'reducible' to an outworking of neoliberalism or simply historically wrong even if it does seem that way. I still have some sympathies with some fairly traditional modes of historical criticism and I am aware that there are strands of Jesus scholarship, and biblical scholarship, which can at least be felt threatening to power. Outside historical Jesus studies, the work of Keith Whitelam and Nadia Abu el-Haj caused both writers all sorts of problems and lies were told about both because they challenged the dominant understandings of Israel, particularly in relation to modern understandings of the state of Israel and Palestine.[26] This seems to me to be at a different subversive level than the increasingly common suggestions that Jesus' sayings were politically radical in their attitude towards ruling powers. They certainly could have been, but let us not assume that simply writing about it is a particularly subversive scholarly enterprise. As a rule of thumb, it might be worth arguing that, as things presently stand, when a significant number of people *openly* (e.g. in print) believe roughly the same thing to be true in historical Jesus scholarship, and scholarship more generally, then it probably is not subversive, if that is not tautology.

As I argued in *Jesus in an Age of Terror*, and will argue in a different way elsewhere in this book, what might be perceived as radical in scholarship can be, so to speak, dealt with. Noam Chomsky spoke of what is perceived as the radical left in universities. He argued that it is possible to enter academia and be radical as long as the questions asked remain at least relatively incomprehensible or the dangerous questions of contemporary politics are not systematically addressed head-on and clearly. The scholar may feel like they are not selling-out by acting as, for instance, a Marxist economist, but in reality the individual has been neutralized and can keep working without being much of a danger to anyone.[27] This seems to be a similar process to what is happening with Jesus-the-radical in scholarship. By pushing criticism of imperialism back to the days of the Romans and Herodians, the effectiveness of criticism of the present has a tendency to be nullified (though I appreciate that there are honourable exceptions among activist biblical and historical Jesus scholars), historically accurate though it may (or may not) be.

Let me give two clear, contrasting illustrations. N. T. Wright always provides numerous entertaining examples, but one of his best concerns Jesus' bodily resurrection. Wright claims that 'in the real world... the tyrants and bullies (including intellectual and cultural tyrants and bullies) try to rule by force, only to discover that in order do so they have to quash all rumours of resurrection, rumours that would imply that their greatest weapons, death and deconstruction, are not after all omnipotent.'[28] Are the writings of a former English Bishop of Durham (and a relatively prominent cultural figure) really a threat to any tyrant? Do tyrants really care? Even though his books sell extremely well, it seems unlikely, does it not? Is his radical Jesus really a threat to imperialism *now*? It seems unlikely if in the sense of academics writing about such matters in learned books. Where there is a danger is when people follow their convictions. Liberation theology is the most obvious example, particularly when put into practice by siding with workers and destitute people against the powers of oppression. Liberation theologians have not only been controversial figures within the Catholic Church hierarchy but also a potential threat for those in more immediate power, including a number of figures being assassinated. It is worth ending this section with Chomsky's assessment:

> In the 1980s, the United States fought a vicious war in Central America primarily against the Catholic Church – and that means European priests, not just priests from indigenous origins – because the Church had started working for what they called 'the preferential option for the poor,' therefore they had to go. In fact, when Americas Watch did their wrap up study on the 1980s, they pointed out that it was a decade framed by the murder of the Archbishop in 1980 and the murder of six

Jesuit intellectuals in 1989, both in El Salvador...the Catholic Church became the main target of the U.S. attacks in Central America because there was a radical and very conscious change in critically important sectors of the Church (including dominant elements among the Latin American bishops) who recognized that for hundreds of years it had been a Church of the rich and the oppressors...they decided to finally become a Church in part devoted to the liberation of the poor – and they immediately fell under attack.[29]

Notes

1. E. S. Fiorenza, *Jesus and the Politics of Interpretation* (New York and London: Continuum, 2000), p. 15.
2. W. Blanton, 'Neither Religious Nor Secular: On Saving the Critic in Biblical-Criticism', in R. Boer (ed.), *Secularism and Biblical Studies* (London and Oakville: Equinox, 2010), pp. 141–61 (141).
3. E.g. R. S. Sugirtharajah, *Asian Biblical Hermeneutics and Postcolonialism: Contesting the Interpretations* (Sheffield: Sheffield Academic Press, 1998); Fiorenza, *Jesus and the Politics of Interpretation*; S. Kelley, *Racializing Jesus: Race, Ideology and the Formation of Modern Biblical Scholarship* (London and New York: Routledge, 2002); W. Arnal, *The Symbolic Jesus: Historical Scholarship, Judaism and the Construction of Contemporary Identity* (London and Oakville: Equinox, 2005); W. Blanton, *Displacing Christian Origins: Philosophy, Secularity, and the New Testament* (Chicago: Chicago University Press, 2007); J. G. Crossley, *Jesus in an Age of Terror: Scholarly Projects for a New American Century* (London and Oakville: Equinox, 2008); H. Moxnes, W. Blanton and J. G. Crossley (eds.), *Jesus beyond Nationalism: Constructing the Historical Jesus in a Period of Cultural Complexity* (London and Oakville: Equinox, 2009).
4. E.g. C. Marsh, 'Quests of the Historical Jesus in New Historicist Perspective', *BibInt* 5 (1997), pp. 403–37; M. Casey, 'Where Wright Is Wrong: A Critical Review of N.T. Wright's *Jesus and the Victory of God*', *JSNT* 69 (1998), pp. 95–103; M. Casey, 'Who's Afraid of Jesus Christ? Some Comments on Attempts to Write a Life of Jesus', in J. G. Crossley and C. Karner (eds.), *Writing History, Constructing Religion* (Aldershot: Ashgate, 2005), pp. 129–46; M. Casey, *Jesus of Nazareth: An Independent Historian's Account of His Life and Teachings* (London and New York: T&T Clark, 2010), pp. 1–59; S. Porter, *The Criteria for Authenticity in Historical Jesus Research* (Sheffield: Sheffield Academic Press, 2000), pp. 28–62; D. C. Allison, *Resurrecting Jesus: The Earliest Christian Tradition and its Interpreters* (London and New York: Continuum, 2005), pp. 1–26; F. Bermejo Rubio, 'The Fiction of the "Three Quests": An Argument for Dismantling a Dubious Historiographical Paradigm', *JSHJ* 7 (2009), pp. 211–53.
5. Bermejo Rubio, 'The Fiction of the "Three Quests"', pp. 238–53, suggests some plausible reasons for the construction of the quests, especially the All-New-Third-Quest, most notably the idea of the triumphal march of History and

Wright's attempt to take the sting out of the challenge to orthodox Christian theology provided by Sanders's *Jesus and Judaism* (I would add Vermes's *Jesus the Jew* – a key influence on Sanders – but the point stands) and accommodate a trend in which Wright was playing a role.

6. Allison, *Resurrecting Jesus*, p. 18. For such an attempt, see e.g. Marsh, 'Quests of the Historical Jesus.'
7. Kelley, *Racializing Jesus.*
8. G. Bornkamm, *Jesus of Nazareth* (London: Hodder & Stroughton, 1960), pp. 102, 223.
9. Bermejo Rubio, 'The Fiction of the "Three Quests",' p. 240.
10. R. T. McCutcheon, *Manufacturing Religion: The Discourse on Sui Generis Religion and the Politics of Nostalgia* (Oxford: Oxford University Press, 1997), p. 7.
11. S. Prothero, *American Jesus: How the Son of God Became a National Icon* (New York: Farrar, Straus and Giroux, 2003).
12. Prothero, *American Jesus*, pp. 7–10.
13. Allison, *Resurrecting Jesus*, pp. 133, 135, 137, 138, 147.
14. A. Marr, 'Interview with Noam Chomsky,' *The Big Idea* (BBC2, 14 February, 1996), http://video.google.com/videoplay?docid=-4827358238697503#.
15. Blanton, *Displacing Christian Origins*, p. 7.
16. G. Lukásc, *History and Class Consciousness: Studies in Marxist Dialectics* (London: Merlin Press, 1971). Cf. e.g. T. Eagleton, *Ideology: An Introduction* (London and New York, Verso, 1991; updated version, 2007), p. 99; M. Perry, *Marxism and History* (London: Palgrave, 2002), p. 81.
17. A. Toscano, *Fanaticism: On Uses of an Idea* (London and New York: Verso, 2010).
18. S. Žižek, 'Why We All Love to Hate Heider,' *New Left Review* 2 (March–April, 2000), pp. 37–45.
19. R. Littlejohn, 'Why I Wouldn't Go on Question Time with the Unsavoury Nick Griffin,' *Daily Mail* (20 October, 2009).
20. C. Murray, *Murder in Samarkand: A British Ambassador's Controversial Defiance of Tyranny in the War on Terror* (Edinburgh and London: Mainstream Publishing, 2006), pp. 270–82.
21. R. Williams, 'A Hundred Years of Culture and Anarchy,' *The Spokesman* 8 (December, 1970), reprinted in R. Williams, *Culture and Materialism* (London and New York: Verso, 1980), pp. 3–8.
22. As Eagleton (*Ideology*, p. 101) put it in a slightly different context (reducing ideology to class), 'Social classes do not manifest ideologies in the way that individuals display a particular style of walking: ideology is, rather, a complex, conflictive field of meaning, in which some themes will be closely tied to the experience of particular classes, while others will be more "free floating", tugged now this way and now that in the struggle between contending powers. Ideology is a realm of contestation and negation, in which there is constant busy traffic: meanings and values are stolen, transformed, appropriated across the frontiers of different classes and groups, surrendered, repossessed, reinflected.'

23. B. D. Ehrman, *Jesus, Interrupted: Revealing the Hidden Contradictions in the Bible (and Why We Don't Know about Them)* (New York: HarperOne, 2009), p. 2.
24. B. D. Ehrman, *Jesus: Apocalyptic Prophet of the New Millennium* (Oxford: Oxford University Press, 1999), p. ix.
25. It is notable that in much of the storm surrounding Ehrman's popularizing work, the repeated refrain is that it is sensationalist (especially his publications on text criticism) and behind the sensationalism is some fairly conventional views held by many scholars. Indeed.
26. For discussion, see Crossley, *Jesus in an Age of Terror*, pp. 143–94.
27. N. Chomsky, *Understanding Power* (New York: New Press, 2002), p. 242.
28. N. T. Wright, *The Resurrection of the Son of God* (London: SPCK, 2003), p. 737.
29. Chomsky, *Understanding Power*, p. 154. See further, J. G. Crossley, *Reading the New Testament: Contemporary Approaches* (London and New York: Routledge, 2010), pp. 159–61. Cf. Blanton, 'Neither Religious Nor Secular', p. 142, who writes of 'the salvaging of that unruly, risky energy of critique, the scandal of which once meant lost jobs, ecclesiastical outrage, and official governmental censure'.

Part I

From Mont Pelerin to Eternity? Contextualizing an Age of Neoliberalism

Powerful ideological influences circulated through the corporations, the media, and the numerous institutions that constitute civil society – such as the universities, schools, churches, and professional associations...the capture of certain segments of the media, and the conversion of many intellectuals to neoliberal ways of thinking, created a climate of opinion in support of neoliberalism as the exclusive guarantor of freedom.

– David Harvey[1]

Chapter 2

Neoliberalism and Postmodernity

> I tell you, to all those who have, more will be given; but from those who have nothing, even what they have will be taken away. (Lk. 19:26)

Introduction

In *Jesus in an Age of Terror*, I focused on developments in historical Jesus and Christian origins scholarship since the 1967 Six Day War and the intensification of Anglo-American Orientalism since the 1970s. I looked at how broad and hugely influential cultural trends relating to issues surrounding Israel and (neo-) Orientalism have had a profound impact on the rise of the emphasis on 'Jesus the Jew' and the construction of 'the (contemporary) Arab world', the latter at times becoming synonymous with 'the Mediterranean' in influential social-scientific approaches to the New Testament. In a different but complementary way, William Arnal argued that the rise of debates over Jesus' 'Jewishness', and the scholarly construction of a fixed Jewish identity, ought to be seen as a reaction against the economic uncertainties and fractured identities associated with globalization and postmodernity.[2] Whether we can more precisely connect postmodernity with the political trends in Anglo-American culture may well be impossible to establish with an absolute degree of certainty (though, as I will hopefully show, I do think the general case is a strong one), but I certainly think it can be argued that the historically contemporaneous rise of postmodernity and its economic counterpart have also had, as might obviously be expected, a profound impact on the ways in which the historical Jesus has been constructed in scholarship. Here I want to push the influence of postmodernism and postmodernity further and look at the influence of its economic counterpart, neoliberalism. This will provide the broad contextual basis for analysing some of the ways in which Jesus has been constructed in scholarship and beyond in recent decades.

Economics and Postmodernity

Before we turn to certain specific political traits of our 'postmodern condition', it is helpful to summarize key points concerning postmodernism and postmodernity and their relationship to free markets and neoliberalism, not least because such issues are hardly common in historical Jesus scholarship despite their great importance for understanding scholarly trends and movements. First, as a general definition of 'postmodernism' and 'postmodernity', the following from Terry Eagleton will be broadly assumed here:

> The word postmodernism generally refers to a form of contemporary culture, whereas the term postmodernity alludes to a specific historical period. Postmodernity is a style of thought which is suspicious of classical notions of truth, reason, identity and objectivity, of the idea of universal progress or emancipation, of single frameworks, grand narratives or ultimate grounds of explanation. Against these Enlightenment norms, it sees the world as contingent, ungrounded, diverse, unstable, indeterminate, a set of disunified cultures or interpretations which breed a degree of scepticism about the objectivity of truth, history and norms, the givenness of natures and the coherence of identities... Postmodernism is a style of culture which reflects something of an epochal change, in a depthless, decentred, ungrounded, self-reflexive, playful, derivative, eclectic, pluralistic art which blurs the boundaries between 'high' and popular' culture, as well as between art and everyday experience.[3]

What we generally call postmodernism started to emerge in the 1960s and from the 1970s onwards it is reasonable enough to speak in broad and general terms of the 'postmodern condition', at least in the West.[4] But what is often seen as a cultural and intellectual trend is as embedded in its historical, political and economic contexts as anything else. When we think of pop art, fashion, a bombardment of media images, indeed the overlapping worlds of art and advertising, the complexities of urban life, and the much vaunted shift from the repetitive high modernist architecture to the apparently playful, eclectic, parodying and/or kitsch (ironic or otherwise) postmodern architecture then it is not difficult to appreciate how much postmodernism can be seen as very much an integral aspect of cultural, economic, social and political life. One of the most famous assessments of the 'postmodern condition' summarizes the collapse of space and time alongside the corporate-based cultural mixes and consumption: 'Eclecticism is the degree zero of contemporary general culture: one listens to reggae, watches a western, eats

McDonald's food for lunch and local cuisine for dinner, wears Paris perfume in Tokyo and "retro" clothes in Hong Kong; knowledge is a matter for TV games.'[5]

It is not, of course, simply the case that postmodernism is deeply embedded in capitalist culture; it is, to use Jameson's famous description, the cultural logic of so-called *late* capitalism (roughly synonymous with 'multinational capitalism' for Jameson, among other things).[6] Here David Harvey's often complementary work comes into its own as he points out that the aesthetic and intellectual forms of postmodernism came to the fore in the context of the crisis of accumulation that began in the late 1960s and came to a head in 1973 (an important date for Harvey's analysis),[7] leading to a significant surface-level shift in the appearance of capitalist accumulation since 1973.[8] The sharp recession of 1973, accompanied by oil crises, marked the end of a period of growth and led to attempts to halt inflation in Western economies. Union power declined post-1973 with labour now restructured to face market volatility and increasing competition with stable employment patterns giving way to increasing part-time and temporary contractors and specialist workers. A rise in service employment (especially finance, insurance, estate) was paralleled by the decline in manufacturing and industry.[9] And between the early 1960s and the mid-1980s, unemployment steadily rose in the USA and Europe.[10] Most importantly for understanding the rise of postmodernity, the late 1960s and early 1970s marks the shift from the economic rigidity of the post-war Fordist–Keynesian consensus to the rise of neoliberalism and flexibility of accumulation and labour, paralleled in a shift from high modernism to postmodernism and a shift in cultural attitudes, consumption and practices since 1970:

> The relatively stable aesthetic of Fordist modernism has given way to all the ferment, instability, and fleeting qualities of a postmodernist aesthetic that celebrates difference, ephemerality, spectacle, and the commodification of cultural forms...the more flexible motion of capital emphasizes the new, the fleeting, the ephemeral, the fugitive, and the contingent in modern life, rather than the more solid values implanted under Fordism.[11]

Following the groundbreaking work of Jameson, Harvey and others,[12] it is worth summarizing further links between market and cultural change. Accelerated turnover time was and is matched by accelerated consumption in mass markets (e.g. fashion, pop music) and innovations in electronic banking and finance. Assisted by the rise of mass media and communications – with the widespread use of the colour television from the 1970s onwards being a particularly crucial moment for the postmodern[13] – the image has become more prominent than ever before, from the sharp rise in personal image consultants in the 1980s to numerous youth cultures, with business keen to cash in and contribute. Image is, obviously, crucial in business, from named branding and advertising through to sponsoring the right events. The dramatic fall of the jewellers Ratner's in the UK is, after all, typically attributed to Gerald Ratner labelling his own product 'total crap'. Perhaps superficial imaging has become most notable in politics, certainly as Harvey would have it, from the Kennedy–Nixon debate onward, with PR firms an integral part of party politics. In the USA, Reagan and Clinton would be obvious examples but we should not forget the remarkable rebranding of the elite-educated George W. Bush as a Texas cowboy. In the UK, Thatcher and Blair, not to mention the often-favoured PR firm Saatchi and Saatchi, would be obvious examples and we should recall that Gordon Brown was believed by some to be a PR disaster which, apparently, cost votes (whether or not this is a fair assessment is another matter). That image-making in politics masks harsher political realities hardly needs spelling out. A not unrelated point would be that causality often takes a back seat in this world of intense superficial imaging with effect triumphant (so Baudrillard), and so is the right sort of context for the rise of deconstructionist thinking.

The ways in which certain strands of postmodernism mask power and the causes of socio-economic change is as significant as its much-hyped unmasking of power, and will be discussed further below. Prime examples of these seemingly contradictory tendencies might be the well-known deconstructionist critique of power functioning alongside postmodern complicity with the market, most notoriously in the numerous near-hagiographical treatments of the 'material girl' Madonna and her MTV stage. Or again, for all the trumpeting of cultural relativism in certain strands of postmodernist thought, at least of a more popular variety, the idea that we ought not to be so 'ethnocentric' as to pass judgment on other cultures 'leaves our own culture conveniently insulated from anyone else's critique'.[14] To fast forward a little, we might think of scholars such as Richard Rohrbaugh and Bruce Malina who tabulate difference and/or talk of the 'Mediterranean', which too often blurs into the (contemporary) 'Middle East', in descriptions of the social world of Jesus and the New Testament, and rebuke scholarship for repeatedly imposing 'ethnocentric' misunderstandings on the Other.[15] We might be wary of pushing such views too hard. The Malina-inspired line has the force, does it not, of protecting the opposite in its grand geographical and ethnic constructs (usually 'the West' or, just to remind us where power really lies, 'North America') from similar criticism, namely that it would be 'ethnocentric' for anti-Westerners to complain about the ways in which 'our' corporations and governments work?

Excursus: Marxism and Postmodernism

This is emphatically not to say that all things postmodern are about buying into the logic of late capitalism and here I would also add briefly, but emphasize strongly, some qualifications of the Marxist approaches associated with Harvey, Eagleton, Jameson and others. The challenges to contemporary capitalism, including those associated with the cultural phenomenon of postmodernism, have not simply come from Marxism – the opposite impression can just as easily be taken from reading some of the leading theorists – but a range of ideological perspectives which are not necessarily Marxist, such as human rights activism, direct action, anarchism (a not insignificant influence on radical postmodernist thinking), environmentalism, certain feminist movements, animal rights activism, certain church and religious movements and so on. Intentional or otherwise, one overall *effect* of the important work of Harvey, Eagleton, Jameson and others is that Marxism has provided the *only* challenge. Indeed, it is a notable feature of Harvey's excellent analysis that he downplays the long-term oppositional significance of the events of 1968 and sees the rhetoric of freedom as one of the factors in the emergence of postmodernism and its connections with contemporary manifestations of capitalism (see below). There may also be an element of the historic rivalry between anarchism and Marxism (and if the left is good at one thing it is, of course, falling out). It is interesting to compare the comments of the Marxist historian Eric Hobsbawm from 1969 where his condescension towards a significant anarchist presence in the events of 1968 are as much about his surprise as his disdain for anarchism and his loyalty to orthodox Marxism:

> the main appeal of anarchism was emotional and not intellectual... Admirable but hopeless...the monumental ineffectiveness of anarchism which, for most people of my generation...determined our rejection of it... Spanish anarchism [was] a tragic farce...anarchism as a revolutionary movement has failed...the revival of interest in anarchism today seems so unexpected, surprising and – if I am to speak frankly

> – unjustified...anarchism has no significant contribution to socialist theory to make.[16]

However, the rise to prominence, or re-emergence, of those groups listed above (anarchists, human rights groups etc.) is due in no small part to the events of 1968 and the social changes of the 1960s more generally. More recently, Seattle, May Day protests, the increasing critiques of foreign policy and corporate media, and the almost instant and large protests against the Iraq war were not predominantly Marxist, even if there were plenty of overlapping sympathies. Part of the dominance of Marxism, and the perception of an all-embracing critique of postmodernity, may well be due to Marxism's implicit, though not necessary, totalizing claims, the most extreme form found in the Stalin regimes and 'red bureaucracies' long predicted by Bakunin.[17] However right though Bakunin was in terms of historical developments, a more plausible reason for the dominant Marxist explanation would be that the rise of major thinkers positively inclined to the postmodern, notably Lyotard, was a reaction against Marxist metanarratives in particular. In turn, Jameson provided a major Marxist response and critique. In many ways, the key debates turned on what is to be done with Marxism.[18]

Neoliberalism and Postmodernity

With these qualifications in mind, I think we can accept the general point that there is a link between postmodernity and contemporary forms of capitalism. As should already have been implied, and as Harvey's later work in particular has shown, the emergence of neoliberal thought has at least complemented the emergence of postmodernism, so much so that Harvey can talk of the 'the neoliberalism of culture'.[19] It is not difficult to see why neoliberalism can go hand-in-hand with postmodernity. Neoliberalism advocates individual property rights and free trade, promotes the private sector over the public sector, supports deregulation of the market, challenges traditional manifestations of state power, urges virtually every aspect of human existence to be brought into the market, encourages individual responsibility, downplays systemic problems as a cause of individual failure, and emphasizes the importance of the market for the common good, human freedom, elimination of poverty and creation of wealth, all of which generally complement postmodernism, even if we should always recall that we are working with generalizations and even if the overlaps and influence do not, so to speak, go all the way.[20] It is probably not going too far to suggest that neoliberalism is now the dominant global economic model, with even China seemingly moving in this direction, albeit with a distinctive spin.

There are, however, many tensions within neoliberalism, particularly when put into practice. Its form of individual freedom involves liberty and rights but real decision making is left in the hands of experts and unelected bodies such as the IMF. Individual freedom does not necessarily extend to freedom to form strong collective movements challenging the market (e.g. trade unions) and corporate power has more than shown its capabilities for removal of individual freedom and rights.[21] Moreover, propaganda (see, as ever, Herman and Chomsky), surveillance and force are used to suppress opposition to the market and neoliberalism, from Seattle and Genoa to the controversial 'kettling' tactic used by British police in the 2009 G20 demonstrations and the November 2010 student protests. It follows naturally that the state can play a key role in protecting the interests of the market (why else would there be corporate lobbyists?). It also follows that neoliberalism does not always endorse the idea of the freedom to fail.[22] We need only think of the 2008 international recession and how governments bailed out certain banks. Paradoxically, then, state intervention can become a key feature of a philosophy hostile to state intervention. As Chomsky points out concerning the Reagan era, 'if market forces had been allowed to function, the United States would no longer have an automobile industry, or a microchip industry, or computers, or electronics, because they would have been wiped out by the Japanese'.[23]

It should, perhaps, be less of a surprise, then, that we find nationalism, jingoism, imperialism and war taken up by neoliberal states to promote or provoke, directly or indirectly, neoliberalism (think of the Falklands or the Iraq war).[24] This tension between non-intervention and state intervention partly explains why neoconservatism has come to the fore in the past decade. Neoconservatism has not only provided vigorous support for neoliberal economics but has positively revelled in the possibilities of militarization, authoritarianism and threats to the order (whether real or otherwise). We could go as far as suggesting (as Harvey does) that this is paralleled in states such as China where neoliberal economics can emerge alongside authoritarianism.

State intervention and violence have in fact been one of the ways in which neoliberalism became established in certain contexts, infamously in the American-backed economic experimentation in 1970s Chile. The IMF, just as infamously, has directly imposed neoliberal conditions on numerous occasions. In America at the turn of the 1970s, there was the discussion of top-down planning , at least for the widespread promotion of free enterprise in schools, media, publishing and so on, with universities singled out for particular attention because they were deemed centres of anti-corporate and anti-state thinking.[25] Universities were also important in the rise of neoliberalism because they always provide a pool of potentially very useful privileged and affluent people, in certain cases people with strong neoliberal pedigree, most influentially Milton Friedman and the 'Chicago Boys'.[26]

However, the most famous manifestations of neoliberalism in the USA and UK under Reagan and the Hayek-fuelled Thatcher were developed through democratic and cultural mechanisms. In their own particular ways, Chomsky, Harvey and others, often via Gramsci, have shown how the manufacture of consent took place and became a cultural norm, or the Gramscian common sense. The 1970s, for instance, saw the emergence of the neoliberal Centre for Policy Studies and the Adam Smith Institute, and high profile converts in the media, such as *The Wall Street Journal* and the Murdoch press, most notably *The Sun* in the UK which in the pre-Murdoch era was *The Herald*, a newspaper associated with the working-class left. By the 1980s, the Conservative-dominated media in the UK were leading relentless attacks on 'benefit scroungers', single mothers and an opposition labelled the 'loony left'.

Since the 1970s, neoliberalism has worked its way into the mass media, think tanks, intellectual schools, corporations, universities, schools (I recall deeply boring classes at school called 'Enterprise' which consisted of lessons on how to be business savvy with students developing their own mini-businesses, usually and predictably a sweet shop) and so on. In universities, neoliberalism has become dominant in leading economic departments and business schools and, in the case of the USA at least, this would involve training international students who would export these ideas, whether to Chile and Mexico or to the IMF, World Bank and UN.[27] By the 1980s, coupled with the economic crises of the 1970s, Thatcher and Reagan were able to ride on the wave of a developing neoliberal movement and impose vigorous neoliberal agendas. The accompanying rhetoric, especially the rhetoric of Thatcher, and later of Blair and Cameron (both desperate to win the blessing of Murdoch), was that there was 'no alternative'.

Various cultural and intellectual explanations also played their part in this manufacturing of common sense, with support coming from right to left. Youth movements and cultural upheavals of the 1960s, including the events of 1968, would provide a sharp challenge to traditional class structures and feed into the consistent suspicion of power so integral to postmodernism and deconstruction. The classic sixties rhetoric of freedom would be taken in different directions, probably both partially tied in with the increasing awareness of, and reaction to, the terror and failures of the Soviet-led regimes. On the one hand, the rhetoric of freedom would go one way in the development of social justice movements, as it did with anarchist, libertarian-Marxist, environmental, human rights, diverse direct action and ever-increasing anti-war movements since Vietnam (see above).[28] On the other hand, the rhetoric of freedom could go in the direction of an intense anti-solidarity individual freedom (so Harvey). This could include the intense individualism of the sort willingly taken up by the devotees of Thatcher and Reagan where 'meritocracy' settled as a buzzword for the decades to come, even if it merely justified the class system rather than provided any genuine widespread opportunities for social mobility.[29] Mention might also be made of that old, not wholly accurate (or inaccurate) cliché of hippies and the generation of '68 becoming our cuddly business leaders: revolution, the people cried, not knowing that we would end up with Ben and Jerry's and Richard Branson.

The scene was set for further dissemination and the spread of neoliberalism. The Republican Party were the political class of neoliberalism raising formidable financial resources and developing an electoral base consisting of, among others, the Christian Right, so much so that no post-Carter president would dare admit to being anything other than a committed Christian. Furthermore, by the Clinton era, Democrats had deemed it crucial to support capitalist class interests, even at the expense of their traditional electoral base. The Republican mobilizing of the Christian Right is a particularly notable achievement for the corporate classes as many among the white working class were voting against their material and economic interests in favour of nationalism and religion. Put another way, as Chomsky did in light of the 2004 US elections, 'As for "moral values," we learn what we need to know about them from the business press the day after the election, reporting the "euphoria" in board rooms – not because CEOs oppose gay marriage.'[30]

In the UK, Thatcher launched a full-scale attack on the unions, major industries (steel, shipbuilding, coal) and anything smacking of traditional working-class culture. Her most notable action was the devastating Miners' Strike of 1984–85 and the destruction of the National Union of Mineworkers and numerous mining communities. To this day, the fear of Thatcher partly prevented the Conservative Party from getting an outright majority against a heavily weakened Labour Party in the 2010 General Election. Privatization intensified under Thatcher and by the time she left office there had been, unsurprisingly, a sharp decline in strike action, due not least to the Conservatives carefully planning to destroy union power in the UK. While there was, equally unsurprisingly, deep hostility towards Thatcher, she developed a strong middle-class base and the lure of strong middle-class values as a basis for consent. One of her crucial moves was the selling off of council houses to tenants thereby increasing homeownership and contributing to a decline in traditional working-class identities and values.[31] In this context, Thatcher also fostered an entrepreneurial culture, parodied in hugely popular television shows such as *Minder* and *Only Fools and Horses*. But only gently parodied: the main entrepreneurial characters of strongly working-class backgrounds were also created extremely sympathetically. By the time Labour returned to power in 1997, now rebranded New Labour, neoliberalism was deeply embedded and part and parcel of party political culture, so much so that Blair could introduce policies Thatcher never could (e.g. tuition fees for university students).[32] The way was eventually paved in 2010 for the Cameron-led Conservative-Liberal Democrat 'progressive' coalition to intensify the work of Thatcher now that they, with the help of the 2008 recession, had been gifted the opportunity to cut the public sector in ways Thatcher could only dream about.

Neoliberalism has, of course, not always had its own way and it continues to have its staunch opponents: Thatcher did not have the popular support Reagan could muster, large parts of the British electorate were (as we saw) hostile to her neoliberal 'reforms' and it is by no means clear what would have happened to Thatcherism had she not reversed her low poll ratings through the Falklands War. However, there is not the space here for counterfactual history (memorably described by E. P Thompson as '*Geschichtswissenschlopff, unhistorical shit*').[33] Neoliberalism now has such a major cultural presence in many countries that key parts of its agenda can appear as 'natural' as anything else in contemporary culture. When, in the UK, no party won the 2010 General Election outright and the coalition negotiations were underway, a repeated refrain in the mainstream media was that there had to be a quick resolution because the *markets* needed one.

Mission Accomplished

It is perhaps fitting to end this section on a catty teleological note by pointing out that neoliberalism-neoconservatism had its own 'mission accomplished' moment thanks in part to Francis Fukuyama's pseudo-prophetic prediction of 'the End of History' and then the Iraq war. Unfortunately for Fukuyama, and helped in no small part by his former colleagues in the Project for the New American Century, the 'End of History' turned out to be as useful a judgment as 'Mission Accomplished' (we need only think of the Balkans, September 11, al Qaeda, Afghanistan...), though lacking the perverse comedic element of Bush's moment. Indeed, it is tempting to tweak Žižek's application of Marx's dictum to September 11 and then the recession by replacing it with reference to 'the End of History' and then 'mission accomplished': first as tragedy, then as farce.[34]

This overview of dominant and influential political, cultural and economic contexts since around 1970 complements the contexts in which I placed contemporary historical Jesus and New Testament scholarship in *Jesus in an Age of Terror*. In that book, as mentioned, I looked at the ways in which the geopolitics involved in Anglo-American foreign policy, particularly those involving the Middle East, and the cultural and intellectual support amassed in the forms of dangerous stereotyping, have had a profound impact on the ways in which scholars construct Christian origins. These are precisely the sorts of topics which concern Herman and Chomsky's more recent applications of their Propaganda Model to the manufacture of consent in the mass media, education and politics, the main approach which underpinned my analysis of contemporary scholarship. Furthermore, what is crucial to the Propaganda Model and the manufacturing of consent is the role of corporate (and sometimes state) power effectively owning the mass mainstream media and so, as pointed out in chapter 1, any disagreements will tend to reflect disagreements among the elite and powerful.

That issues surrounding, for instance, the Iraq war complement neoliberal (and, of course, neoconservative) agendas ought to be obvious enough. To give one such obvious example: the plans laid by the Coalition Provisional Authority (CPA) under Paul Bremner in 2003. Part of the pre-war planning by the Bush administration, the CPA would push for privatization, deregulation, low taxes, foreign investment and general (neo-) liberalization of the Iraqi economy and yet accompanied by an authoritarian attitude toward the formation of unions and the right to strike.[35] All the neoliberal contradictions (though, obviously, not necessarily a contradiction for the neoconservatives) are present in this war and its aftermath where the cultural stereotyping of Arabs and Muslims (as well as the confusion and convenient blurring of both categories) played a not insignificant cultural role (just think of the images from Abu Ghraib, the death of Baha Mousa and the economic experimentation on Iraqis).

Liberal and Credible

I finally want to develop the analysis of the sort of liberalizing line mentioned in chapter 1, partly with reference to work on the manufacturing of consent. This time I particularly want to develop further the idea of the liberal and 'credible' masking, deflecting and justification of power, an approach tackled more broadly by Wendy Brown.[36] The critique of liberal masking of power has a long intellectual history, not least in Marxist circles, and has recently been given a distinctive updating by Slavoj Žižek, among others, for a postmodern age. According to this view, liberal diversions or surface-level changes might include things like: New Age movements; 'Western Buddhism' ('it enables you to fully participate in the frantic capitalist game while sustaining the exception that you are not really in it'[37]); so-called 'political correctness'; 'politically correct' narrative twists (Žižek gives the example of *Shrek* with the caring dragon and the beautiful princess turning into a ordinary girl after the fairy-tale kiss); performance of symbolic mandates (Žižek gives the example of fatherhood) by not taking them seriously with accompanying ironic comments and yet still performing them; and so on. Žižek's critique partly functions as an attack on a postmodern penchant for praising displacements, reinscriptions read as potentially 'subversive', and replicating ever more 'sites of resistance' to include even films like *Shrek*. Instead, the old story is simply being repackaged for a new age but now with added credibility. In terms of the dominant liberal democratic consensus, 'When we think we are making fun of the ruling ideology, we are merely strengthening its hold over us.'[38] This is not dissimilar to the criticism (from the right and the left) often levelled at political satire.

I want to develop this point in more detail and with more evidence in order to show just how deeply embedded this liberal diversion is in our contemporary culture because it is crucial to both this book and *Jesus in an Age of Terror*. And the examples are endless. Anti-Bush jokes and images were easily turned into something that sold. More bizarre still, and in the shadow of the invasion of Iraq, Levi's Europe decided to embrace the popular anti-war feeling by releasing a limited edition teddy bear with a peace symbol on its ear, hardly an effective form of protest but certainly one which might aid Levi's profits and give them a distinctive image in a largely anti-Iraq war Europe.[39] Perhaps the most prominent corporate example for our times is the Buddhist, vegetarian and casually clothed Apple CEO, Steve Jobs, advertising his iProducts as the machinery of the casually clothed, cool creative types in contrast to PCs and the BlackBerry which only boring corporate types would use.[40]

A different kind of example for our times might be that great leveller, the open-plan office. In contrast to his elite-educated predecessors, the head of the Civil Service in the UK, Gus O'Donnell, who was state and Warwick University educated and from a lower middle-class background, believes in the importance of having women, people from ethnic minorities and disabled people among the ranks of the Civil Service. Upon taking the top Civil Service job, he decided to move from his wood-panelled office into an open-plan office for at least one day a week.[41] This may sound a democratizing move (albeit limited) carried out with the best of intentions, but, let us put it this way, would *you* want *your* boss *that* close, no matter how remarkable his interpersonal skills? While hardly claiming that things are no different from the days when plenty of people from non-traditional backgrounds were excluded from jobs, it remains clear enough that the underlying structure of power does not change with moves towards diversity and humility.

The most serious examples concerning imperialism and foreign policy have been catalogued by Richard Seymour in *The Liberal Defence of Murder*.[42] Seymour looks at the historic roots of the importance of 'credible', 'moderate', liberal and socialist support for imperialism. Seymour's history takes us right up to contemporary figures such as Bernard-Henri Lévy and other purveyors of 'humanitarian barbarism' in their support of the 'war on terror' and with their emphasizing of the rhetoric of pure intentions in American foreign policy while making out enemies to be wholly evil.[43] Those familiar with the UK media need only recall how liberal-left commentators, such as David Aaronovitch, Julie Burchill, Nick Cohen and Johann Hari, along with the liberal centre-left newspaper, *The Observer*, were all cheerleaders for the Iraq war, with their 'common sense', pragmatism and love for humanity, even if those such as Hari have repented somewhat since. And is there a more flamboyant example of the 'liberal defence of murder' (and almost anything else) than that walking contradiction, the neoliberal and neoconservative apologist, dogmatic anti-religionist and self-proclaimed voice of both liberalism and Trotsky, Christopher Hitchens?

Many people now look back in disbelief over the past decade, and the roles of Bush and Blair in particular. But now we have Obama, the great liberal figure of our time. While we can acknowledge that certain things have been different from his predecessor,[44] too much faith in 'change we can believe in' can have that same function of masking power. In Obama's famous 2009 speech in Cairo he addressed America's relationship with Arabs and Muslims past and present and using not only the Bible but also the Talmud and Qur'an, effortlessly harmonizing the Abrahamic religions under the suitably vague term 'God' and the one rule that transcends all, that 'we do unto others as we would have them do unto us' (cf. Mt. 7:12; Lk. 6:31).[45] Yet, beneath the high rhetoric, Obama rarely deviated from standard American positions on the Middle East in recent years and provided minimal detail. And, in the heart of an anti-democratic police state with an unfortunate human rights record, he spoke of peaceful governments governing with respect and how Islam is part of a promoting of peace. Behind the kindly vague language of religious tolerance, there was, in terms of US interests, little difference from the famous Bushisms, 'you're either with us or against us' and 'the coalition of the willing', as he stood shoulder-to-shoulder with Mubarak,[46] an issue which is apparently best forgotten now that the Western media could no longer avoid showing Mubarak for what he is.

Notes

1. D. Harvey, *A Brief History of Neoliberalism* (Oxford: Oxford University Press, 2005), p. 40.
2. W. Arnal, *The Symbolic Jesus: Historical Scholarship, Judaism and the Construction of Contemporary Identity* (London and Oakville: Equinox, 2005), pp. 39–72.
3. T. Eagleton, *The Illusions of Postmodernism* (Oxford: Blackwell, 1996), p. vii.
4. This is not, of course, to suggest that what we call postmodernity (or any other related name) has no antecedents, but rather that a number of ideas began to crystallize into something distinctive enough to earn itself this much-used term. On the history and crystallization of all things postmodern see P. Anderson, *The Origins of Postmodernity* (London and New York: Verso, 1998), pp. 3–46.
5. J.-F. Lyotard, *The Postmodern Condition: A Report on Knowledge* (Manchester: Manchester University Press, 1984), p. 76.
6. F. Jameson, 'Postmodernism, or, The Cultural Logic of Late Capitalism', *New Left Review* (July–August, 1984), pp. 53–92; F. Jameson, *Postmodernism, or, The Cultural Logic of Late Capitalism* (London and New York: Verso, 1991).

On 'late capitalism' see Jameson, *Postmodernism*, pp. xviii–xxii. The key influence on Jameson's use of 'late capitalism' was E. Mandel, *Late Capitalism* (London: Verso, 1975).

7. See also Jameson, *Postmodernism*, pp. xx–xxi.
8. D. Harvey, *The Condition of Postmodernity* (Oxford: Blackwell, 1989), e.g. pp. 189, 327–28.
9. See also Jameson, *Postmodernism*, pp. 3–6, 260–78.
10. Harvey, *Condition of Postmodernity*, pp. 147–51.
11. Harvey, *Condition of Postmodernity*, pp. 156, 171.
12. In addition to Jameson, *Postmodernism* and Harvey, *Condition of Postmodernity*, see esp. Harvey, *Neoliberalism*. See also D. Harvey, *The New Imperialism* (Oxford: Oxford University Press, 2003); D. Harvey, *The Enigma of Capital and the Crises of Capitalism* (London: Profile Books, 2010). For a general introduction to related approaches see Anderson, *Postmodernity*, pp. 54–81.
13. Anderson, *Postmodernity*, pp. 88–89.
14. Eagleton, *Illusions of Postmodernism*, p. 124.
15. See further J. G. Crossley, *Jesus in an Age of Terror: Scholarly Projects for a New American Century* (London and Oakville: Equinox, 2008), pp. 25–52, 58–142.
16. E. Hobsbawm, 'Reflections on Anarchism (1969)', in idem, *Revolutionaries* (New York: New Press, 2001), pp. 97–108 (98–100, 105). The reflections on 1968 of Chomsky, a serious thinker strongly influenced by anarcho-syndicalism and who came to prominence as arguably the major critic of American and corporate power in the aftermath of 1968, are more nuanced, though not uncritical. See N. Chomsky, 'Noam Chomsky on 1968', *New Statesman* (8 May, 2008), http://www.newstatesman.com/politics/2008/05/iraq-war-chomsky-1968-vietnam.
17. E.g. M. Bakunin, *Selected Works* (New York: Alfred A. Knopf, 1972), pp. 283–84.
18. Cf. e.g. Anderson, *Postmodernity*, pp. 27–36, 53–54.
19. Harvey, *Neoliberalism*, p. 47. Cf. Jameson, *Postmodernism*, pp. 261, 263, 265–66, 278.
20. Again, there is much more to the definition and origins of neoliberalism than can be discussed here. See further e.g. D. Plehwe, B. J. A. Walpen and G. Neunhoffer (eds.), *Neoliberal Hegemony: A Global Critique* (London: Routledge, 2007). On the intellectual origins of neoliberalism see P. Mirowski and D. Plehwe (eds.), *The Road from Mont Pelerin: The Making of the Neoliberal Thought Collective* (Cambridge, MA: Harvard University Press, 2009).
21. Harvey, *Neoliberalism*, pp. 41–44, 69–70; N. Chomsky, *What We Say Goes: Conversations on U.S. Power in a Changing World* (New York: Metropolitan, 2007), pp. 38–39.
22. Harvey, *Neoliberalism*, pp. 67–81.
23. N. Chomsky, *Understanding Power* (New York: New Press, 2002), p. 256.
24. For further details see e.g. N. Klein, *The Shock Doctrine: The Rise of Disaster Capitalism* (London: Allen Lane, 2007), pp. 136–40. Cf. Jameson, *Postmodernism*, p. 5: 'this whole global, yet American, postmodern culture is the internal and superstructural expression of a whole new wave of American

military and economic domination throughout the world: in this sense, as throughout class history, the underside of culture is blood, torture, death, and terror'. On imperialism beyond nationalism see M. Hardt and A. Negri, *Empire* (Cambridge, MA and London: Harvard University Press, 2000).
25. Harvey, *Neoliberalism*, pp. 43–45.
26. See further Klein, *Shock Doctrine*, pp. 49–128.
27. See Harvey, *Neoliberalism*, pp. 40–41.
28. A point effectively avoided in the all-too-convenient history in P. Blond, *Red Tory: How Left and Right Have Broken Britain and How We Can Fix It* (London: Faber and Faber, 2010).
29. Cf. R. Seymour, *The Meaning of David Cameron* (Winchester and Washington: Zero Books, 2010), pp. 45–61.
30. N. Chomsky, '2004 Elections', *ZNet* (November 29, 2004), http://www.zcommunications.org/2004-elections-by-noam-chomsky. See also N. Chomsky and G. Achcar, *Perilous Power: The Middle East and U.S. Foreign Policy* (Boulder and London: Paradigm Publishers, 2007), p. 31.
31. Compare Eric Hobsbawm's punchy analysis (while perhaps turning a blind eye to his traditional Marxist partisanship) on one reason for the rise of Thatcherism: 'It was moved not only by the justified belief that the British economy needed a kick in the pants but by class feeling, by what I called "the anarchism of the lower middle class"' (E. Hobsbawm, *Interesting Times: A Twentieth Century Life* [London: Abacus, 2002], p. 273).
32. See also Seymour, *Cameron*, pp. 67–73.
33. E. P. Thompson, *The Poverty of Theory and Other Essays* (London: Merlin Press, 1978), p. 300.
34. S. Žižek, *First as Tragedy, Then as Farce* (London and New York: Verso, 2009).
35. For the tragic and devastating consequences of the neoliberal-neoconservative approach to the reconstruction of Iraq see the accounts in N. Klein, 'Baghdad Year Zero: Pillaging Iraq in Pursuit of a Neocon Utopia', *Harper's* (September 2004), pp. 43–53; Klein, *Shock Doctrine*, pp. 323–82.
36. W. Brown, *Regulating Aversion: Tolerance in the Age of Identity and Empire* (Princeton: Princeton University Press, 2006) shows, among other things, the links between tolerance, liberalism, terror and empire. On neoliberalism and individualism see e.g. pp. 17–19.
37. Žižek, *First as Tragedy, Then as Farce*, p 66. Compare also Žižek's (in)famous analysis of Buddhism in idem, *The Puppet and the Dwarf: The Perverse Core of Christianity* (Cambridge, MA: MIT Press, 2003), e.g. pp. 20–33.
38. S. Žižek, *Welcome to the Desert of the Real! Five Essays on September 11 and Related Dates* (London and New York: Verso, 2002), p. 71. See more generally S. Žižek, *The Sublime Object of Ideology* (London and New York: Verso, 1989).
39. N. Klein, 'Put Away the Cuddly Toys. Now It's Time to Get Tough', *Guardian* (3 March, 2003).
40. P. Elkind, 'The Trouble with Steve Jobs', *CNN Money* (5 March 2008), http://money.cnn.com/2008/03/02/news/companies/elkind_jobs.fortune/index.htm.
41. A. Grice, 'Sir Gus O'Donnell: "People Make Better Policy Advisers If They Have Been on the Front Line"', *Independent* (19 December, 2005); M.-A. Sieghart, 'Radio 4 Profile: Sir Gus O'Donnell, Cabinet Secretary', *BBC News* (2 March, 2010), http://news.bbc.co.uk/1/hi/uk_politics/8543950.stm.

42. On the underlying logic of what follows see the complementary M. Dillon and J. Reid, *The Liberal Way of War: Killing to Make Life Live* (New York and London: Routledge, 2009).
43. R. Seymour, *The Liberal Defence of Murder* (London and New York: Verso, 2008).
44. Cf. Žižek, *First as Tragedy, Then as Farce*, pp. 104–10.
45. B. Obama, 'Remarks by the President on a New Beginning', The White House: Office of the Press Secretary (2009), http://www.whitehouse.gov/the-press-office/remarks-president-cairo-university-6-04-09.
46. See further J. G. Crossley, *Reading the New Testament: Contemporary Approaches* (London and New York: Routledge, 2010), pp. 126–28.

Chapter 3

Biblioblogging: Connected Scholarship[1]

For those who may still be in the dark, 'biblioblogging' is a popular phenomenon in the world of biblical scholarship. The term simply refers to the activities biblical scholars, ranging from interested amateurs through to famous professors, blogging on the Bible (known collectively as 'bibliobloggers') which took off in the previous decade. Biblioblogs now number, remarkably, in the hundreds.[2] They also seem to be popular among biblical scholars, and not simply because people regularly encounter biblical scholars who read blogs. By August 26, 2008, Mark Goodacre's NT Blog received four million visits since 2 September, 2003.[3] Biblioblogging is one of the most helpful ways of showing the connections between scholarship and contemporary cultural trends partly for the reason of a tendency towards explicitness on a range of topics. Through biblioblogging, the conventional constraints of academic publishing are considerably looser and it means bloggers can be overtly political and engage with a whole range of cultural and current events. Furthermore, it is intimately tied in with the tendencies of the mainstream media and it regularly mimics and replicates the very style of (for instance) newspapers, the online versions of which also typically have a number of blogs. At the same time, blogging is still part of the public persona of the scholar (and here I would contrast it with personal politics) and so it becomes an ideal collection of material for testing the role of ideology and cultural trends in contemporary scholarship.

I examined this in detail in *Jesus in an Age of Terror* with particular reference to Herman and Chomsky's propagandist approach to the mass media.[4] The Propaganda Model was largely designed to analyse the traditional mainstream mass media and show how the press is not really an important tool of democracy and it is not significantly disagreeable, argumentative or subversive of corporate and state power. The function of the mass media, according to Herman and Chomsky, is to provide support for the special interests dominating the state and private activity. Although individuals may hold very different views from the agendas of the mass media – and this 'contradiction' is a crucial point, as we saw in chapter 1 and will develop again in part III – these views will not be seriously reflected in the overall agendas. Fundamental dissent is largely missing from the press: it is more likely to be squeezed towards the back pages or left to some marginalized press. Censorship effectively becomes self-censorship behind the rhetoric of free and open debate. Thus, Herman and Chomsky borrow the loaded phrase 'manufacturing consent'.

When this approach was developed with reference to biblioblogging, it was clear that the dominant trends in the American mass media concerning US foreign policy (e.g. Israel and Palestine, 'war on terror' and so on) were replicated among the bibliobloggers, even though, obviously, the corporate backing is only really found in the mainstream media. There were a very small minority of exceptions, but these were typically marginalized or ignored. What I want to test in this chapter are the ways in which the neoliberal dominance (and the relevant cultural tendencies) of the contemporary mass media is replicated on the biblioblogs. In particular, there are two issues which involve some of the key topics on neoliberalism and postmodernity that we covered in the previous chapter. The most serious concerns the horrific 2010 earthquake in Haiti which killed over 100,000 people and which brought about some thoughtful reactions on the biblioblogs, but also a covering up of the effects of neoliberalism which appear to have played no small part in the disastrous aftermath. In particular, this masking involved the ways in which vague concepts relating to 'religion', 'Scripture' and 'God' can be brought in to cover over some of the uncomfortable issues surrounding external involvement in human suffering.

The second case concerns what might seem at first sight a highly unusual moment in the history of critical biblical studies: the brief but spectacular online blog run by the pseudonymous biblioblogger, N. T. Wrong. Wrong is significant for a number of reasons, but for our purposes Wrong is primarily significant because this blogger explicitly brought forward a number of views challenging the dominant political and ideological tendencies on the biblioblogs. The reactions among some of the other biblioblogger are crucial because not only is further masking of political tendencies apparent, but the emphasis is clearly shifted to those most postmodern of concerns: the body, personal surveillance and a shifting of the radical to the cheekily subversive.

'Religion', 'Scripture' and 'God': The Importance of Being Vague

With ideas of manufacturing consent also hovering in the background, Russell McCutcheon has pointed out an ideological function of defining 'religion'.[5] The prioritizing of an 'inner' religion over 'external' practices, no matter how well masked by scholars of religion, is a significant move. Not only can it remove the involvement of that thing we call 'religion' from the messier worlds of society and history, it also buys into a discourse of liberal democracy and Western capitalism, hence popular phrases like 'true Islam' function to extract only those things deemed palatable. In other words, we have an echo of Žižek's analysis of the Other welcomed but without the nasty bits, an issue we will discuss further in chapters 5 and 6. Here 'religion' functions as something that has to be private and non-threatening.

A notable twist on this view of 'religion' comes via Richard Dawkins no less. At first his approach seems very different, but on closer inspection has an obviously related ideological function which we will explore further in chapter 7. On 15 September, 2001, just four days after the attacks on the Twin Towers, Dawkins provided an analysis of the motivations.[6] Getting people to kill themselves in such a way is extremely difficult in itself. Rational human beings, Dawkins argues, do not do such things. Dawkins surmises that this can only be explained by 'religion', a 'ready-made system of mind-control' with a devaluing effect on the life of others. By Dawkins's rationale, if we could accept that death is the end, the rational agent would not be so keen to risk their life and the world would be a safer place. According to Dawkins, 'Religion is also, of course, the underlying source of the divisiveness in the Middle East which motivated the use of this deadly weapon in the first place.' This is a common use of 'religion' (compare the old cliché, 'religion causes all wars') in New Atheist circles and it is constantly used at the expense of history and the socially embedded nature of 'religion'.[7] If we want a fuller explanation of September 11, presumably we need to turn to a whole complex of socio-historical and geo-political explanations: the specifics of Saudi Arabian contexts, the decline of secular nationalism in North Africa and the Middle East, US foreign policy in the Middle East and so on. Dawkins's 'religion' covers over the sheer complexities underlying murderous acts and, potentially, any complicity on 'our' part.

In such instances, then, 'religion' functions as a sufficiently vague category which can manufacture consent and cover over those political issues which are problematic in terms of the Propaganda Model. This ideologically significant use of vague categories is echoed in related concepts such as 'Scripture' and even 'God'. The dominant use of 'Scripture' in contemporary American political discourse (and beyond) is part of what Yvonne Sherwood calls the 'Liberal Bible', an interpretative tradition developing since the sixteenth and seventeenth centuries.[8] The Liberal Bible is a Bible supportive of 'freedom of conscience', 'rights', law and consensus, and marks a shift from the Absolute Monarchist's Bible where decisions made by the monarch were to be seen as proof of divine power. It usually follows from this perspective that the Bible and Jesus are more representative of democracy than the Qur'an and Muhammad and so, predictably, the Liberal Bible is able to support actions against its constructed opposite (undemocratic, tyrannical and terroristic). Perhaps because of no obvious link with modern democracy in the Bible, and functioning as a way of concealing its early modern origins, another significant development of the Liberal Bible is that (successful) readings are consistently vague and difficult to pin down.[9]

Vagueness is important because no major politician *really* uses the Bible for key foreign policy decisions and so a (successful) allusion to the Bible can woo certain voters and deflect attention from the more difficult issues.[10] As we have seen and will continue to see throughout this book, it is frequently in liberal rhetoric and liberal circles where power is credibly maintained, covering over and deflecting as well as any other mode of discourse. This vague use of liberal biblical reference can, of course, be developed with reference to that arch liberal, Barak Obama, where, as we saw in the previous chapter, rather than a mere Liberal Bible, we got something like Liberal Holy Writings covering three faiths and more! And this scripturally laden speech, we recall, was delivered in a then-American-backed police state.

The 2010 Haiti Earthquake and Theodicy

In fear of over-emphasis, what the vague concepts of 'Scripture', 'religion' and 'God' are effective at doing, then, is brushing over any problematic politics and providing ideologically convenient narratives for consumption. This can be effective when it comes to natural disasters. Alice Bach makes reference to 'Bush's Bible' in the aftermath of Hurricane Katrina where Bush spoke about a natural disaster in the hands of God.[11] God, Bush claimed in a speech to the National Cathedral in New Orleans, works in mysterious ways, suffering is mysterious, God's purposes are sometimes impossible to know, but God will always care.

Bach points out that a lack of human preparedness was a major problem in the flooding of the streets and Bush said nothing about governmental inaction and contribution to human suffering. Resort to God, it seems, means blame can be shifted to a vague generalization about mystery with which many believers would not disagree in the abstract.

We can find similar things happening in the reflection on the tragic events surrounding the Haiti earthquake. The broad narrative found in the mainstream media is well summarized by Roland Boer: 'depictions of the disaster have mostly fallen into set patterns: the poorest nation in the hemisphere, chaos, looting, collapsed infrastructure, loony fundamentalists blaming the Haitians for the punishment for their sins, heroic salvage efforts by altruistic states, the collapse of government, the need for external forces to reassert law and order'.[12] These set patterns are, to some extent, replicated on the biblioblogs, though it is worth adding that there was nothing like the widespread conclusion in the media that looting in Haiti was part of a mysterious violent streak in Haitian history, a view brilliantly satirized by Charlie Brooker.[13] It is certainly clear that bibliobloggers were, as would be expected, deeply moved by the earthquake.[14] April DeConick's reaction was perhaps the simplest but no less poignant for it.[15] She expressed her horror and great concern before immediately giving a link and suggestions for people to provide aid. Others blogs, however, were not quite as forthright in terms of practical advice and one of the notable reactions, and probably predictable given the high number of Christian bibliobloggers, was much soul searching on the age-old question of theodicy. As with the above concepts of religion, Scripture and God, vagueness helps guide the reflections.

On a more overtly theological blog, *Metanoia*, Craig Uffman asked a question repeated on biblioblogs, 'where was God in the earthquake?', before giving the best answers to an impossible question.[16] Steve Wiggins likewise discussed a world where many innocent suffer, as well as many guilty, and 'how a loving God and divine fairness fit into such a warped and corrupted system presents questions often left unanswerable'.[17] Even with Job, he conceded, the 'best that the narrator can offer is that Yahweh made a bet with the Satan and Job came out on the losing end. Not much hope for justice there.' In the context of Haiti, 'this poorest of western hemisphere nations', the 'question of where God is amid all this tragedy, perhaps 100,000 dead, pensively teeters in minds sensitive to the human condition.' Celucien Joseph even wrote a poem on Haiti ('Haiti: the Land of bitter tears!'), questioning why Haiti had to suffer again and raised the usual theodicy problems but ultimately wrote of 'God of our forgotten trial, / Unconditional mercy and unreserved love… / Upon the Lord above, in hope our soul shall rest / Standing tall at thy summit… / Lest we forget Thee… / Lead us into thy Light… / Toward freedom we shall march… / Oh God of our weary years'.[18] Ben Witherington also asked the questions relating to 'Where was God in all this?' He weighed in against the idea 'of some sort of automatic correlation between disaster and one's moral condition or beliefs' (Lk 13:8; Jn 9:1–5), arguing that causation in suffering is complex. He also turned to Elijah, pointing out that God was not present in the natural disasters seen by Elijah but God is present among his followers rushing to aid people. After a lengthy discussion, Witherington was at pains to point out that God does care and that humans can cause suffering but ultimately concluding, 'more than this we do not know, and cannot rightly say'.[19] Ultimately, then, we are back to a caring God moving in mysterious ways.

Questioning the Dominant Narrative

What we have in these examples is something similar to what Alice Bach saw in Bush's use of 'God' in the aftermath of Katrina, though we can say that, unlike Bush (or his team) these biblioblogger's hearts were more likely to be in the right place. In terms of the Haiti earthquake, there was little in the way of opposing narratives or analysis of the ideological function of the dominant media narratives. Jim Linville came close with something along the lines of a broader critique of dangerous cultural constructions of a corporate guilt tied in with religious language, but did not go as far as applying it to the politics of Haiti.[20] In his poem, Celucien Joseph did write of '200 years of failed justice and false hopes / Of foreign uses and abuses of Ayiti Cherie', but, no doubt partly constrained by the poetic form, there was no further elaboration.

Ben Witherington was certainly critical of the US role, emphasizing as he does the causal role of humanity in suffering, but it is a critique which has more bark than bite:

> Haiti has been a disaster happening and waiting to happen for ever. Had most of the buildings in Port au Prince been strengthened or rebuilt to withstand such disasters, literally millions of people would have been less likely to be harmed in that city by what has just happened. And we have known about these problems in our own backyard for decades. For decades now the U.S. would rather throw good money after bad on military adventures in the Middle East and elsewhere when in fact with a fraction of what we have spent in the last decade on war the entire country of Haiti could have been rebuilt and given decent housing!!

> Yes its [sic] true. And these are our backdoor neighbors. But of course they do not have oil and other commodities to offer us, so we as a nation have largely ignored them and their cries for help, hoping that the piecemeal efforts of small U.N. and Christian agencies would pick up the slack – which they have been unable to do, so overwhelmed have they been by the grinding indigenous poverty and needs of that whole country, not to mention governmental corruption over many decades.[21]

While hardly wanting to downplay the problematic role of the USA in the Middle East, it is significant that Witherington does not, in the specific case of Haiti, extend this critique to direct *outside* involvement in Haiti, which is known, not least due to the overthrow of Jean-Bertrand Aristide's government in 2004. Witherington's mention of 'indigenous poverty' seems too undefined to be useful, though it clearly helps deflect any issues of outside impact on poverty, while 'governmental corruption' appears to reference the Haitian rather than outside governments. But Witherington's analysis of the politics reveals little new. A more explicit conclusion is that of John Hobbins. Hobbins cites a *New York Times* article by David Brooks which argues for unashamed paternalism.[22] While other countries have faced colonialism, Brooks adds, Haiti is still worse off. And so he echoes an argument used to describe the Middle East: the reason cannot really be socio-economic or political; it must be something else, like...'voodoo'. This curious blend of Pat Robertson (see below) and Richard Dawkins (see above) is then developed by Hobbins, who claims:

> Brooks goes on to point out that voodoo religion is a contributing underlying cause to the unfolding tragedy. An inconvenient truth: not all religions are created equal. Some religions are moralistic and demanding and uplift their adherents. Other religions have more in common with party politics. They are about handicapping the other guy, and giving yourself an unfair advantage. They breed what Brooks calls 'social mistrust' and irresponsibility.[23]

By contrast, the clearest example of a critique of the dominant positions came from Roland Boer: 'Depressing, isn't it? Not just the havoc wreaked on a nation battered by neo-colonialism, but the way depictions of the disaster have mostly fallen into set patterns...the need for external forces to reassert law and order...with 10,000 troops!! That's an invasion.'[24] What is significant about the remarks of Boer is that they are an isolated phenomenon across the biblioblogs, not dissimilar to those rare bibliob-logging voices deeply critical of American foreign policy I previously discussed. Boer provided three blog entries and there were some comments left in the comments section (2, 8 and 2, respectively, though a total of 5 from Boer himself). As might be expected, these are lower numbers than those generated on other blogs (compare 107 comments on Witherington's post!).

Interestingly, Boer also made reference to one of those dissenting voices now creeping into the mainstream media, at least in the UK, namely Peter Hallward, an expert on Haitian politics. Hallward published a grim account of the problems in Haiti.[25] His account did not brush over the politically problematic. We might add that Chomsky, who has also been writing on, and involved with, Haiti for years, was also providing a different analysis of the situation along similar lines.[26]

Hallward argued that this most calamitous disaster in Haitian history 'is best understood as another thoroughly manmade outcome of a long and ugly historical sequence'. He argued that the long-term impact of the 2010 earthquake will include the result of a long-term history of 'deliberate impoverishment and disempowerment' in what is regularly called the 'poorest country in the western hemisphere'. This harsh poverty is the direct legacy of 'perhaps the most brutal system of colonial exploitation in world history, compounded by decades of systematic postcolonial oppression'. Moreover, the 'international community', with its concerns for humanitarian aid, has played its part in the suffering. The USA and allies have consistently been involved, sometimes violently, in Haitian history since the US invasion and occupation in 1915. Working conditions are terrible. Hallward notes that the best evidence suggests around 75 per cent of the population lives on less than $2 per day and 56 per cent on less than $1, and how neoliberal intervention has 'robbed its government of any significant capacity to invest in its people or to regulate its economy'. Since the 1970s, neoliberal policies have forced tens of thousands of small farmers into overcrowded urban slums and too many inhabitants of Port-au-Prince live in 'desperately sub-standard informal housing, often perched precariously on the side of deforested ravines'. The basic infrastructure of Port-au-Prince, including running water, electricity and roads, is minimal, hardly the best start for disaster relief. Tellingly, the storms which killed so many Haitians in 2008 also hit Cuba, which has not had the impact of neoliberal reforms, but killed 'only' four people.[27] With Hallward's comments in mind, Chomsky's perception of the US media portrayal following the earthquake is unsurprising ('It's been mainly awful') and the 'worst part is ignoring our own disgraceful role in helping to create the catastrophe, and consequent refusal to react as any decent person should – with massive reparations, directed to popular organizations.'[28]

The analyses of Hallward and Chomsky obviously paint a detailed and more disturbing picture of the suffering in Port-au-Prince and one of the functions of the media portrayals of the disaster (intentionally or not) is largely to brush over such issues and focus on vague metaphysical questions of why humans suffer, sometimes followed by the narrative that the subsequent looting was the result of something violent in Haitian history, thereby allowing neoliberal ideology to continue without any serious questioning. We should now recall what we have read on some of the reactions among the biblioblogs. While there was, obviously, genuine concern for human suffering, we typically saw general thoughts on humans causing suffering in abstract terms, the role of God among aid workers, the not-unexpected soul searching and concern to defend (or attack) God's role, and even blaming (a certain form of) religion for poor infrastructure. Plenty of 'why questions' were asked on the blogs, mostly of God, instead of looking for answers closer to home. Earnest reflections on God, religion and Scripture continue to be excellent ways of covering over the more gruesome and uncomfortable details of this terrible tragedy.

Why We All Love to Hate Pat Robertson

In chapter 1, we saw, with reference to figures such as Jörg Haider and Nick Griffin, a key ideological function of the far right: to bolster the benevolence and credibility of the centre and the liberal consensus. In the case of Haiti, the hate figure was the right-wing American evangelical, Pat Robertson. Robertson infamously claimed as a 'true story' that the Haitians 'swore a pact to the Devil' to drive out the French and ever since they have been cursed.[29] Like the widespread media reporting of this somewhat 'distinctive' take on history, there was strong condemnation across several biblioblogs with plenty of further condemnation in the comments sections.[30] Terri, on *Wheat among Tares*, not unfairly pointed out that Robertson is 'always reliable for inappropriate, stupid responses to natural disasters', and concluded bluntly, 'Where is that spontaneous bolt of lightning from heaven when it's needed?'[31] Steve Wiggins fired at 'drivel, based on hearsay history and implicit racism, does not justify a loving, or even neutral, God' and 'idiotic platitudes that only drive mourning theists closer to the other side.'[32] This deity of the Religious Right has been truly revealed as 'racist, supersessionist, arrogant, and uncaring'. Scott Bailey, who spoke of his rage when reading Robertson's comments, suggested that we should see Satan as Robertson's theological mentor and he would have been happy for someone to punch Robertson hard. In the face of the huge number of lives lost and the destruction of lives and families, Bailey, with obvious justification, let fly with the polemic.[33]

From the 'secular'/atheist wing of biblioblogging, the polemic was, unsurprisingly, no less fierce, and again not dissimilar to Dawkins's construction of 'religion'. Jim Linville spoke of Robertson's comments as 'vile' and looked at the history being interpreted by Robertson. Linville suggested that Robertson might be picking up on an old tradition that Haitian spiritualists once made sacrifices in their bid for freedom from the French. Robertson annoyed Linville on a number of levels. Linville did not like the 'smug-ass self-righteous apocalyptic world-view in which everything happens happens to prove him right' and the idea of corporate guilt for the sacrifice of a couple of animals two-hundred years ago. True to his atheist background, Linville was also scathing of the role of religion which claims 'an illusory "higher purpose" that does nothing [to] alleviate suffering but to help people ignore it, or, worse, enjoy it when it happens to others'. Furthermore, Linville believes (again, not unreasonably) that by 'merely mentioning that Robertson is "controversial" and not a total fucking wack-job, the mainstream media lets him get away with it'. For good measure, Linville even put a picture of a horse's arse with Pat Robertson's name beneath it to illustrate his point![34] John Loftus, consistently more aggressive towards Christianity than the more playful Linville, decided that Robertson's comments were 'Reason 1,937 why I want nothing to do with Christianity'.[35]

This is not, of course, to defend Robertson in any way nor even to disagree with the general view on the biblioblogs – Robertson's 'thinking outside the box' is hardly the greatest contribution to understanding Haiti. Again, the point is to look at his ideological function. The constant criticisms of Robertson played their part in the manufacturing of catastrophe, a part of the established narrative, as Boer pointed out. It is, again, part of the role that the conveniently vague constructions 'God', 'Scripture' and 'religion' play deflecting the issues well away from the ongoing destruction of Haiti and the involvement of an aggressive neoliberal agenda and colonial powers up to and including the present. In more general terms, this manufacturing of catastrophe among bibliobloggers replicates the ways in which both the mainstream media constructs stories to reflect neoliberal interests and the ways in which biblioblogging has also bought into broader patterns in the mainstream media on the issue of the subtle neoliberal consensus. As ever, what is important to stress is that the more direct corporate backing for the mainstream media is not present in biblioblogging, so, while the replication of the mainstream media may well continue indefinitely, it is by no means a necessity. But with the function of academia and its own fuzzier connections with state and corporate power, major change is hardly guaranteed. For such reasons, the connections between biblioblogging, conventional scholarship and neoliberalism remain significant.

We will continue this analysis of masking but, in addition to seeing the ways in which the more challenging views are ostracized, we will look at how biblioblogers (presumably unconsciously) deal with direct confrontation of more politically radical views and how radical gets blunted to become culturally subversive.

*N. T. Wrong and the Biblioblogger*s

> **Jim West**: What, may I ask, are your professional goals?
> **N. T. Wrong**: To reconfigure the manner in which biblical studies is carried out in the entire world.[36]

Biblioblogging tends to be conservative in both intellectual and religious terms, with scholars such as N. T. Wright, Walter *Brueggemann*, Bruce Malina and John Meier being perennial favourites and with the bloggers being generally white, middle class, aged 20s-40s and male,[37] though there are a number of both intellectual and religious blogs we might deem more 'liberal' (see below). While possibly a white, middle class, male aged between 20 and 50, for all that is known, in April 2008 the very antithesis of the archetypal biblioblogger, at least in terms of intellectual and religious ideas, burst on to the scene with an array of satirical, humorous and sometimes controversial posts before finally bowing out in February 2009. I am speaking, of course, of the infamous pseudonymous blogger N. T. 'Tom' Wrong.[38]

The identity of Wrong has been the subject of some debate (some serious, some humorous) and with this in mind I should point out right now that I am emphatically *not* Wrong, as much as I wish I had thought of the idea. Without wanting to continue the quest for the historical Wrong, some comments on Wrong's online personality can be made without establishing the true identity of this pseudonymous blogger. Wrong is happily blasphemous (or at least happily prepared to mock the sacred), regularly swears (unlike most biblioblogers), discusses topics most bloggers might deem risqué (more on that later, fear not) and pokes fun at numerous biblical scholars (e.g. Eisenmann, Dever, Witherington and, of course, N. T. Wright). I would guess that Wrong is a non-believer but it is certainly fair to say that religion and fundamentalism (of whatever religion) were and are frequently teased. Wrong is no atheist apologist though. Of Hector Avalos, author of the controversial and provocative book, *The End of Biblical Studies*, Wrong claimed, 'Once a fundie always a fundie. He's just batting for the other side, now... Avalos is a fundie in manner and to a lesser extent in content. In manner, he is doctrinaire about his own beliefs, with a tendency to generalise about the opposition.'[39]

Wrong is comfortable with broader interdisciplinary work, including that of Talal Asad, Walter Benjamin, Slavoj Žižek and Edward Said, and areas such as postcolonialism and critical theory in general, along with ideological critiques of scholarship. Wrong is just as comfortable with more traditional historical critical approaches to the Bible as well as ancient Near Eastern archaeology and is clearly what is conventionally labelled 'minimalist' ('maximalist' was deemed a swear word by Wrong). Wrong seems to be an expert in Hebrew Bible and early Judaism but is still in the comfort zone in New Testament studies, with posts ranging from topics such as the *pistis christou* debate to Jesus' resurrection. It is highly likely that we are dealing with a trained biblical scholar (a point admitted by Wrong in an interview[40]) and easily one of the most broadly learned and intellectually sophisticated of any of the bibliobloggers.

Surveillance and the Politics of Wrong

> Surveillance has become ubiquitous and taken for granted in today's world. It appears in many sectors of life, not necessarily in some developmental order, but in each certain features are displayed: rationalization, the application of science and technology, classification and knowledgeabilty of subjects...the internet provides games and spaces where surveillance may be explored as well as experienced... In the worlds of theme parks and shopping malls, too, surveillance is not merely an external process but something participatory. The overlapping and cross-cutting cultures of surveillance may be reinforced and normalized by their interactions with entertainment media... Because of the widespread, systematic and routine ways in which personal data are processed in the twenty-first century, it is appropriate to talk of the 'surveillance society'.
>
> – David Lyon[41]

This sort-of-biographical material is important because, as we will see, it becomes part of the focus of the controversies surrounding N. T. Wrong in the world of biblioblogging, in contrast to what might be considered to be controversial, namely, Wrong's politics. Wrong's political output has been highly critical of the 'war on terror' and the cultural support it has amassed in the form of a 'hideously emboldened Orientalism'.[42] Wrong has also been fiercely critical of uncritical support for Israeli state policies towards Palestinians.

Wrong's openly expressed politics are at odds with almost all the world of biblioblogging. As mentioned in passing above, when I discussed the function of political trends among bibliobloggers in *Jesus in an Age of Terror*, key areas of the contemporary application of the Propaganda Model were covered, such as Iraq, the Middle East, the 'war on terror', the myth of unique suffering, stereotyping of Muslims and Arabs, and Israel and Palestine. In each case, biblioblogging overwhelmingly came down in support of dominant positions in the Anglo-American mass media and among the supportive political and intellectual elites, though not infrequently in direct contrast to views of the general public. This support included: endorsement or avoidance of the Iraq war; a strongly pro-Israeli line over against Palestinians; highlighting of the suffering of British and Americans with no expressed concern for the suffering of victims of American power in the 'war on terror', in some cases even when bibliobloggers were confronted directly with such evidence; and even somehow placing the explicitly anti-Bush N. T. Wright on the side of George W. Bush, alongside 'maximalist' scholars of the Hebrew Bible, and against scholars deemed too intellectually and politically liberal, including the 'minimalist' scholars of the Hebrew Bible! Alternative views were typically either ignored or rejected.[43]

These ideas can now be developed further, particularly as ever-new means of media communication related to blogging (e.g. Facebook, Twitter) are being used by biblical scholars. In particular, it is helpful to see those mundane ways in which cultural and political power is maintained and developed and the subtle ways in which propaganda infuses democratic states.[44] As we have seen, and will develop further in part III, part of the Propaganda Model is the idea that journalists, intellectuals, academics and so on are not necessarily intentionally buying into the system (though some might) and that as individuals they may well hold different views from the propaganda system, but it typically remains true that the dominant ideological positions are perpetuated.

With such ideas relating to the unintentional in mind, we might recall ideas about societal and cultural surveillance from the previous chapter and how they have been rapidly developing in our age of neoliberalism, neoconservativism and postmodernity.[45] Surveillance is central to modern societies and democratic systems for categorizing, group shaping, boundary guarding, social control, social predicting (are you a *potential* suspect?) and an ever-increasing observation of the individual or the group in an array of cultural contexts. These contexts might include: endless political debates over 'liberties' versus 'security'; the controversial USA Patriot Act; the ever-increasing use of CCTV surveillance cameras on British high streets; the use of GPS from hikers to concerned parents; loyalty cards (perfect for establishing consumer profiles); the rise and rise of the reality television genre (e.g. *Big Brother*); celebrity-driven tabloids and magazines; and even the academic categorization and 'overview' such as that given by this author.[46]

Further in line with our postmodern age, and indeed within certain strands of neoliberalism, are those often unintentional and highly personalized forms of surveillance. One of the most popular academic examples of what David Lyon calls 'postmodern surveillance' is bodily surveillance, the most notable examples of which involve fitness, calorie counting, weights, running times, muscle development and so on, a general phenomenon rising dramatically from the 1980s onwards.[47] But probably one of the most remarkable instances (at least in terms of success) of unintentional conformity to a general system of surveillance has to be the emergence of social networking and micro-blogging sites such as Facebook and Twitter. With such examples we can find not only masses of personal details stored about countless and often willing individuals – infamously convenient for marketing purposes – but also a means of keeping an eye on the whereabouts of the individual and monitoring of employees by employers. Online gossiping behind the boss's back is now riskier than ever, as a certain ambitious English footballer has found out to his dismay, though another was able to manipulate Twitter in order to orchestrate a big-money move to another club, no doubt aware his bosses would read his disgruntled 'tweets' (as it turned out they did)![48] And this issue has only continued to grow.

In terms of bibliobloggers we can, should we wish, regularly monitor the travel plans, eating habits, locations, swimming times and sporting interests, alongside the latest updates on biblical scholarship and biblioblog entries, on Facebook and Twitter.[49] On the biblioblogs, Michael Bird gave the most regimented daily timetable imaginable, from waking up at 7.00am and getting in to work at 8.15am, through German practice, prayer readings and collecting various pious writings at 8.30–8.50am, 8.50–9.00am, and 9.00–9.10am respectively, right up to an evening of book reviews, articles, research, devotionals, blogging and winding down, each given their allotted time.[50] This might be an extreme example, as some fellow bloggers pointed out, but others have still posted their timetables and many still blog where they have been, who they have seen, what they will be doing and what their precise short-term career and travel intentions are.[51] These are extremely common features on the biblioblogs.

It is now worth analysing Wrong in light of the above conclusions on propaganda and surveillance. Wrong does not fit into this model in terms of a pandering academic; quite the opposite, in fact. As Wrong has said to me in an email conversation (and, yes, I am blissfully aware of the absurdity), this character is 'a photo negative, more or less'.[52] In terms of surveillance, Wrong's identity remains a mystery and our masked hero has managed to escape capture and identification, which may account for much of the hostility towards Wrong. At best the person behind the mask seems to have been physically present at International SBL 2008 in Auckland, and at least promised to be physically present at Annual SBL 2008 in Boston, but these remain teasing because of the mystery person lurking behind the mask and his non-conformity to being precisely monitored has hardly gone unnoticed.[53] Even when some serious attempts by other bibliobloggers were made to find out who was behind the mask through tracing IP addresses and comparing Wrong's ideas and humour to known academics, Wrong stayed silent on any precise allegations of location and identity, adding,

> This was one of the most absurd things I've seen in a long time. There were dozens of posts dedicated to discovering N. T. Wrong's identity, thousands of words written, with greater or lesser degrees of seriousness. I loved it. I felt like I was watching from the box-seat at the theatre of the absurd. It was pure pathos at its most Pythonesque. Like waiting for Godot – who you deep down know will never come, but that's not the point. Brilliant. Thanks to all who orchestrated it, and to those – even more absurdly – who took it seriously.[54]

Wrong's anonymity provided an obvious means of avoiding the surveillance of the person behind Wrong, even inverting the surveillance by gazing at those trying to monitor the whereabouts and identity of the person behind Wrong, and thus constantly maintaining the 'photo negative' image, not least through what must be one of the oldest forms of those resisting being caught: taunting.

We can take this idea of a 'photo negative' further by analysing the key areas taken from the Propaganda Model when we look at Wrong's politics in more detail and when compared with other bibliobloggers. N. T. Wrong critiqued capitalism and resource exploitation in relation to the Middle East, satirized negative stereotyping of Arabs and Muslims in the American media and popular culture, a key area in the contemporary application of the Propaganda Model, and referenced arguments about how such stereotyping is part of the ways in which American soldiers tortured and abused Iraqi citizens.[55] Closer to biblical studies, Wrong ridiculed a picture used by Yigael Yadin with the caption 'A girl from North Africa felt "at home" operating the two grinding stones, which are over 3,000 years old.' Wrong, echoing Said, argued that such views suggest that the 'Arab world is unchanging, permanent, in contrast to Western progress and change'.[56] During the recent Israeli invasion of Gaza, Wrong wrote of

> any number of Hollywood terrorist films, American television shows, etc, in which the problem is always portrayed as crazed individuals arriving *ex nihilo* (or rather, arriving, from the primeval chaos out East) and the solution is conversely portrayed as the action of smart and justice-restoring individuals. The former is unglorified and complex; the latter is hyped, simplified to the level of the (dangerously widespread) shit-for-brains lowest common denominator of a viewer.[57]

Perhaps the most sensitive issue of all within the contemporary application of the Propaganda Model is that of Israel and Palestine. Yet Wrong was similarly forthright in his politics. Wrong, for instance, has fired at Christian Zionism and its uncritical support for Israel.[58] In terms of biblical studies, or related areas, he has been strongly critical of the alliance of Eilat Mazar, the Christian 'fundamentalism' of the unaccredited Armstrong College and support for Israeli nationalism through so-called 'biblical archaeology' in the discovery of a tunnel in Jerusalem which was tied in with the story of David (2 Sam. 5:6–8; 1 Chron. 11:4–6).[59] Wrong also defended Jewish groups in the UK, as well as a Palestinian group, opposed to Israeli policies towards Palestinians manifest in their Christmas carols attacking Israeli policy. Wrong defended certain members of the Church of England for allowing such an event to take place while mocking criticisms made by the Israeli ambassador and a number of what Wrong called 'bandwagon-riding half-arses' such as the former Archbishop of Canterbury George Carey.[60]

We might contrast this with one example of the pressure to conform (and there are plenty of others), namely, Chris Tilling and his nine-part series on Christian Zionism.[61] Tilling has been critical of Christian Zionism and was initially keen to show that it was not merely a theological curiosity because it 'impacts world politics'. He wrote explicitly of political issues surrounding the British Mandate, the founding of the State of Israel, Christian Zionist involvement in Israeli politics and so on. Tilling received plenty of emails and comments and it became clear that there was increasing pressure from Christian Zionists and others for him to not be critical (even before Tilling had made any judgment in some cases!), and so Tilling had to emphasize that he was more interested in theology and hermeneutics rather than politics. Eventually, the political issues were abandoned by Tilling and it seems to be that this was due to the pressure placed on him.

Presumably, applying such pressure on someone like Wrong would be difficult enough under normal circumstances and even more so given that it is a pseudonymous blog. As Wrong put it,

> It [blogging pseudonymously] gives you a degree of freedom to say what you really think, without worrying about what those who might employ you think. I encourage everybody to do it. In fact, most books should be published pseudonymously, too. Who doesn't want to write a scathing refutation of what they wrote ten years ago? I think it could encourage more open writing. It might also make it easier for people to approach works without bias against the author. It wouldn't help with The Man's academic publishing requirements – but you know what they can do.[62]

However, what I would argue is that Wrong was the exception that proves the 'rule', and only partly because the blog was pseudonymous and that this meant an alleviation of the pressures to conform and an ability to poke fun at attempts at surveillance. Wrong boosts the success of using the Propaganda Model for the analysis of blogging because his political output was more-or-less ignored. Certainly, there were occasional comments left on the blog, but Wrong's explicit politics were effectively 'dealt with' by other bloggers largely refusing to engage with them. It might be argued that biblioblogging is really only concerned with biblical studies and religion but we should not forget that there is a widespread concern for politics and political discussion, including almost immediate reactions to certain high profile news events. Wrong did not, therefore, *have* to be ignored because blog topics were supposedly too off-topic. It is in this sense that Wrong fits a pattern of political (non-) biblioblogging in the pre-Wrong years. This ignoring was seen, for instance, when the case of Falluja was raised and in the ways in which the July 7 murders in London were handled whereby any question of the possibility that foreign policy was involved was ignored and the British government was praised. On the July 7 murders (and Falluja for that matter), biblioblogers reflected the responses in the British press and by the British government but, notably, in direct contrast to the views of the majority of the British public.[63]

The Wrong Controversies

What also makes Wrong all the more significant for our purposes is the simple fact that there is now no ongoing N. T. Wrong blog, even though Wrong still lurks online. It is also possible to factor in some of the hostility towards Wrong's pseudonymous identity which frequently arose in comments sections on blogs (including Wrong's blog), alongside, perhaps, the quests for the real identity of Wrong and Stephen Carlson's raising of various potential problems for the career of pseudonymous bloggers.[64] Perhaps if Wrong's true identity were to have been revealed, the controversial posts would have been difficult to maintain. Some people may well have explicitly wanted to 'out' Wrong and/or get rid of Wrong, but we might speculate that this fits into the arguments made above in that, if successful, it would effectively contribute to the marginalizing of his views.

Perhaps. But whatever the reasons, we can certainly say that the overall effect of the reception of Wrong certainly marginalized his political views. This is especially highlighted by the ways in which Wrong has caused controversy and where he has made a number of bibliobloggers take note. Wrong, with tongue partly in cheek, listed 129 biblioblogs on a five-point scale from 'very conservative' to 'very liberal' using the following criteria:

1. Very conservative: You probably hold to the doctrine of inerrancy, or some version close to it. You can name a number of heresies offhand. And you have DA Carson, FF Bruce, or an Apollos Commentary in your bookshelf.
2. Fairly conservative: The Bible is 'The Word of God' in some sense. You have spent time wondering whether 'emergent' or 'emerging' better describes yourself. You have an NT Wright or James Dunn book in your bookshelf.

3. Conservative liberal: You really like the Jesus Seminar, and believe that what Jesus was really on about was people loving each other rather than condemning people. You have books by Marcus Borg and John Spong on your bookshelf.
4. Liberal: You esteem the Bible for the work it is. You spend a lot of time working out ways to read the Bible which can liberate it for different readers. You have a book on queer readings of the Bible on your bookshelf.
5. Very Liberal: You approach biblical books like any other books, taking the good stuff with the bad shit. You often stop and wonder why you bother with a field riddled with so many apologists. You have Foucault, Said, and Philip Pullman on your bookshelf.[65]

What John Lyons labelled 'an inspired burst of pedantic and nerdish endeavour',[66] this comical playing around with surveillance and categorization caused a notable amount of interest in both the comments section (42 comments on the first post, 40 comments on the follow up post) and on other blogs, many biblioblogers not a little touchy about their allotted label.[67] However, probably the most controversial legacy of N. T. Wrong was one word mentioned in his interview with Jim West:

> **JW**: What do you enjoy doing in your spare time?
> **NTW**: I read fiction. I recently quite enjoyed Darkmans by Nicola Barker. I quite like music such as Nick Cave, Conor Oberst, Iron & Wine, and Lily Allen. I like a good movie, too – I recently blahed out on Tom Tykwer movies on DVD. I do a bit of gardening, and aim to create a self-sufficient vegetable garden, and am currently preparing soil for the upcoming season. I also enjoy the occasional subversive art attack on cityscapes.
> **JW**: Do you have any secret hobbies or interests that our readers might find surprising?
> **NTW**: Fisting.

This *Brüno*-esque moment led to what can only be described as moral outrage or a defence against moral outrage. Some, such as David Ker, did not see this merely as a joke:

> It's one thing to slaughter a pig on the sacred altar. It's quite another to fall down and worship it. But that's in fact what has occurred at Biblioblogs.com. This august blog highlighting the best of Biblical scholars has featured a reprobate heretic and pervert as their featured blogger of the month… He confessed in the interview with Jim West that he has a special addiction for the most reprehensible sexual practice while claiming to be a husband and father… Who is this supposedly

> note-worthy blogger? Who should we as bloggers interested in the finest in Biblical studies look to as the apex of academia? It is the pseudonymous NT Wrong. NT Wrong is an excellent writer. He is a scholar of some distinction... He is vulgar in the extreme. Not satisfied to pepper his post with the most disgusting language, Wrong actually wrote a summary post proudly listing his wretched vocabulary...he [Jim West] positively slobbers all over a flaming pervert and two-bit scholar who does not even claim to be a believer in the Bible or the God of the Bible![68]

Mark Goodacre was not as outraged. He liked the interview but still had a notable reservation:

> The interview is actually very entertaining, and the anti-bishop reveals a bit more of his voice. He is clearly enjoying trying to see what he can get away with, though, since there is an obscenity of the kind that is surprising (and frankly not entirely welcome) in an academic venue.[69]

Goodacre later added,

> in linking to an article that includes an obscenity, I think it is important to mention the fact to my readers given that, by linking to it, I am encouraging them to go there. My general rule about blogging is that I avoid saying anything that I would not say in the classroom. That is my rule of thumb. I quite understand, of course, that others would feel differently.[70]

To underscore the controversial nature of this topic, a discussion of the controversy generated 145 comments both for and against, and about which Goodacre claimed we must be dealing with 'the longest comment thread of all time on the biblioblogs'.[71] Not only does the ability to shock such academics speak volumes about social locations and intellectual restrictions of biblioblogers, and perhaps biblical scholarship more widely, but it also shows that bloggers certainly do get heated and emotional about both personal and wider issues. This only amplifies the deafening volume of the silence on the political issues. Put one way, the aforementioned penetrative act is not, as far as I am aware, a topic which crops up in the Bible. Put another way, however, we could say that a concern with what biblical texts deem sexual immorality does, but then so do issues of Israel and the Other, as well as imperialism and Empire. Why does the sexual issue provoke all the debate and the political one not?

Here we have effectively seen the unintentional blunting of the politically radical edge of N. T. Wrong's blog so that for the bibliobloggers he becomes more subversive in the postmodern sense and does so by the switching of the focus to the body and those ruder parts of the body in particular. And 'by subversive in the postmodern sense', I am echoing Eagleton's critique of the more subversive scholarship in postmodernity: 'Conference papers entitled "Putting the anus back into *Coriolanus*" would attract hordes of excited acolytes who knew little about the bourgeoisie but a good deal about buggery... The radical impulse would not be abandoned; but it would shift gradually from the transformative to the subversive.'[72] Unfortunately, not even the great N. T. Wrong could prevent the combined might of cultural trends and the bibliobloggers from shaping what was to be done with his blog.

But one person can hardly overturn the system alone. So, at the same time, let us not be too disheartened: we should at least doff our caps before anyone who can wind up so many with consummate ease. After that poll of over 70 bibliobloggers asking for their top five most influential scholars, the results were collected and a top ten was compiled. N. T. Wright and Walter Brueggemann were one and two respectively in a top ten which also included James Dunn, Peter Enns, Gordon Fee and Bruce Malina.[73] With this celebration of conservatism in mind, Wrong's satirical blogging was like something from another, much more entertaining and provocative planet, not least for its attacks on the not infrequent pomposity of the blogging and academic worlds. More analytically, Wrong is also important for political analysis because of the highlighting of the sensitive points in the manufacture of consent. Moreover, Wrong shows it is possible to disturb the dominant views, irrespective of whether we think this is a good or bad thing, and Roland Boer's Stalin's Moustache, Deane Galbraith's Remnant of Giants and, in his own indomitable way, Jim West (presently of Zwinglius Redivivus) are certainly filled with the spirit of Wrong. Yet as things stand they remain exceptions that prove the 'rule' and Boer's blog typically attracts those sympathetic to Marxist critique and critical theory rather than part of the wider discussions across the still very conservative (intellectually and religiously) biblioblogs.

A 'Very Conservative' Defence of Murder?

However, ignoring Wrong is not through a lack of effort on Wrong's part and it is not as if Wrong has been *entirely* ignored. Wrong has attempted to make bibliobloggers explain their political statements, most notably the Hebrew Bible/Old Testament scholar John Hobbins, and this in direct relationship to the Propaganda Model. On my own work on the political locations of scholarship, Hobbins made various polemical claims about *Jesus in an Age of Terror*, not to mention his puzzling claim of the 'politics of the Copenhagen/Sheffield school of "postcolonial Biblical Studies"', even though, by his own admission, it turned out that he had not even seen a physical copy of the book, never mind actually having read it![74] Roland Boer was unimpressed: 'Ths [sic] stuff from Hobbins is plain stupid – a mish-mash of political bullshit and biblical comments – and he seems to know little about both. I don't [know] why you grace it with a response.'[75] Niels Peter Lemche commented, 'So far I haven't seen any argument from this Hobbit, but nevermind, we do not normally see that from the conservative part. Just assertions. I believe that people over here do not really care. It's a N-American discourse – utterly uninteresting.'[76]

Whatever we may or may not think about Hobbins's views, I still think there is a case to be made to take them more seriously, albeit in a different sense to the sentiments expressed by Boer and Lemche. In the world of blogging, Hobbins is now a known biblioblogger, often referenced among other biblioblogers, and has co-run a website which has held interviews with biblioblogers and has provided a quasi-'canonical' list of biblioblogers. His voice is certainly heard within the world of biblioblogging, irrespective of his argumentative abilities. Of course, we might again say, 'why bother?', but with the ever-expanding biblioblogs, such people may well be making up a notable section of the guild and, even if they do not make a splash (some will and some have), they will still write books and publish articles (as many have), support consensus views (at least if their scholarly tastes are anything to go by) and so on. For such reasons biblioblogers are, I think, to be taken seriously, irrespective of the validity of their ideas.

Back to Hobbins, what is significant is that he repeatedly engages in dismissal without dealing with the details of a given argument, as Wrong repeatedly pointed out. Dismissal without substance or argument is part of the Propaganda Model and Chomsky, more than most, has suffered with slurs ranging from Holocaust denial to irrelevance.[77] Of Chomsky, and without any engagement with the details of Chomsky's argument (and let us not forget the voluminous output of Chomsky), Hobbins dismissed his detailed and heavily supported work. According to Hobbins, Chomsky 'is in fact a starry-eyed dreamer of sorts, a Zionist of the old school. It's charming in a way. But it does not make for precise analysis.'[78] Of Wrong, Hobbins claimed,

> Like Chomsky, I can only assume at this point that you are a de facto supporter of Hezbollah and Hamas... I think you expose yourself rather often, though not as blatantly as Chomsky, to the accusation that you must be a supporter of Hezbollah and Hamas. I appreciate your disclaimers to the effect that you are not.

This was in response to Wrong's claim about 'Palestine, invaded by Israelis (after forcing the majority of the land to be given to a minority 6% of the population)', a 'little box or two for Palestinians to "live" within', and the issue of Israeli troops killing Palestinians, before asking if there is a case to be made for this sort of apparently benign imperialism.[79] Obviously, this does not make Wrong a supporter of Hezbollah and Hamas and the substance-free dismissal of Wrong gives a good insight into the political agenda underlying Hobbins's rhetoric.

In doing this, Wrong, thanks unintentionally to Hobbins, too, was able to highlight an additional feature and development of the work of Edward Herman and Noam Chomsky in line with the general arguments implied in the previous chapters, namely the role of former leftists and communists, or those deemed leftists but who are supportive of state-approved invasions, because they give greater and 'liberal' credibility to a brutal system or have seen the darker side and apparent lack of pragmatism of those in opposition to certain wars. Edward Herman, for instance, speaks of the value for the mainstream media of a figure such as Christopher Hitchens and his polemical assertions and substance-free arguments:

> Christopher Hitchens is a real asset to the war party... His value is enhanced by the fact that he is a 'straddler', that is, a man in transition from an earlier left politics to apologetics for imperial wars, but with a foot still in The Nation's door and a harsh critic of Kissinger and Pinochet. He is therefore presentable as a member of the 'rational left' or left that has 'seen the light'. Such folks are much honored by the mainstream media.[80]

In some detail, Richard Seymour, in his book, *The Liberal Defence of Murder*, looks at the historic roots of the importance of 'credible' and intellectual liberal and socialist support for imperialism right up to contemporary figures such as Christopher Hitchens and Bernard-Henri Lévy and other purveyors of 'humanitarian barbarism' in their support for the 'war on terror', with their emphasizing of the rhetoric of pure intentions in American foreign policy while making out enemies to be wholly evil.[81] Wrong's interaction with Hobbins has highlighted a similar role for Hobbins. Indeed, one response by Hobbins is particularly important in seeing how he can be brought in line with the Hitchenses of this world, namely, Hobbins's connections with Italian communism: 'Yet the only political party I've ever actually belonged to, the Italian Communist Party (to be precise, the successor party thereto), supported the US-led bombing of Serbia. That's because, in the real world, Isa 2:1–5 remains a distant horizon.'[82]

Concluding Remarks

These two test cases provide us with instances of how scholarship can explicitly react with key issues associated with neoliberalism and postmodernity, and contribute in its own small way to the sometimes silent perpetuation of neoliberal ideology. Radical alternatives to dominant narratives of power were, intentionally or otherwise, deflected, be they away from the causes of suffering in the aftermath of the Haiti disaster or the critiques of standard understandings of the 'war on terror'. We have seen how liberal credibility and 'extremism' function both in terms of the tragedy of Haiti and in the role of a convert from communism. We have also seen how biblioblogging, and related social media, buys into some very contemporary modes of surveillance, from surveillance of the body to willingly providing various personal details for all who are prepared or able to read. What is significant about the role of biblioblogging is that it is, strictly speaking, by and large removed from the direct backing of private or public power (unlike, say, an academic when producing work for a university) yet still replicating the trends of the mainstream mass media. Biblioblogging clearly shows the strong connections between scholarship and its contemporary cultural contexts, a point which if it was not so widely ignored would not have to be made in such detail, and ought to be advocated as an important medium for any comprehensive analysis of contemporary scholarship.

With a broader neoliberal context now established, and the general connections with biblical scholarship, we can turn to some general points concerning the role of historical Jesus scholarship in a capitalist context and then more specifically an age of neoliberalism, before moving on to more detailed case studies in part II. I will begin by showing how deeply embedded the role of Jesus scholarship is in that most Thatcherite of cults: the cult of the individual.

Notes

1. Blog posts inevitably contain a number of typographical errors but, in the interests of representing bloggers as fairly as possible, I have tried to quote them as accurately as possible and so kept the typographical errors.
2. Anonymous, 'Complete List of Biblioblogs', Biblioblog Top 50, http://biblioblogtop50.wordpress.com/biblioblogs/. For overviews of biblioblogging, including the origins of the terms 'biblioblogger' and 'biblioblogging' see J. R. Davila, 'Assimilated to the Blogosphere: Blogging Ancient Judaism', *SBL Forum*, http://www.sbl-site.org/Article.aspx?ArticleId=390; J. G. Crossley, *Jesus in an Age of Terror: Scholarly Projects for a New American Century* (London and Oakville: Equinox, 2008), pp. 20–25; R. Boer, 'Editorial', *Bible and Critical Theory* 5 (2009), p. 1; J. West, 'Blogging the Bible: A Short History', *BSR* 39 (2010), pp. 3–13.
3. M. Goodacre, 'Four Million Visits', NT Blog (26 August, 2008), http://ntweblog.blogspot.com/2008/08/four-million-visits.html.
4. E. S. Herman and N. Chomsky, *Manufacturing Consent: The Political Economy of the Mass Media* (London: Vintage, 1988); Crossley, *Jesus in an Age of Terror*, pp. 20–55.
5. R. T. McCutcheon, *Religion and the Domestication of Dissent: or, How to Live in a Less Than Perfect Nation* (London and Oakville: Equinox, 2005).
6. R. Dawkins, 'Religion's Misguided Missiles', *Guardian* (15 September, 2001).
7. Crossley, *Jesus in an Age of Terror*, pp. 82–100; W. T. Cavanaugh, *The Myth of Religious Violence: Secular Ideology and the Roots of Modern Conflict* (Oxford: Oxford University Press, 2009).
8. Y. Sherwood, 'Bush's Bible as a Liberal Bible (Strange Though That Might Seem)', *Postscripts* 2 (2006), pp. 47–58.
9. See also M. Krejci, 'An Atheist's Dilemma: Should We Bend the Bible for Justice?', *SBL Forum* (2008), http://sbl-site.org/Article.aspx?ArticleID=779; J. Berlinerblau, *Thumpin' It: The Use and Abuse of the Bible in Today's Presidential Politics* (Louisville: Westminster John Knox, 2008).
10. See again Krejci, 'An Atheist's Dilemma'; Berlinerblau, *Thumpin' It*.
11. A. Bach, 'Bush's Bible: A Wild Beast Loosed upon the World', *Postscripts* 2 (2006), pp. 109–25 (119).
12. R. Boer, 'Tag: Haiti', Stalin's Moustache (January 2010), http://stalinsmoustache.wordpress.com/tag/haiti/.
13. C. Brooker, *Newswipe*, episode 3, first aired 2 February, 2010 (BBC/Zeppotron), available at http://www.youtube.com/watch?v=0cNsxTfyVEo.
14. J. F. McGrath, 'Who Is the Wisest? Jesus, Solomon or Pat Robertson? (Biblioblogging and the Haitian Earthquake)', Exploring Our Matrix (January 2010), http://exploringourmatrix.blogspot.com/2010/01/who-is-wisest-jesus-solomon-or-pat.html.
15. A. DeConick, 'Tragedy in Haiti', The Forbidden Gospels (January, 2010), http://forbiddengospels.blogspot.com/2010/01/tragedy-in-haiti.html.
16. C. Uffman, 'Where Was God in the Earthquake?', Metanoia (January, 2010), http://www.craiguffman.com/2010/01/where-was-god-in-the-earthquake.html.

17. S. A. Wiggins, 'Theodicy versus Idiocy', Sects and Violence in the Ancient World, http://sawiggins.wordpress.com/2010/01/14/theodicy-versus-idiocy/.
18. C. Joseph, 'Haiti: The Land of Bitter Tears!', Christ, My Righteousness (January 2010), http://christmyrighteousness9587.wordpress.com/2010/01/14/haiti-will-survive/.
19. B. Witherington, 'Haiti – Where Was God?', Bible and Culture (January 2010), http://blog.beliefnet.com/bibleandculture/2010/01/haiti---a-case-study-for-theodicy.html.
20. J. Linville, 'What Disaster Will God Send to Punish T.V. Land for Pat Robertson?', Dr Jim's Thinking Shop and Tea Room (13 January, 2010), http://drjimsthinkingshop.com/2010/01/13/what-disaster-will-god-send-to-punish-t-v-land-for-pat-robertson/.
21. Witherington, 'Haiti – Where Was God?'
22. D. Brooks, 'The Underlying Tragedy', *New York Times* (14 January, 2010).
23. J. F. Hobbins, 'The Unnatural Natural Disaster: What We Need to Learn from Haiti', Ancient Hebrew Poetry (January, 2010), http://ancienthebrewpoetry.typepad.com/ancient_hebrew_poetry/2010/01/the-unnatural-natural-disaster-what-we-need-to-learn-from-haiti.html.
24. Boer, 'Haiti'.
25. P. Hallward, 'Our Role in Haiti's Plight', *Guardian* (13 January, 2010).
26. N. Chomsky, 'Haiti Post-Earthquake', *ZCommunications* (11 March 2010), http://www.zcommunications.org/haiti-post-earthquake-by-noam-chomsky.
27. Hallward, 'Haiti's Plight'.
28. Chomsky, 'Haiti Post-Earthquake'.
29. D. Shea, 'Pat Robertson: "Haiti 'Cursed' by 'Pact to the Devil'" (Video)', *Huffington Post* (13 January, 2010), http://www.huffingtonpost.com/2010/01/13/pat-robertson-haiti-curse_n_422099.html.
30. J. Watts, 'Pat Robertson: Haiti "Cursed" after "Pact to the Devil" (Video)', The Church of Jesus Christ (January 2010), http://thechurchofjesuschrist.us/2010/01/pat-robertson-haiti-cursed-after-pact-to-the-devil.
31. Terri, 'Ugh', Wheat among Tares (January, 2010), http://wheatamongtares.blogspot.com/2010/01/ugh.html.
32. Wiggins, 'Theodicy versus Idiocy'.
33. S. Bailey, 'Satan Is Pat Robertson's Theological Mentor', Scotteriology (14 January, 2010), http://scotteriology.wordpress.com/2010/01/14/satan-is-pat-robertsons-theological-mentor/.
34. Linville, 'Pat Robertson'.
35. J. W. Loftus, 'Reason 1,937 Why I Want Nothing to Do with Christianity: Pat Robertson on Haiti's Disaster', Debunking Christianity (January 2010), http://debunkingchristianity.blogspot.com/2010/01/reason-1937-why-i-want-nothing-to-do.html.
36. J. West, 'Jim West Interviews Bishop N.T. Wrong', Biblioblogs (February, 2009), http://www.biblioblogs.com/featured-blogs/2009-02/.
37. This is a repeated topic on biblioblogs and there was even a heated discussion at an SBL session on biblioblogging in Philadelphia, 2005, as to why this sort of person was attracted to biblioblogging. For a summary with links to the discussion on the biblioblogs see S. C. Carlson, 'Sans-Biblioblogue?',

Hypotyposeis (25 November, 2005), http://www.hypotyposeis.org/weblog/2005/11/sans-biblioblogue.html.

38. N. T. Wrong Blog, http://ntwrong.wordpress.com/.
39. N. T. Wrong, 'Hector Avalos Blogs', N. T. Wrong Blog (5 August, 2008), http://ntwrong.wordpress.com/2008/08/05/hector-avalos-blogs/.
40. J. West, 'Jim West Interviews Bishop N.T. Wrong', Biblioblogs (February, 2009), http://www.biblioblogs.com/featured-blogs/2009-02/.
41. D. Lyon, *Surveillance Studies: An Overview* (Cambridge: Polity, 2007), pp. 1, 6, 7.
42. On this phrase see D. Gregory, *The Colonial Present: Afghanistan, Palestine, Iraq* (Oxford: Blackwell, 2004), p. 18.
43. Crossley, *Jesus in an Age of Terror*, pp. 20–52.
44. Herman and Chomsky, *Manufacturing Consent*, p. 302; N. Chomsky, *Media Control: The Spectacular Achievements of Propaganda* (New York: Seven Stories Press, 2nd edn, 2002), pp. 20–21
45. From Foucault's famous analysis of the Panopticon to the various forms of bodily surveillance (and, notably, bodily surveillance under empire), various ideas concerning surveillance are now being analysed in biblical scholarship, e.g. D. Reis, 'Surveillant Discipline: Panoptic Vision in Early Christian Self-Definition,' *The Bible and Critical Theory* 4 (2008), pp. 23.1–23.21; C. V. Stichele and T. Penner, *Contextualizing Gender in Early Christian Discourse: Thinking beyond Thecla* (London: T&T Clark/Continuum, 2009), e.g. pp. 63–71.
46. On recent surveillance studies see especially Lyon, *Surveillance Studies*. For related work see e.g. D. Lyon, *Surveillance after September 11* (Cambridge: Polity, 2003); D. Lyon, *Theorizing Surveillance: The Panopticon and beyond* (Cullompton: Willan, 2006); K. D. Haggerty and R. V. Ericson (eds.), *The New Politics of Surveillance and Visibility* (Toronto and London: University of Toronto Press, 2006). The ideas on surveillance used in this chapter were also helped in no small part through discussion with Todd Penner and a paper of his which touched on issues of surveillance, categorization and historical criticism in '"Home Is Where the Heart Is" – A Concluding Methodological Prescript', unpublished paper delivered to the 'Holy Land as Homeland?' seminar, University of Oslo, 6–8 March, 2009.
47. Lyon, *Surveillance Studies*, p. 55.
48. S. McMillan, 'Facebook furore as Palace youngster reveals his plan to millions', *Guardian* (8 July, 2008); G. Caulkin, 'Darren Bent in Foul-mouthed Twitter Controversy', *Times* (31 July, 2009).
49. Arguably the most prominent is Mark Goodacre. See e.g. http://twitter.com/goodacre.
50. M. Bird, 'On Writing (1): Finding Time to Write', Euangelion (1 February, 2007), http://euangelizomai.blogspot.com/2007/02/on-writing-1-finding-time-to-write.html.
51. For discussion and links see J. Lyons, 'A More Sensible Regime!', Archives of Reception of the Bible (9 February, 2007), http://receptionofthebible.blogspot.com/2007/02/more-sensible-regime.html.
52. Email dated 24 January, 2009.

53. E.g. in July 2008 Wrong posted five reports from Auckland SBL on various genuine sessions. On SBL Boston see J. Lyons, 'Official Notice from the Office of Bishop N.T. Wrong,' Archives of Reception of the Bible (Thursday, 13 November, 2008), http://receptionofthebible.blogspot.com/2008/11/official-notice-from-office-of-bishop.html.
54. West, 'Jim West Interviews Bishop N. T. Wrong.'
55. N. T. Wrong, 'At the Airport for SBL,' N. T. Wrong Blog (16 November, 2008), http://ntwrong.wordpress.com/2008/11/16/at-the-airport-for-sbl/; N. T. Wrong, 'Burke Lecture 2008: The Challenge of Islamophobia,' N. T. Wrong Blog (4 July, 2008), http://ntwrong.wordpress.com/2008/07/04/burke-lecture-2008-islamophobia/; N. T. Wrong, 'Capitalism, Middle East Invasions, Resource Exploitation, Advertised as "Civilized Christianity" versus "Terrible Islam" – 1922,' N. T. Wrong Blog (18 October, 2008), http://ntwrong.wordpress.com/2008/10/18/1922-cartoon/.
56. N. T. Wrong, 'Yigael Yadin, the Bible, Archaeology, and Orientalism – When Captions Precede Their Photos,' N. T. Wrong (10 November, 2008), http://ntwrong.wordpress.com/2008/11/10/yigael-yadin-the-bible-archaeology-and-orientalism/.
57. J. G. Crossley, 'Starting Points and the Attack on Gaza,' Earliest Christian History (9 January, 2009), http://earliestchristianhistory.blogspot.com/2009/01/starting-points-and-attack-on-gaza.html.
58. N. T. Wrong, 'History of Christian-American Zionism,' N. T. Wrong Blog (21 June, 2008), http://ntwrong.wordpress.com/2008/06/21/american-christian-zionism/.
59. N. T. Wrong, 'Eilat Mazar Uses Fundamentalist Christian Cult to Link Archaeological Finds to "King David",' N. T. Wrong Blog (2 January, 2009), http://ntwrong.wordpress.com/2009/01/02/eilat-w-mazar-biblical-archaeology/.
60. N. T. Wrong, 'Anti-Israel Christmas Carols Prove Effective in Provoking Israeli Arseholes,' N. T. Wrong Blog (11 December 2008), http://ntwrong.wordpress.com/2008/12/11/anti-israel-christmas-carols/. For further criticisms of Israel see e.g. N. T. Wrong, 'Israel: "Profundity" of Ideas as Justification for Colonialism; Bodily Desire as Justification for Dispossession,' N. T. Wrong Blog (24 November, 2008), http://ntwrong.wordpress.com/2008/11/24/israel-balfour/#comments; N. T. Wrong, 'Israeli David and Arab Goliath,' N. T. Wrong Blog (13 August, 2008), http://ntwrong.wordpress.com/2008/08/13/israeli-david-and-arab-goliath/.
61. For full discussion of this and several other examples see Crossley, *Jesus in an Age of Terror*, pp. 31–48. For Tilling's nine-part series on Christian Zionism see http://www.christilling.de/blog/2007/02/my-christian-zionism-series.html.
62. West, 'Jim West Interviews Bishop N.T. Wrong.' See also S. C. Carlson, 'Ethical Considerations Relating to Pseudonymous Biblioblogging,' Hypotyposeis (14 February, 2009), http://www.hypotyposeis.org/weblog/2009/02/ethical-considerations-relating-to.html.
63. Crossley, *Jesus in an Age of Terror*, pp. 31–36.
64. Carlson, 'Ethical Considerations.'
65. N. T. Wrong, 'On Conservative and Liberal Biblioblogs,' N. T. Wrong Blog (30 October, 2008), http://ntwrong.wordpress.com/2008/10/30/on-conservative-and-liberal-biblioblogs/. This was the follow-up to N. T. Wrong, 'List

of Bibliobloggers – Conservative or Liberal?', N. T. Wrong Blog (29 October, 2008), http://ntwrong.wordpress.com/2008/10/29/list-of-bibliobloggers/.

66. W. J. Lyons, 'What Kind of Blogger Are You?', Archive of Reception of the Bible (29 October, 2008), http://receptionofthebible.blogspot.com/2008/10/what-kind-of-blogger-are-you.html.
67. For a selection see the links given by P. G. McCullough, 'Wrong Has Fun with Labels', kata ta biblia (31 October, 2008), http://patmccullough.com/2008/10/31/nt-wrong-has-fun-with-labels/.
68. D. Ker, 'It's One Thing to Slaughter a Pig on the Sacred Altar', Lingamish (2 February, 2009), http://lingamish.com/2009/02/its-one-thing-to-slaughter-a-pig-on-the-sacred-altar/. See also D. Ker, 'So, What's Going on Here?', Lingamish (15 February, 2009), http://lingamish.com/2009/02/so-whats-going-on-here/.
69. M. Goodacre, 'Biblioblogging Top 50 for January and Other Wrongs', NT Blog (3 February, 2009), http://ntweblog.blogspot.com/2009/02/biblioblogging-top-50-for-january-and.html.
70. J. G. Crossley, 'Fishing-gate', Earliest Christian History (3 February, 2009), http://earliestchristianhistory.blogspot.com/2009/02/fishing-gate.html.
71. M. Goodacre, 'N T Wrong: Transmission Cut?', NT Blog (17 February, 2009), http://ntweblog.blogspot.com/2009/02/n-t-wrong-transmission-cut.html. For the comments see Crossley, 'Fishing-gate'. Some of the comments were irrelevant to the topic, but without these the number still well exceeds 100.
72. T. Eagleton, *The Illusions of Postmodernism* (Oxford: Blackwell, 1996), pp. 4–5.
73. K. Brown, 'Biblioblog Top 10 Most Influential Authors and Books', C. Orthodoxy (20 June, 2009), http://corthodoxy.wordpress.com/2009/06/20/biblioblog-top-10-most-influential-authors-and-books/.
74. J. F. Hobbins, 'Good and Bad Imperialism', Ancient Hebrew Poetry (23 March 2009), http://ancienthebrewpoetry.typepad.com/ancient_hebrew_poetry/2009/03/good-and-bad-imperialism.html; J. F. Hobbins, 'What's Wrong with N. T. Wrong's Anti-Imperialism', Ancient Hebrew Poetry (24 March, 2009), http://ancienthebrewpoetry.typepad.com/ancient_hebrew_poetry/2009/03/whats-wrong-with-n-t-wrongs-antiimperialism.html. These links include detailed responses to Hobbins as does J. G. Crossley, 'John Hobbins, Jesus in an Age of Terror and Imperialism', Earliest Christian History (23 March, 2009), http://earliestchristianhistory.blogspot.com/2009/03/john-hobbins-jesus-in-age-of-terror-and.html. As Niels Peter Lemche pointed out, 'And thank you for lumping me among the post-colonialists. If only I had earned this label.' See J. West, 'John Hobbins on the Politics of Imperialism: Defending the Far Right', Dr Jim West (23 March, 2009), http://jwest.wordpress.com/2009/03/23/john-hobbins-on-the-politics-of-imperialism-defending-the-far-right/#comments [now unavailable].
75. Crossley, 'Jesus'.
76. West, 'John Hobbins'.
77. See Crossley, *Jesus in an Age of Terror*, pp. 128–41, with bibliography.
78. Hobbins, 'What's Wrong'.
79. Hobbins, 'What's Wrong'.

80. E. Herman, 'Christopher Hitchens and the Uses of Demagoguery', *ZMag* (22 September, 2002), http://www.zmag.org/znet/viewArticle/11646.
81. R. Seymour, *The Liberal Defence of Murder* (London and New York: Verso, 2008).
82. Hobbins, 'What's Wrong'. For his past engagements with Marxism see also J. F. Hobbins, 'A First Reading in Marxism for Students of the Bible', Ancient Hebrew Poetry (27 March, 2009), http://ancienthebrewpoetry.typepad.com/ancient_hebrew_poetry/2009/03/a-first-reading-in-marxism-for-students-of-the-bible-.html.

Chapter 4

'Not Made by Great Men'? The Quest for the Individual Christ

> The one who is more powerful than I is coming after me; I am not worthy to stoop down and untie the thong of his sandals. (Mk 1:7)

In this chapter I want to establish a general context for analysing understandings of the historical Jesus in contemporary contexts. In particular, I hope to show that a dominant feature of the quest for the historical Jesus – Jesus as Great Man – works in harmony with a dominant capitalist understanding of causality, particularly the importance of a freely acting autonomous individual with little concern for material conditions as a historical mover. The peculiarities of New Testament studies will mean that theological concerns also have to be factored in. This will supply the general scholarly context for the rest of the book. In the following chapter, I will narrow the chronological range further by looking at more specifically contemporary manifestations of liberal capitalism, particularly, of course, the contexts of neoliberalism and postmodernity, as well as multiculturalism.

Great Men

Georg Lukásc argued that atomized and individualized (bourgeois) history, including the 'Great Man' view of history, with its emphasis on establishing facts over historical development, not only avoids a more totalized view of history and explanations of historical change, but effectively justifies the normality of capitalism as part of the mysterious or eternal laws of nature.[1] As a useful generalization, this argument still stands today. One of the more remarkable examples of this 'bourgeois history' has to be Margaret Thatcher's infamous claim (or at least the reception of the claim) that 'there is no such thing as society. There are individual men and women, and there are families.'[2] Today, many of us will be all-too-familiar with the ways in which we are supposed to be in awe of the great individual. Some of the rhetoric of the past decade, with the wars in Afghanistan and Iraq particularly in mind, has involved the importance of great leaders and figures being *required*, from endless references to Churchill and the need to avoid changing a Commander-in-Chief during a time of war to the negatives such as the sentiments that it is nothing more than a few bad apples responsible for rotten corporations or torture in Abu Ghraib. We might also make dishonourable mention of the increasing obsession with celebrity and rich lists ('the top 50- most powerful women', 'the top ten most influential...'). As Wendy Brown put it,

> An identification of belief, attitude, moral fiber, and individual will with the capacity to make world history is the calling card of the biographical backstories and anecdotes that so often substitute for political analyses and considerations of power in American popular culture...from mythohistories to mythobiographies, we are awash in the conceits that right attitudes produce justice, that willpower and tenacity produce success, and that everything else is, at most, background, luck, or accidents of history. It is a child's view of history and politics: idealist, personal, and replete with heroes and villains, good values and bad.[3]

The kind of individualistic history critiqued by Lukásc, Brown and many others is alive and well in the study of the historical Jesus and beyond and deeply embedded in the history of scholarship.

For instance, Halvor Moxnes and Dieter Georgi, among others, have shown how ideas of Jesus as the outstanding genius of his time, or as the supreme historical actor of his time, reflect broader trends in Western bourgeois thought, notably the role of the Great Man, at the time historical Jesus studies were beginning to emerge in Europe.[4] Moxnes shows how Schleiermacher's interest in the historical Jesus involved writing a biography, a popular form in nineteenth-century bourgeois German circles, and the description of ideal figures who incorporated the values of society, values that were distinct from the more traditional power structures; in other words, the biographies of Great Men. In particular, Schleiermacher saw the individual in relation to people, land and nation, and, in terms of the study of the historical Jesus, to write the life of Jesus as a biography was to write it by using categories carrying meanings within an 'imagined' German land, people and nation. Jesus represented a particularly great type of person who had influence over 'all peoples and all ages', and so his relation to people, land and nation served as an ideal. Moxnes makes the more general and significant point that historical Jesus studies emerged at the same time as the growth of nationalism in Europe and in many ways we will see that this link with nationalism remains strong, albeit modified for our times.

Indeed, the idea of Jesus as Great Man is something that has united great swathes of historical Jesus scholarship. As Georgi points out in his wide-ranging survey,

> The view that Jesus had been a genius of sorts became a dominant view in the late eighteenth, nineteenth, and twentieth centuries, not only in Germany but also in western Europe and North America, among both Protestants and Catholics. The differences between conservative and liberal Christology in this respect were of minor importance.[5]

I want to spend the rest of this chapter showing how these forms of individualism are manifested in different ways in contemporary Jesus scholarship, and from a range of perspectives. The rest of this book will partly be an attempt to show *some* of the ways (and only *some* of the ways) in which Jesus is now constructed as a late twentieth-/early twenty-first-century equivalent of the nineteenth-century Great Men biography, with updated concerns for people, land, state and so on. Jesus still serves as the great ideal in scholarship.

Yet while individualism and the cult of the individual have faced some resistance in the historical reconstructions by historians in history departments, such resistance has not had a major impact on contemporary mainstream historical Jesus studies. There are several reasons for this, but two obvious ones involve biography and faith. In terms of biography, lives of Jesus are, obviously, about one man and therefore it is understandable that emphasis is on the words and deeds of this man. In terms of faith, Jesus is the central figure in the Christian faith and in theology and the overwhelming majority of New Testament scholars are practising, or at least lapsed, Christians. Therefore it is understandable that the words and deeds of the individual Jesus are analysed so heavily. As I have argued elsewhere, we must also recognize that such differing assumptions will inevitably have some impact on the results and approaches of the disciplines of history and New Testament/Christian origins studies.[6]

Consequently, there are countless portraits of Jesus that have become famous: the Cynic-like figure, the revolutionary, the charismatic, the eschatological prophet, the sage, the rabbi, the social critic and so on. Underlying all these is a serious scholarly fact-finding mission. One of the most famous things for which E. P. Sanders's groundbreaking books on Jesus are remembered is the establishment of basic *facts* about Jesus (born c. 4 BCE, grew up in Nazareth, baptized by John the Baptist, preached the kingdom of God, executed under Pilate etc.).[7] In this sense, one of Sanders's key aims is to shift away from theological concerns and interpret as a conventional historian, the sort of historian that might be found (say) in a history or ancient history department. But note how Sanders locates himself in the tradition of historical biography in order to analyse what the subjects *thought*:

> I shall discuss Jesus the human being, who lived in a particular time and place, and I shall search for evidence and propose explanations just as does any historian when writing about history... Jesus' own theology and the theologies of his first followers are historical questions, which are to be explored in the same way as one studies what Jefferson thought about liberty, what Churchill thought about the labour movement and the strikes of 1910 and 1911, what Alexander the Great thought about the union of Greek and Persian in one empire, and what their contemporaries thought about these great men while they still lived... The historian who studies a great human being, and reports fully on his or her findings, will almost certainly write at least a few things that some admirers would rather not read. People whose image of Jefferson has been created by imagining the character of the author of the Declaration of Independence may be shocked by a study of his love life and consumption of alcohol... This is not a warning that I am going to 'expose' something truly shocking about Jesus, such as sexual promiscuity... I shall not only write about how nice he was, nor shall I ignore the aspects of his life and thought that many of his most ardent admirers wish would go away.[8]

All this is typical of the agendas of many reconstructions of Jesus' life. In many ways poles apart from Sanders are the American Jesus Seminar. Yet their concerns are still with the facts about Jesus and what Jesus *thought* or *believed*, as can be seen in not only the subtitle to their flagship book (*The Search for the Authentic Words of Jesus*) but also their famous colour coding:

> red: Jesus undoubtedly said this or something like this.
> pink: Jesus probably said something like this.
> gray: Jesus did not say this, but the ideas contained in it are close to his own.
> black: Jesus did not say this; it represents the perspective or content of a later or different tradition.[9]

Harking back, like Simon Schama's popular histories, to the grand nineteenth-century historical narratives, and with echoes of Renan,

Bruce Chilton's *Rabbi Jesus*, seemingly so unusual in historical Jesus studies, actually reads more like a conventional biography than any other recent scholarly work on Jesus (note the sub-title: *An Intimate Biography*). Here we even get exclusive snapshots of Jesus as a *kabbalah*-loving Galilean celebrity, a once adolescent geek whose weight fluctuated when he grew up and whose hair was ever diminishing:

> Jesus was thin and scraggly, hungry much of the time...he never reached his natural height as patristic writers knew...
>
> The young man who stood on their doorsteps was shorter than average height... But he was broader in the chest than the scrawny adolescent they remembered. His beard had filled out and he had a new self-confidence...
>
> Jesus grew heavier over the years... The emerging paunch only strengthened his voice, however, and his thick beard and thinning hair made for the impression of *gravitas*. Shorter than the norm, overweight, and tending to baldness...
>
> He was not the man they remembered from Capernaum. He was much thinner, almost gaunt, with a distracted air about him...
>
> His paunch was gone. He was fit, lean, his face etched by sun, a harsh regime, and the rigors of his meditative practice.[10]

The concern with establishing facts gets taken to another kind of extreme – more *Encyclopedia Americana* than Churchill's *Marlborough* – in the massive multi-volume work on the historical Jesus by John Meier. If the celebrity biographer is interested in all things gossipy, then it may be fair to say that Meier is interested in the more sober hard facts. In Meier's own words,

> this book operates on a very fundamental level as it asks what, within the Gospels and other sources available, really goes back to the historical Jesus. The primary goal of this book is the detection of reliable data. Inevitably, interpretation will accompany the assemblage of data, if for no other reason than that the selection and compiling of such data already involve a certain degree of interpretation. But every attempt will be made to keep interpretation to an absolute minimum. Our goal will be primarily the ascertaining of reliable data...what we seek in this book are precisely the particular data needed for historical reconstruction of individual persons and events in a very narrow time frame.[11]

Countless more scholarly examples could have been chosen, right up to and including the recent penchant for memory studies ('liberal' or, more usually, 'conservative'),[12] but doing so would just be to keep repeating the obvious: the study of the historical Jesus is overwhelmingly concerned with fact finding,[13] or even in the case of memory studies biographical details are merged with remembrance, and with description and descriptive interpretation in its various forms, with little concern for questions such as *why* the Jesus movement emerged when and where it did and *why* this movement subsequently led to a new religion. By Eric Hobsbawm's standards most of these historical Jesus writers would come perilously close to being guilty of 'antiquarian empiricism' and more than one historical Jesus scholar might be guilty of writing what Hobsbawm dismissed as the 'Victorian tome' so typical of conservative biography opposed to history, which asks the 'big questions'.[14] If we were to be kinder, some of the historical Jesus books are perhaps more akin to the modern-day biography of literary figures (though, of course, the subject left nothing in writing) than historical biography.

In terms of historical explanation, such detail must at least imply that the individual Jesus of Nazareth is thought to be the most significant figure (and factor?) in the emergence of subsequent Christianity. Indeed, several historical Jesus scholars are keen to show the connections between Jesus and the Christian movement that followed. Sanders and Wright, for instance, virtually make this a methodological necessity. Indeed, Wright has been fiercely critical of those like the members of the American Jesus Seminar for reconstructing a Jesus which cannot account for emergent Christianity. In contrast, Sanders famously saw the connection between Jesus and the early Christians in the matter of eschatology. The very first Christians had problems with the 'troublesome fact' that the kingdom had not yet come and so, Sanders argues, it is 'almost impossible to explain these historical facts on the assumption that Jesus himself did not expect the imminent end or transformation of the present world order'.[15]

For all Wright's analysis of Jesus' theology, he also makes connections with subsequent Christianity. With reference to Jesus' storytelling, Wright notes that it is both similar and dissimilar to the Jewish context and the early Christian world. If we recognize this *double dissimilarity*, he argues, 'when something can be seen as credible...within first century Judaism, and credible as the implied starting-point...of something in later Christianity, there is the strong possibility of our being in touch with the genuine history of Jesus'.[16] But here again we remain in the realm of *description*, without any serious discussion of social and economic trends that are invariably present in historical change and developments and that may have aided and abetted the shift from Jesus to early Christianity. When Wright does look beyond the surface level events and stories he bypasses the route of social and historical causes by taking (rightly or wrongly) a historically bizarre turn with an intensified individualism or supernatural individualism to explain the 'blind forces' of historical change, claiming that the 'proposal that Jesus was bodily raised from the dead possessed unrivalled power to explain the historical data at the heart of early Christianity'.[17]

This is not to say such scholarship is necessarily wrong (to repeat: in many ways that is another issue). On one basic level it should be obvious that there would be little if any useful socio-economic analysis if there were not a significant amount of factual data and reconstruction of ideas and beliefs. The issue I find slightly troubling is that the sheer amount of 'factual' detail given in scholarship over socio-economic causal explanations runs the dangerous risk of giving the impression that there is little more to religious or historical change than a suitably large enough amount of people being convinced by an argument based on the benefits of the god of Jesus over against others. In terms of broader historical trends, a very obvious-but-useful analogy might be the argument that the Second World War happened not simply because of what Hitler did but because of a whole host of social and economic factors, most obviously including the economic conditions in Germany after Versailles. Thematically closer to home, no radical comment is being made in suggesting that the Jewish War happened due to deep rooted socio-economic problems and not simply because of a few hot-headed radicals. We can certainly apply the idea to Christian origins that broader historical change frequently happens because something is going on beneath the surface, but for now we should note that this important socio-economic emphasis is ignored in favour of a form of the Great Man view of history and a history which seems strangely detached from material realities.

As alluded to earlier, the major *over*-emphasis on the role of an individual at the expense of explaining historical change has not been typical practice among historians more generally, and so I suspect it is not going too far to suggest that a major reason for this is that many practitioners believe God is ultimately in control of history and that Jesus, obviously from this perspective, had a significant impact on human history and historical change.[18] We might say that where a classic individualist history can give the impression of free-floating actors, certain histories of Christian origins have the invisible supernatural or theological hand guiding the apparent chaos of activity. It is also no surprise that apocalypticism and eschatology have been dominant contexts in which Jesus has been analysed; as Ernst Käsemann famously stated, apocalyptic is 'the mother of all Christian theology'.[19] Though, with many scholars, we might argue that apocalypticism and eschatology both provide crucial ways of analysing Jesus' *theology*, there are further grounds to suspect deeper reasons for their popularity than just historical plausibility. As John Kloppenborg points out, since the Second World War, eschatology became a central theological category among leading Protestant theologians (e.g. Moltmann, Pannenberg) and is intimately tied in with Christology. Consequently, it is difficult to see that its acceptance in historical Jesus studies is simply for reasons of detached historical research.[20] Compare, for instance, the comments of Dale Allison in an article on eschatology in the Gospel tradition which ties several features of the above together: 'the heart of eschatology is not when or what but who, not a schedule or a plan but a person. The Gospels move us to contemplate the future not by giving us a blueprint but by relating all to Jesus, Messiah and Son of man.'[21]

Social Sciences: An Antidote to Individualism?

It might be thought that the ever-increasing use of social sciences could provide an alternative way forward.[22] I have already suggested that this can indeed be the case, but much use of the social sciences has been either descriptive or feeds into the idea of individual influence. The idea of Jesus as charismatic leader – the social scientific model of the individual *par excellence* – shows no signs of losing its popularity and, probably more than any other social-scientific model, it highlights Jesus as notably different from his social context, not to mention the model's descriptive importance by placing Jesus as a 'type'.[23] There have been historical Jesus studies grounded in social and economic histories – such as those of Richard Horsley, William Herzog, Halvor Moxnes, John Dominic Crossan and my own – that have the potential for wide-ranging, causally based explanations for the emergence of the Jesus movement and subsequent Christianity, but ultimately, whether intended or not, the reception of such works tends to involve discussions of theology and description. For all Horsley's application of Marxist-influenced social sciences, it is the resulting Jesus that becomes the object of scrutiny. Wright's problems with Horsley, for instance, involve Jesus' *attitudes* toward violent revolution and social outcasts.[24] In a similar way, Dale Allison's problem with the work of Herzog and others is that it is a 'secular reading' in that such interpretations 'shove our attention away from traditional theological, christological, and eschatological concerns...

[but] Jesus himself was a deeply religious personality, who interpreted everything in terms of an unseen world'.[25]

Perhaps more than anyone it is Crossan who has sought to systematize the social sciences in the study of the historical Jesus. For all of Crossan's creative use of causality in social sciences, and his attempts at explaining the shift from Jesus to the birth of Christianity, his portrayals of Jesus and subsequent Christianity still, at least in the reception of Crossan's work, ultimately remain a theological and descriptive enterprise (compare Crossan's own stress on Jesus as social revolutionary, the split between the 'life' and 'death' traditions etc.) and not without one eye, as his critics frequently point out, on contemporary relevance.[26] As Crossan says of himself in a passage which I suspect may one day attain the hallowed status of 'oft-quoted', his scholarly work was not 'just a study of the past', but, like Jesus' teaching, 'a critique of the present'. Crossan then calls this 'a way of doing necessary open-heart surgery on Christianity itself'.[27]

It is, therefore, no surprise that in the reception of Crossan's work we get emphases on the individual, the descriptive, the exegetical and/or the theological. Crossan's work ultimately makes Jesus scholars chatter because he portrayed Jesus as a Cynic-like peasant preacher and used all sorts of weird and wonderful texts to make his case.[28] The idea of who Jesus was and what the texts really mean feeds into the reception of Crossan's use of social sciences. For example, on one level Wright appreciates Crossan's use of social sciences. He thinks that social anthropology must be part of 'the equipment of the historian' and helps avoid anachronisms 'by recognizing that different societies operate with different worldviews and social norms'. Wright gives a brief application of this to the story of Mary and Martha (Lk. 10:38–42) with the conclusion so typical in historical Jesus and New Testament studies that 'a subversive note is struck'.[29] This seems a clear indication that social sciences have a descriptive and exegetical function. But is making Wright's religion better/subversive really the best social sciences can offer?

Donald Denton's detailed analysis of Crossan's work has a more nuanced take. He makes the following suggestion:

> We can take from Crossan the important gains that are reflected in his macro- and mesocosmic levels of historical work. There is a particular need in Jesus studies to catch up with the larger historiographic world in accounting for the data within the contexts provided by sociology; Crossan's attention to this area is an example to emulate.[30]

Yet again it is significant, though not wrong in itself, that the (qualified) positive side of Denton's evaluation of Crossan's use of social sciences is ultimately grounded in how Jesus is *portrayed* and how Jesus-the-individual acts:

> He is successful in interpreting the data in light of sociological models, without reducing historical events or actions to instances of ideal types... Within pan-Mediterranean sociological constructs, Jesus remains a first-century religious figure with genuine religious sensibilities and a historical agent whose actions are intentional, and not reducible to a confluence of environmental factors. But it is to this area of his method, where I believe Crossan is most successful, that he devotes the least amount of methodological discussion.[31]

To some extent these reactions to Crossan's work are inevitable: Crossan largely (but not exclusively) deals with how social conditions influence or help explain the *teaching* of the historical Jesus and subsequent Christianity, with masses of exegesis and discussion of tradition history.[32] To do this in a discipline dominated by, and obsessed with, exegesis and the traditional historical-critical method makes the response predictable. Once again, I am *not* saying such approaches are necessarily wrong, but they do, once again, illustrate that explaining historical change is not high on the agenda and that individualism, or at least a certain kind of individualism, is.[33]

It didn't have to be this way. Scholars could have focused more on Crossan's use of socio-economic reasons for historical change as well as critiquing his actual portrait of Jesus and use of sources.[34] After all, Crossan and Reed signal a statement of intent by introducing a book with the words, 'Why did Jesus happen when and where he happened? Why then? Why there?... Why not another time? Why not another place?'[35] And, of course, recall that there has also been a long tradition in history departments of scholars engaging in broader-ranging, causal socio-economic explanations.[36] Closer to home (perhaps) was it simply impossible for New Testament scholars to engage more with Marxist explanations of Christian origins, from Friedrich Engels and Karl Kautsky through to virtually unknown (at least in terms of New Testament studies) Marxists of the mid-twentieth century?[37]

Biography does not have to be the way of the typical historical Jesus book either. Some historians have not been particularly impressed with a basic historical-biographical approach to history. E. H. Carr was particularly scathing of the perspective, stretching from the ancient world to the present, that individuals are the decisive factor in history. For Carr, history was all about seeing the role of the human in society. So while he was more than happy to see biographies concerned with individual behaviour and eccentricities as a different genre to 'history', Carr could recognize those biographies which located the individual in broader social trends as 'serious contributions to history', citing Isaac Deutscher's biographies of Stalin and Trotsky.[38] Even Hobsbawm, who like Carr is attracted to broader historical patterns, is not wholly hostile to writing about individual figures and has in fact done so (e.g. Harold Laski, Roy Cohn, Salvatore Giuliano, Karl Korsch).[39] But Hobsbawm consistently tries to see how the individual illuminates broader historical trends, how successfully the individual reacted to historical conditions in the broader sweep of historical change, and how ideas are intermingled with socio-economic context. We have now more or less arrived at Marx's famous and widely accepted saying from *The Eighteen Brumaire of Louis Bonaparte*: 'Men make their own history, but they do not make it just as they please; they do not make it under circumstances chosen by themselves, but under circumstances directly encountered, given and transmitted from the past.'[40]

For those more biographically inclined, there are similar possibilities raised in a recent defence of the biographical form as serious history by the late Ben Pimlott.[41] Pimlott was anything but a member of the sex-obsessed gossipy school of biographical writing, best represented, perhaps, by Andrew Morton's *Diana: Her True Story*, and he would not even entirely side with the all-too-common lengthy and meticulously researched descriptions of someone-or-other's life. In fact, he remained upbeat about those factors that Hobsbawm and others think should play a primary role in historical research. As Pimlott put it, 'far from underplaying social factors, the good biographer highlights them, to give added precision to the story', adding that 'good biography' will make connections across periods of time.[42]

As this implies, we are moving beyond the use of social sciences for mere description. Indeed, though writing in a context critical of certain outdated forms of social historical explanation, Pimlott even referred to the 'stress on the role of the individuals' as 'old-fashioned'.[43] From the perspective of at least one prominent figure in biographical writing, then, it follows that there should be nothing contradictory about writing about specific historical figures with a concern for explaining social change.[44]

We are now into the heart of a major well-worn debate among historians: the role of the individual in historical change. This is a massive area, but a brief and slightly caricatured overview should give some indication of just how one-sided and odd looking the study of the historical Jesus and Christian origins actually has been. On the one hand, the humanities have had the Victorian historians stressing the role of the great individual in history, epitomized (misleadingly, some would say) by Thomas Carlyle's famous sentence, 'The History of the world…is but the Biography of great men.'[45] On the other hand, the humanities have had a major twentieth-century alternative in various social historians, Marxist historians and *Annalists* like Fernand Braudel, who famously claimed that the human is a prisoner of environment and mind and that human events were superficial, like the froth of the ocean tossed around by deeper, slower moving currents – that is, social, geographical and economic trends discernable only over long periods of time.[46] In terms of the quest for the historical Jesus, not to mention its relationship to Christian origins, if there are very few followers of Braudel, there must be countless followers of an apparently misinterpreted Carlyle.

This needs one brief qualification for our present purposes. In some ways, the re-emergence of narrative histories and micro-histories have meant that the history of the good and the great remain, but these kinds of history have also welcomed histories from below and sought out forgotten and marginalized individuals.[47] While Jesus and Paul can be, and sometimes are, seen as figures from traditionally marginalized backgrounds, at the same time they will still play a structurally similar role to the good and the great in history, even if in a differently romanticized form. This may mean that history grounded in the role of the individual has a long shelf-life in the historical study of Christian origins. Jesus as Great Man, genius, or even enlightened Beckett-like sage, is not only deeply embedded in the discipline but he may also be here to stay for some time.

Concluding Remarks

What this discussion of Jesus the individual has done is to show, hopefully, that the Great Man view of history is as alive as it ever was in the quest for the historical Jesus. Jesus is no doubt placed at the centre of historical change because he is, obviously, so theologically important. This is perhaps best shown by the ways in which social sciences are used by scholars such as Crossan to explain change differently, but the reception of such works typically brings the individual to the fore and relegates the possibilities of broader trends in historical change. There is a quirkier side to this, too, with the God of the gaps sometimes on hand to guide the path of history. The work of Wright has led to a great deal of attention being paid to that strangest of areas in historical Jesus studies and historical change: the resurrection and the role of the supernatural in historical change. This means that it would not be wise to ignore the role of the resurrection in ideological analyses of historical Jesus scholarship and, as I have argued elsewhere, scholarship on the resurrection conveniently brings various ideological strands together.[48] But we are now getting ahead of ourselves. As this Great Man style of individualism has been, as Moxnes and Georgi have shown, an indicator of broader cultural and political values, we first need to be more precise in our contextualization of the contemporary quests for the historical Jesus in order to show what he represents. And as the idea of individualism has, of course, been widely highlighted as typical of capitalist thought, not least because it has the positive (and convenient) connotations of freedom, though it can also (just as conveniently) blame the individual for their plight rather than any deeper rooted societal issues. But this merely establishes a general context of individualism as dominant in Jesus studies; it is to specific manifestations of capitalist individualism that I now turn in more detail.

Notes

1. G. Lukásc, *History and Class Consciousness: Studies in Marxist Dialectics* (London: Merlin Press, 1971), e.g. pp. 46–55. Cf. pp. 10–11: 'When the ideal of scientific knowledge is applied to nature it simply furthers the progress of science. But when it is applied to society it turns out to be an ideological weapon of the bourgeoisie. For the latter it is a matter of life and death to understand its own system of production in terms of eternally valid categories: it must think of capitalism as being predestined to eternal survival by the eternal laws of nature and reason.'
2. M. Thatcher, 'Aids, Education and the Year 2000!', *Woman's Own* (31 October, 1987), pp. 8–10.
3. W. Brown, *Regulating Aversion: Tolerance in the Age of Identity and Empire* (Princeton and Oxford: Princeton University Press, 2006), p. 18.
4. D. Georgi, 'The Interest in Life of Jesus Theology as a Paradigm to the Social History of Biblical Criticism', *HTR* 85 (1992), pp. 51–83; H. Moxnes, 'What Is It to Write a Biography of Jesus? Schleiermacher's *Life of Jesus* and Nineteenth-Century Nationalism', in H. Moxnes, W. Blanton and J. G. Crossley (eds.), *Jesus beyond Nationalism: Constructing the Historical Jesus in a Period of Cultural Complexity* (London and Oakville: Equinox, 2009), pp. 27–42.
5. Georgi, 'Life of Jesus Theology', p. 76.

6. For recent discussion see e.g. J. G. Crossley, *Why Christianity Happened: A Sociohistorical Account of Christian Origins (26–50CE)* (Louisville: Westminster John Knox, 2006), pp. 1–34.
7. E. P. Sanders, *Jesus and Judaism* (London: SCM, 1985), p. 11; idem, *The Historical Figure of Jesus* (London: Penguin, 1993), pp. 10–11.
8. Sanders, *Historical Figure*, pp. 2, 4–5. It should be pointed out that Sanders's concerns as an ancient historian over against theologian have brought significant benefits to New Testament studies. On this see Crossley, *Why Christianity Happened*, pp. 29–32.
9. R. W. Funk, R. W. Hoover and the Jesus Seminar, *The Five Gospels: The Search for the Authentic Words of Jesus* (New York: Schribner, 1993), p. 36.
10. B. Chilton, *Rabbi Jesus: An Intimate Biography* (New York: Doubleday, 2000), pp. 47, 104, 138, 193, 225.
11. J. P. Meier, *A Marginal Jew: Rethinking the Historical Jesus*. I. *The Roots of the Problem and the Person* (New York: Doubleday, 1991), pp. 10–11.
12. Recent examples include: J. D. G. Dunn, *Jesus Remembered* (Grand Rapids: Eerdmans, 2003); R. Bauckham, *Jesus and the Eyewitnesses: The Gospels as Eyewitness Testimony* (Grand Rapids: Eerdmans, 2006); A. Le Donne, *The Historiographical Jesus: Memory, Typology, and the Son of David* (Waco: Baylor, 2009); R. Rodriguez, *Structuring Early Christian Memory: Jesus in Tradition, Performance, and Text* (London and New York: T&T Clark/ Continuum, 2010); D. C. Allison, *Constructing Jesus: Memory, Imagination, and History* (Grand Rapids: Baker, 2010).
13. Cf. H. Moxnes, 'The Historical Jesus: From Master Narrative to Cultural Context', *BTB* 28 (1999), pp. 135–49 (138–43); W. R. Herzog, *Prophet and Teacher: An Introduction to the Historical Jesus* (Louisville: Westminster John Knox, 2005), pp. 1–24.
14. Quoted in B. Pimlott, 'Brushstrokes', in M. Bostridge (ed.), *Lives for Sale: Biographers' Tales* (London and New York: Continuum, 2004), pp. 165–170 (166; cf. 168). Cf. E. J. Hobsbawm, *On History* (London: Abacus, 1997), p. 248: ' If we leave aside deliberate historiographical conservatives or neo-conservatives such as the British "antiquarian empiricists"...those historians who continue to believe in the possibility of generalizing about human societies and their development continue to be interested in "the big *why* questions"... No doubt there are historians who have abandoned such attempts, and certainly there are those who combat them, perhaps with zeal increased by ideological commitment.'
15. Sanders, *Historical Figure*, p. 183.
16. N. T. Wright, *Jesus and the Victory of God* (London: SPCK, 1996), p. 132. The subtitle of one of Wright's popular books on Jesus also stresses biographical importance, *The Original Jesus: The Life and Vision of a Revolutionary* (Oxford: Lion, 1996).
17. N. T. Wright, *The Resurrection of the Son of God* (London: SPCK, 2003), p. 718.
18. Cf. Georgi, 'Life of Jesus Theology', pp. 76, 80–83.
19. E. Käsemann, *New Testament Questions of Today* (London: SCM, 1969), p. 102.

20. J. S. Kloppenborg, 'As One Unknown, without a Name? Co-opting the Apocalyptic Jesus', in J. S. Kloppenborg with J. W. Marshall (eds.), *Apocalypticism, Anti-Semitism and the Historical Jesus: Subtexts in Criticism* (London and New York: T&T Clark/Continuum, 2005), pp. 19–21.
21. D. C. Allison, 'Eschatology', in J. B. Green, S. McKnight and I. H. Marshall (eds.), *Dictionary of Jesus and the Gospels* (Downers Grove and Leicester: IVP, 1992), pp. 206–209 (209).
22. Cf. Moxnes, 'Historical Jesus', pp. 143–49.
23. The *theological* danger of supposedly reducing Jesus to any old charismatic leader is recognized by S. C. Barton, 'Historical Criticism and Social-Scientific Perspectives in New Testament Study', in J. B. Green (ed.), *Hearing the New Testament: Strategies for Interpretation* (Grand Rapids: Eerdmans, 1995), pp. 61–89 (76). For critical analyses of the charismatic leader in historical Jesus studies from perspectives less concerned with theological dangers see e.g. B. J. Malina, *The Social World of Jesus and the Gospels* (London: Routledge, 1996), p. 123; cf. 124–42, 217–41.
24. Wright, *Victory*, pp. 156–58.
25. Allison, *Resurrecting Jesus*, pp. 22–23.
26. As ever, note the biographical relevance of the subtitles of Crossan's books on Jesus: *The Historical Jesus: The Life of a Mediterranean Jewish Peasant* (San Francisco: HarperCollins; Edinburgh: T&T Clark, 1991) and *Jesus: A Revolutionary Biography* (San Francisco: HarperCollins, 1994).
27. J. D. Crossan, *A Long Way from Tipperary* (San Francisco: HarperSanFrancisco, 2000), p. 175.
28. Cf. D. L. Denton, *Historiography and Hermeneutics in Jesus Studies: An Examination of the Work of John Dominic Crossan and Ben F. Meyer* (London and New York: T&T Clark/Continuum, 2004), p. 11: 'if Crossan's Jesus portrait is an easy target, his method is not'.
29. Wright, *Victory*, p. 52.
30. Denton, *Historiography*, p. 77.
31. Denton, *Historiography*, pp. 77–78. After analysing the methodological approaches of Crossan and Ben Meyer, Denton then proceeds to give his own, based on holistic approaches to the historical Jesus married with narrative approaches to history (*Historiography*, pp. 154–92). While I believe that Denton's narrative approach has a lot to offer, it still remains generally in the area of description and theological understanding of the individual (see below).
32. Cf. Denton, *Historiography*, pp. 57–78. As Denton observes (67), 'It is to the microcosmic level that Crossan devotes most of his attention in methodological discussion, because, as he says, method stands or falls with how one handles the sources'.
33. Similar comments can be made for the use of social-sciences in the genre of 'New Testament history'. B. Witherington, *New Testament History: A Narrative Account* (Carlisle: Paternoster; Grand Rapids: Baker, 2001), p. 10, claims that his New Testament history 'will involve a focus not only on historic individuals and events, but also on social movements and crosscurrents that illuminate those persons and events. The New Testament peoples and their activities must be seen within their proper social and religious contexts if they are to be

understood properly. The Jesus movement as a messianic movement was not an isolated phenomenon on the landscape of early Jewish history. Nor was the rise of the church an example of *creatio ex nihilo*. Things must be seen in their proper contexts.' Yet it remains that there is no causal explanation, while social context is utilized to show what people and groups were 'really like'. It is notable that Witherington, like Wright, also has to resort to the supernatural (resurrection) in explaining historical change: 'a consistent witness to Jesus' resurrection runs throughout our sources, and this provides prima facie evidence that Jesus' resurrection and appearances provide the key historical middle ground between the life and death of Jesus and the birth of the early church' (170).

34. Compare Denton's conclusions (*Historiography*, p. 77), and cited above.
35. J. D. Crossan and J. L. Reed, *Excavating Jesus: Beneath the Stones, behind the Texts* (New York: HarperCollins; London: SPCK, 2001), p. xv.
36. For a useful overview see R. J. Evans, *In Defence of History* (London: Granta, 2nd edn, 2000), pp. 129–90.
37. F. Engels, 'On the History of Earliest Christianity (1894)', in K. Marx and F. Engels, *Collected Works*. XXVII. *Engels: 1890–95* (London: Lawrence & Wishart, 1990), 447–69; K. Kautsky, *Foundations of Christianity: A Study in Christian Origins* (London: Orbach & Chambers, 1925). On the post-Engels/Kautsky Marxist tradition see e.g. P. Kowaliński, 'The Genesis of Christianity in the Views of Contemporary Marxist Specialists of Religion', *Antonianum* 47 (1972), pp. 541–75. These non-Christian Marxist explanations should be distinguished from the more liberationist approaches as the former tend more toward historical causal explanation of the evidence while the latter tend more toward theological interpretation.
38. E. H. Carr, *What Is History?* (London: Penguin, 2nd edn, 1987), p. 46.
39. See e.g. E. J. Hobsbawm, *Uncommon People: Resistance, Rebellion and Jazz* (London: Abacus, 1998) and *Revolutionaries* (London: Abacus, 1999), pp. 183–91. Such issues of the individual in history are also discussed, though with debateable conclusions it must be added, in Hobsbawm's autobiography, *Interesting Times: A Twentieth Century Life* (London: Abacus, 2002), e.g. pp. 265–72.
40. K. Marx, *The Eighteenth Brumaire of Louis Bonaparte* (New York: International Publishers, 1963), p.15.
41. Pimlott, 'Brushstrokes'.
42. Pimlott, 'Brushstrokes', pp. 169–70.
43. Pimlott, 'Brushstrokes', p. 166.
44. Pimlott, 'Brushstrokes', p. 166, talks of E. H. Carr's 'superficially persuasive denunciation of biography in *What is History?*' However, as we saw with the brief look at Carr on biography, it was not a full denunciation and Pimlott's qualifications on the individual in the context of social change echo Carr's qualifications noted above.
45. T. Carlyle, *On Heroes and Hero-Worship and the Heroic in History* (Berkeley: University of California, 1993), p. 13; cf. p. 2. There was, however, more to Carlyle than this. As Carr (*What Is History?*, pp. 49–50) points out, Carlyle saw the massive significance of the plight of the masses over against philosophers and elites underlying the French Revolution and ultimately all revolutions.

For a vigorous critique of the idea that Carlyle was an advocate of great men having absolute power over their historical milieu see e.g. P. Rosenberg, 'A Whole World of Heroes', in H. Bloom (ed.), *Thomas Carlyle* (New York: Chelsea House, 1986), pp. 95–108.

46. F. Braudel, *The Mediterranean and the Mediterranean World in the Age of Philip II* (3 vols.; London: Collins, 1972–73), I, p. 21. As with Carlyle, qualifications ought to be made. As Peter Burke points out, Braudel did, after all, devote several hundred pages of *Mediterranean* vol. III to events. Burke adds that it was Braudel's followers who tended to shift away from event-level history. See P. Burke, 'History of Events and the Revival of the Narrative', in P. Burke (ed.), *New Perspectives on History Writing* (London: Polity, 2nd edn, 2001), pp. 283–300 (286–87).
47. Note that one of the criticisms sometimes aimed at Schama's narrative histories is his tendency to shift away from 'history from below' to more famous figures. For a firm rebuking see M. Steel, *Vive la Revolution* (London: Scribner, 2003), pp. 218–19. The issue of whose history is being told is one worth bearing in mind for those writing lives of Jesus.
48. J. G. Crossley, 'Manufacturing Resurrection: Locating Some Contemporary Scholarly Arguments', *Neot.* 45 (2011), pp. 50–76.

Chapter 5

'Never Trust a Hippy': Finding a Liberal Jesus Where You Might Not Think

> For you always have the poor with you, and you can show kindness to them whenever you wish... (Mk 14:7)

> you discover that, for all the new packaging, the Conservatives are the 'same old Tories' after all – from the expected 50 Tory MPs in the next parliament to be drawn from the City or the financial services industry all the way to the 'no entry' signs on country estates their families have owned for more than 500 years.
>
> – Jonathan Freedland[1]

Image Is Everything: The Quest for the Ephemeral Jesus

One notable aspect of the rapid developments in an international free-market context is the mass spread of a popularized culture, from which Jesus was never going to be immune. According to the veteran historian Eric Hobsbawm,

> the global icons come from popular culture. They might not even be strictly part of it, and they might even be inanimate objects. When Andy Warhol, one of the artists of the century most sensitive to the meaning of popular culture, invented the famous set of global icons, he chose Marilyn, Mao, Che Guevara, and a can of Campbell's soup. The simultaneous availability of these images on a planetary scale made this iconography possible.[2]

The Bible is in many ways a global icon in Hobsbawm's sense, but it is Jesus, in his numerous recognizable manifestations, who is the most readily recognizable human image and persona. To put it another way, it was probably with good reason that John Lennon claimed that The Beatles were bigger than Jesus rather than Campbell's soup. Put yet another way, while most of us instantly recognize Jesus pictures, how many would really recognize even a Paul portrait?

When thinking of the impact of postmodernism/postmodernity on historical Jesus scholarship, we skip the extremely common, relentless and, truth be told, largely pointless assertions that we all have presuppositions (as if that makes everything alright) and that anti-theology is as much a presupposition as theology and so on,[3] by instead pointing to the veritable marketplace of historical Jesuses constructed by scholarship (e.g. Cynic-like philosopher, social critic, apocalyptic prophet, wisdom teacher, rabbi and any combination of the previous and more) in the so-called 'Third Quest' constructed by scholarship whose origins, interestingly enough, have sometimes been dated to 1973.[4] As noted in chapter 2, what scholars have constructed as the Third Quest has involved diversity of approaches and the ideological commitments of the participants. I have explicitly and repeatedly used the word 'constructed' here because, as we saw, there have been recent and accurate challenges to the scholarly periodization of historical Jesus 'quests' with the strong implication that we might not, after all, be seeing something dramatically new since the 1970s. However, the *construction* of the new, the self-identification of being part of a new movement since c. 1973 (give or take a few years either side depending on the scholar), the praising of diversity, and the (rhetorical?) intensification of the marketplace of historical Jesuses is something we can at least say has been buoyant since the 1970s.[5]

A look at certain views associated with the 'big names' of the so-called Third Quest would, perhaps, justify instead a look at quests in an age of postmodernity. One of the most prominent historical Jesus scholars, John Dominic Crossan, was already producing work on the apparent polyvalence and multilayered meanings of Jesus' parables from the early 1970s onwards, which was matching the emerging postmodern cultural mood of the time. By the end of the millennium, and two major books by Crossan relating to the historical Jesus later, historical Jesus scholarship had seen some significant battles between advocates of a Cynic-like Jesus, an apocalyptic or eschatological prophet Jesus, rabbi Jesus, proto-Christian Jesus and so on, each a mass-marketable image as much as the scholars attached to them (as ever, whether scholars know it or not and whether scholars like it or not), each a witness to the hunger of a free-market system yearning for more and more markets. Anyone even generally familiar with historical Jesus scholarship will immediately recognize the following scholar-images (even without the names attached) provided in Mark Allen Powell's introduction to the main players in the (spiritual?) marketplace of scholarship:

> John Meier wins the prize for length... Quantitatively, at least, he has exceeded all other Jesus scholars, ancient and modern... A Catholic priest educated and ordained in Rome, Meier is now professor of New Testament at the University of Notre Dame... When *U.S. News and World Report* sought a catchy caption to distinguish Meier from other Jesus scholars they settled on the phrase 'dogged digger'...
>
> Marcus Borg prefers not to talk about 'the historical Jesus' as a figure of the past who can be studied apart from religious or spiritual concerns... A prominent member of the Jesus Seminar... Although a confessing Christian, he admits that his own faith has been enhanced by studying Buddhism, the writings of Carlos Castenada, and the latter's Indian seer, Don Juan...he had a number of mystical and ecstatic experiences that fundamentally changed his understanding of God, Jesus religion, and Christianity...
>
> It [a degree of celebrity] agrees with him [Crossan]. As comfortable chatting on Larry King Live as he is engaging in academic debates at meetings of the Society for [sic] Biblical Literature... Unlike many scholars, he doesn't mind 'being a personality'...he eschews objectivity as unobtainable and spurious, and offers in its place a more realistic credential for scholarship: honesty.
>
> Even those who have never read any of Wright's volumes may know him as the scholar who spells *god* with a lowercase *g*...[6]

The list could go on but one qualification is worth adding: in the case of Wright we may add that he is also famous for his role as the (now former) Bishop of Durham who will not separate history and theology. But he has also become famous for two counter-images with which he may not be so comfortable: the scholar who thinks it is possible various people really did rise from the dead (Mt. *27:51–53*), because some stories are just so strange they may be true,[7] and the scholar who unintentionally generated, in part, that brilliant online parody: 'Bishop N. T. Wrong'.

And what better manifestation of image and an American form of the acceptable, or idealized face of (neo-)liberalism, than the North American Jesus Seminar? As Stephen Prothero pointed out, 'the Jesus Seminar is quintessentially American. Its method is democratic, its goal is freedom, and its obsession is Jesus.'[8] In its heyday, the Jesus Seminar and its members would actively get involved in the American media (television and printed press) to promote scholarly work, though it attracted controversial headlines, inevitably perhaps with such subject matter and despite the honourable aims of the Jesus Seminar. Even the Hollywood producer Paul Verhoeven could count himself a fellow of the Jesus Seminar who had the intention of making a Jesus film.[9]

We might add the entrepreneurial side of the Jesus Seminar and not least one of the Jesus Seminar's charismatic founding figures, Robert Funk. Funk is notably remembered in what effectively amounts to a myth of the anti-bureaucratic, entrepreneurial, all-American, individual success story for a neoliberal age. Note, for instance, the language used to describe Funk by *a Funk sympathizer and Jesus Seminar fellow, Lane C. McGaughy.* Funk was appointed to chair the Research and Publication Committee of the American Academy of Religion in 1967 because of his 'entrepreneurial talents.' Funk is described as transforming the American Academy of Religion and Society of Biblical Literature into international learned societies partly through 'cutting costs' of flagship journals by 50 per cent. Along with George MacRae, Funk

> decided to tackle the escalating cost of books by publishing works written and edited by AAR and SBL members using the offset method at a fraction of the cost of commercial publishers. The aim was to challenge commercial publishers to lower the price of books by pioneering newer and less expensive forms of production.

Funk established Scholars Press in 1974 with an established 'market for its publications.' Funk also founded Polebridge Press (1981) and the Westar Institute (1986), both famously linked with the Jesus Seminar. *McGaughy* concludes, 'As an entrepreneur, Bob was never quite comfortable with the bureaucratic constraints of either the church or the university... Bob Funk was one of the most influential New Testament scholars of our time, combining solid scholarship with the creative talents of entrepreneurial leadership.'[10]

If we were in any doubt, Jesus scholarship is a not entirely insignificant player in contemporary neoliberal manifestations of capitalism and culture because, put bluntly, Jesus books continue to *sell* (most notably Crossan's massive and *technical* book, *The Historical Jesus*) in a way that, say, books on the Pastoral Epistles do not (yet), and such Jesus books are regularly justified, in part, by publishers for that very reason. Whatever their personal motives (which I again believe to be largely irrelevant to this issue and, for what it is worth, largely honourable), major historical Jesus scholars publish with major publishers. Crossan and Amy-Jill Levine have published major popularizing works with HarperCollins while Sanders published a well-known popular historical Jesus book with Penguin.[11] It might even be worth speculating that SPCK could stop selling all books except those of Wright and still make a comfortable profit for all the massive popularity of his books, not least among certain types of conservative American Christians. Like Crossan before him, Bart Ehrman is something of a media star, appearing on no less than *The Daily Show* and *The Colbert Report* to discuss his scholarly work as a *New York Times* bestselling author.[12] Popular and often highly profitable scholarly partnerships have also emerged based on the famous Jesus-images and image-conscious scholarship (we probably know who represents what): Crossan and Borg; Borg and Wright; Wright and Evans; Bock and Wallace; Bird and Crossley; Levine, Allison and Crossan; and Crossan, Johnson, Dunn and Bock.

Such traits have been reflected in what became the geographical heart of the discipline since around 1970: America. And Funk, perhaps more than any other individual, was responsible for pushing what may have been the inevitable. Funk wanted to promote the history of a specifically American biblical studies tradition and would, for instance, use his presidency of SBL to do just this.[13] Today, the major biblical studies conference, at least in terms of size, is, by a wide margin, the annual SBL meeting held in various locations in North America (though typically the USA) and drawing in scholars from across the planet on a scale seen nowhere else in contemporary biblical studies, attracting at least 5,000 biblical scholars per year, and doubled when held with the American Academy of Religion. By way of contrast, there is the much smaller (delegate numbers are typically counted in their hundreds, not thousands) and significantly named International SBL held in various locations across the world. The growth of the annual SBL meeting since the 1970s has also seen the growth of publisher interest. Hector Avalos recalls his first SBL annual meeting in 1982 when the programme book listed one main book for discussion (Ernest Saunders's history of the SBL) in contrast to 2005 where 24 books were listed for discussion. He adds, 'This is not necessarily a bad thing, but sometimes I wonder how much "agenting", rather than merit or true novelty, is responsible for the selection of the books deemed significant for discussion.'[14] And finally, if we wanted to mention the intellectual aspects of postmodern biblical scholarship, and if we were going to be a touch cynical, then do not Eagleton's following comments, now quoted more fully, bear some resemblance to a steady stream of papers and their presenters, so common at the annual Society of Biblical Literature conference, when he talks of a 'cult of ambiguity and indeterminacy'?

> Conference papers entitled 'Putting the anus back into *Coriolanus*' would attract hordes of excited acolytes who knew little about the bourgeoisie but a good deal about buggery... The radical impulse would

> not be abandoned; but it would shift gradually from the transformative to the subversive, and nobody except the advertisers would speak of revolution anymore… One would continue to dream of a utopian other to the system or regime as such…while grimly insisting on the recalcitrance of power, the fragility of the ego, the absorptive power of capital, the insatiability of desire, the inescapability of the Law, the indeterminable effects of political action… It would not be out of the question to run across people who wished to see the Epoch of Man pass away, and voted Liberal Democrat.[15]

The Return of the Johannine Jesus

Now we can add another, resurrected historical Jesus, only a few years ago long out of step with the world of New Testament scholarship: the historical Jesus via John's Gospel. In recent years, Paul Anderson has been particularly vocal in advocating a 'bi-optic' approach to the Jesus tradition (i.e. using the Synoptic/Markan tradition *and* Johannine tradition) and has been highly active in the ongoing John, Jesus and History project at SBL, with two major publications and more to come.[16] Moreover, Anderson has been pushing this agenda hard beyond the edited volumes: he has been promoting his views on the popular *Bible and Interpretation* website, going as far as implying that the use of John is part of a 'Fourth Quest' (see chapter 1!) for the historical Jesus,[17] has published an online summary for *Zeitschrift für Neues Testament*, 'for the benefit of scholars in Europe and elsewhere',[18] and participated in the lengthy discussion on the Biblical Studies e-list (along with Tom Thatcher).[19]

Anderson is keen on the word 'modern' and 'modernist' in describing lack of concern for John's Gospel in the quest for the historical Jesus: John's signs are 'extremely problematic for a naturalist modernist';[20] there are 'modernist attacks on John's authorship and historicity'; 'whereas the litmus test for the modernist biblical scholar used to be, "in the historicity of John?", the litmus test for the modernist biblical scholar has come to be, "Do you believe in the ahistoricity of John?"'; the criteria of authenticity used in historical Jesus studies (multiple attestation, dissimilarity etc.) are the 'foundation for the majority of modernist Jesus studies'; there is 'the modernist impulse to question John's historicity'; and 'a dialectical approach to historiography may come across as disturbing to a modernist historian'.[21] The rhetorical ploy of labelling (largely) opposing approaches as (overly) 'modernist', along with his 'bi-optic' approach and claims concerning a new Fourth Quest, implies some outdated historical method seemingly used by Anderson's opponents. However, such rhetoric does not get us away from the following basic point: using a source many typically have not in historical Jesus studies (John's Gospel) is merely to add a different *source* and not a different *methodological* approach.

It seems, then, that what we have here is a repackaging of the old story for our 'postmodern' age. This ought to be qualified using Anderson's language because he says explicitly that his intention is not so much to supplant 'modernist criticism with post-modern analysis' as 'to perform the critical task well.'[22] However, Anderson is constructing something, let us say, *post*-Modern and the newness of this is made clear: 'if the modernist platform fails to stand up to critical analyses...critical scholarship at the dawn of the post-Modern era demands an alternative. This is why this study is needed *now*.'[23] If we were to push this logic further we see, unsurprisingly, just how much a part of its postmodernist context Anderson's work truly is, though not necessarily the way Anderson might think.

Indeed, such contextualization becomes clearer when Anderson turns to historical Jesus brands. Based on Marcus Borg's summary of the different possible portraits of Jesus, Anderson suggests that John's Gospel is coherent with the different models. Anderson suggests that John's Jesus is a 'noneschatological prophet...the prophet-like-Moses.' The Johannine Jesus fits 'within the portraiture of a wisdom-imparting sage' and an 'institution-challenging Cynic, in that Jesus cleanses the Temple at the beginning of his ministry, heals on the Sabbath, confronts religious authorities in Jerusalem prolifically, and is willing to challenge the Roman governor in the name of God's transcendent truth and reign.' Anderson adds that Jesus 'comes across with spiritual power, as a holy man in John. While he does not perform exorcisms, the Johannine Jesus is encountered by people epiphanically... Jesus as a holy man cannot be said to be incompatible with the Johannine presentation of Jesus.' Adding to Borg's list, Anderson suggests John's Jesus also comes across as 'an apocalyptic messenger...and the entire ministry of Jesus is presented eschatologically.'[24]

Assuming for the moment the validity of using such disputed categories from historical Jesus scholarship, and that his generalizations do not miss key nuances in the different Gospel traditions, it is questionable whether Anderson's points help us in any significant way in terms of the quest for the historical Jesus. All these interpretations, no matter how conflicting, no matter how contradictory, are somehow valid historically, it would seem. It may, of course, be theoretically possible that there are significant overlaps between different portraits of Jesus, but, for instance, the debates over Jesus as Cynic-like or Jesus as eschatological prophet have been fierce and largely polarizing. The assumption of Anderson is that if most or all of the scholarly portraits of Jesus can be found in John's Gospel then we somehow have an argument for John's Gospel being useful for understanding the historical Jesus. Instead of the aggressively competitive marketplace, are not these kinds of truth claims in line with certain strands of postmodernism with its polite pluralism, interdependence, difference and otherness without judgment, a kind of tolerant, multicultural society for scholarly constructions of the historical Jesus?

Identity, and Lots of It

Turning to the more overt manifestations of postmodernism (and even neoliberalism), we might recall high-profile strands of a distinctive type of postmodern 'political' thinking, particularly the stress on gender, feminism and ethnicity. These stresses may well fit the cultural and political conflicts of our times but they can remain popular because, as Eagleton puts it, 'they are not necessarily anti-capitalist, and so fit well enough with a post-radical age.'[25] Where we might think, for instance, of that particularly common American academic practice of using the third-person pronoun 'she', replacing the masculine form assumed by a generation past, we might also think of a curious analogy in historical Jesus studies: Jesus being nice to women, or at least nicer than his contemporaries. Such concerns for Jesus and women is a notable feature of numerous opposing historical Jesus studies, including those who usually stay away from the more overtly politicized categories.[26]

Some scholars, such as Gerald O'Collins, can note 'the ongoing habit of some male writers of minimizing the testimony of the women' and argue that by 'belittling the empty tomb tradition as a later elaboration, they devalue the witness of women; after all, women, and not men, were utterly central to the empty tomb tradition.'[27] Given that O'Collins is a papal loyalist and a theological thinker close to the Vatican, we can probably assume that his motivations are less an attack on gender inequalities and more about establishing the historical accuracy of the crucial resurrection narrative. But this is clear example of how the new cosy appreciation of women has become so embedded in the discipline that even the more conservative wings openly embrace such credible liberalism.

We might also point out how this sort of thinking is replicated in identity politics and the market. Multiple identities and the combining of identities are typically part of the perpetual capitalist drive for anything new while doing little more than demanding to be another voice to be heard and taken seriously. As Badiou put it more cynically,

> What inexhaustible potential for mercantile investments in this upsurge – taking the form of communities demanding recognition and so-called cultural singularities – of women, homosexuals, the disabled, Arabs! And those infinite combinations of predicative traits, what a godsend! Black homosexuals, disabled Serbs, Catholic pedophiles, moderate Muslims, married priests, ecologist yuppies, the submissive unemployed, prematurely aged youth! Each time, a social image authorizes new products, specialized magazines, improved shopping malls, 'free' radio stations, targeted advertising networks...[28]

Is it perhaps unsurprising, then, that some seemingly radical postcolonial criticism, particularly that stressing hybridity and mixed identities (and indeed complicity of the oppressed), has been increasingly popular in the past 15 or so years? And if we convert this into historical Jesus currency then we have not only a Cynic-like figure, an eschatological prophet, a rabbi, a wisdom teacher, charismatic holy man and so on, but all sorts of combinations which are now being touted by major historical Jesus scholars: Jewish peasant cynic, wisdom teacher *and* eschatological prophet, charismatic holy rabbi, challenger of traditional gender categories *and* social critic and so on. And if *your* Jesus isn't here, one can easily be made up for you, or another category can always be added!

Not dissimilar comments have been made of the disciplinary structure of biblical studies. With particular concern for gender-critical analysis of the discipline, Caroline Vander Stichele and Todd Penner note that the discipline accommodates 'non-normative' feminist agendas, Asian hermeneutics and queer approaches and so we have individuals characterized as such, with the historical-critical centre of the discipline effectively characterized as 'normative' and lacking the cultural, racial and ideological perspectives of those 'others' so typical, we might add, of a postmodern multicultural plural replacing the grand Other. What this structure does is mask power by strengthening its hold. As Vander Stichele and Penner conclude, 'if we take seriously the structure of the guild as outlined here, then the two spheres are rather working in tandem and sustain a larger normativity related to identity and subjectivity, particularly as those intersect with politics, culture, and society in this period of globalized capitalism (and capitalist globalism).'[29] We might modify Vander Stichele and Penner's analysis by adding that this multicultural and tolerant masking has effectively covered over, or worked in tandem with, 'unconscious' dominant political trends in centrist historical Jesus studies in particular, and historical-critical scholarship in general, from implicit narratives of cultural superiority over against Judaism to perpetuating Orientalist agendas concerning the Middle East.

A Sugar-free Historical Jesus (or: Schweitzer's Jesus without Schweitzer)

> On today's market, we find a series of products deprived of their malignant property: coffee without caffeine, cream without fat, beer without alcohol... And the list goes on: what about virtual sex as sex without sex, the Colin Powell doctrine of warfare with no casualties (on our side, of course) as warfare without warfare...up to today's tolerant multiculturalism as an experience of the Other deprived of its Otherness...? Virtual Reality simply generalizes this procedure of offering a product deprived of its substance: it provides reality itself deprived of its substance...just as decaffeinated coffee smells and tastes like real coffee without being the real coffee, Virtual Reality is experienced as reality without being so.
>
> – Slavoj Žižek[30]

While multicultural inclusiveness may at least seem superficially to embrace the Other(s), it is clear this is not necessarily the case in the above examples. As Žižek has argued,[31] this sort of limited inclusiveness is central to liberal Western multiculturalism and our postmodern age, an acceptance of the Other without the Otherness. Put another way, part of the narrative of Western liberalism is to include the Other without the unpalatable bits and extract those bits which are palatable (think of the common debates about what 'true Islam' or 'spiritual Islam' is). Is not the Other deprived of its Otherness a plausible way of describing Anderson's Jesus of John's Gospel, which includes his marketplace of historical Jesuses? After all, all the previously competing Jesuses are now tolerated, with John now invited to join or convene the plurality, while anything that made these Jesuses different, Other and put sharply at odds with one another, is now removed to make sure they all get along. In a related way, and in a debate on the resurrection of Jesus, Michael Bird complains that much of the 'peoples of other cultures in Africa, Asia and South America' do not share Bultmann's Eurocentric, scientific objections to the miraculous.[32] But what does this mean? Bird only really seems interested in backing up his own position on Jesus' miracles and so the Other is simply used when convenient. It is probably not going too far to suggest that many of the aforementioned peoples do not believe half the things Bird believes and many of them will no doubt practice things Bird dislikes. This seems a clear use of the Other in terms of conformity to Bird's position and his multicultural embrace.

We might develop such ideas further with reference to the history of historical Jesus scholarship because this history is a long history, stretching back long before our postmodern age, which has often ensured that Jesus has had the 'malignant property' removed, at least when it comes to key issues. Every now and then a dangerous idea emerges in scholarship. Such ideas are dangerous because they appear to challenge the received view of some idea in scholarship in a profound way and everyone has to deal with the challenge. Such ideas can appear to be challenging to the very core of Christianity itself and yet they manage to gain access to the discipline without, somehow, managing to challenge the very core of Christianity itself. This is because they are neutralized and the harsh element is removed and/or absorbed. This can be done through ignoring the consequences or radically reinterpreting the problematic nature of the challenge. The reasons why such challenges come about may be because the arguments are extremely convincing but, like charisma, they can end up being tamed and consequently providing further credibility for what we might call a decaffeinated or sugar-free Jesus.

One example is the idea of an eschatological Jesus who predicted imminent end times and judgment...and got it wrong. At the end of the nineteenth century and the beginning of the twentieth, Johannes Weiss and Albert Schweitzer made the case and would, especially Schweitzer, become the most influential figures in inspiring the modern mistaken Jesus. However, for many Christian scholars (and this may well describe the majority of New Testament scholars to some degree) this is, for obvious reasons, a problem. A Jesus who made a major error of prediction is potentially difficult to reconcile with the second person of the Trinity, and for certain very liberal Christians this sort of Jesus is potentially difficult to reconcile with contexts promoting modern forms of tolerant open-mindedness, not to mention producing a Jesus who could be used by enemies of the Christian faith to attempt to undermine the Christian faith.

There has also been much scholarly soul-searching and exegesis in trying to deal with the problem, though a tradition of effortlessly incorporating the seemingly problematic into a theological system is also evident. Allison, who has provided detailed referencing of these scholarly reactions to a potentially mistaken Jesus, is part of a long tradition of scholarly 'confession' whereby the scholar comes clean and comes to terms with their own world turned upside down, thanks in this case to the troubling personal impact of a Jesus of imminent eschatology.[33] This only further highlights the idea that a mistaken Jesus of the imminent end times is a dangerous idea. After all, it is difficult to see many scholars emotionally investing so much if Jesus had not been recorded as being so interested in making such predictions or, alternatively, a Tudor historian (Geoffrey Elton aside) suffering anguish if Henry VIII had also been an eschatological prophet.

However, what is clear is that Allison confronts the problem head-on and his confession only heightens the idea that Jesus preaching imminent end times is a serious cultural problem for scholarship.[34] And there is no end to the scholarship which tries to counter this alien Jesus with some serious Otherness. The most cited example of avoiding such a Jesus may well be the Jesus who emerges from the Jesus Seminar (Cynic-like Jesus etc.) and the criticism is regularly made of this Jesus (and others) that a Jesus with apocalyptic teaching or eschatological intentions is a guard against historical anachronism. Repeated uncritically this point may be, but in some ways it is worth heeding because it is a good example of a Jesus with the potentially deeply uncomfortable 'religious' sting taken out.[35] Or, as Deane Galbraith put it differently,

> While the *Jesus Seminar* and other nineteenth-century liberals like to present Jesus as a cuddly wind-up toy whose string you can pull and make him recite any of a few dozen comforting aphorisms (to borrow an image from Joseph Hoffmann), the historical Jesus turns out to be more of a David Koresh-type demagogue with an overinflated estimation of himself than some harmless Cynic philosopher.[36]

However, despite the popularity of an eschatological Jesus, there is a significant scholarly tradition which pushes for this Other Jesus but without the Otherness. For instance, one prominent means of dealing with the problem is to take the sting out of its tail by accepting that, yes, there is lots of language we might call 'eschatological' or 'apocalyptic', but Jesus was not mistaken.[37] The language of end times means, then, *something else*. The most prominent and influential recent historical Jesus scholar to do this is N. T. Wright, who argues that 'apocalyptic' and 'eschatological' language are not about the end of the 'space-time universe' but are more metaphorical reference to socio-political events or, in theological-historical terms, '*the climactic moment of Israel's history*'.[38] But perhaps just as famously, Wright still sees his work as being very much in the tradition of Schweitzer. In an interview with InterVarsity Press, Wright was asked which three or four books he would want on a desert island and one of them was 'Schweitzer's *The Quest of the Historical Jesus*'.[39] If that was not enough academic credibility, Wright also presents Sanders as holding a similar position to his own.[40] Though I think Wright pushes this similarity too hard, does not Sanders, one of the most prominent advocates of a Jesus predicting end times, rightly or wrongly add a small but potentially significant qualification?

> Scholars usually assume that Mark 13 implies the end of the world. We now know that if the stars fell from heaven, the physical universe would be in serious trouble. To ancient people, however, the stars looked fairly close and quite small (as they do to children today until they are taught the basic facts about astronomy). Thus the predictions of cosmic disturbance do not necessarily imply that the universe is about to be destroyed. It is more likely that these sayings simply describe *how* the kingdom will come to an earth that will remain in existence.[41]

While eschatology and Jesus is a perennial problem for historical Jesus scholarship (and no surprise given that it involves Jesus being mistaken), there is another example more specifically suited to our postmodern times, though hardly without precursors in different language for different times. Arguably, the other dangerous idea in historical Jesus studies, and one which will be further discussed in this book, is Jesus the Jew. This needs to be qualified. No one, Nazi and related scholarship aside, denies Jesus was Jewish and today virtually all scholars are delighted to affirm that Jesus was Jewish. So, in the general sense Jesus the Jew cannot be much of a dangerous idea in contemporary scholarship. Instead, I mean that the idea that came to be broadly associated with Geza Vermes (though there were and are others) was and is potentially dangerous, namely that Jesus was a fairly conventional Jewish figure for his time and all his ideas were paralleled in the Judaism of his time (compare Vermes's Jesus as a charismatic Jewish holy man). Indeed, Vermes drew a sharp line between the (Jewish) Jesus of history and the Christ of faith.[42] Again, the potential problem here is that Vermes's Jesus is not sufficiently connected to the Christian faith and is not remotely related to the second person of the Trinity. This sort of Jesus is, if we were to follow Vermes, part of Jewish tradition which otherwise would have recognized him without batting an eyelid if he were not the Christian Messiah.

In one sense, Vermes's Jesus might have provided, for the Christian or non-Jewish academic at least, an experience of the Other with all the Otherness. Yet it would seem that Jesus the Jew has had to be domesticated and rewritten in 'our' terms. While a minority of scholars tried to continue Vermes's line, the dominant line in historical Jesus scholarship has to make sure, it seems, that Jesus transcends some aspect of the scholarly construction of Judaism (e.g. Jesus supposedly broke the Sabbath, or was 'radical' on oaths and so on) to a lesser or greater degree. Or, in the hands of N. T. Wright, we get 'a very Jewish Jesus who was nevertheless opposed to some high-profile features of first-century Judaism.'[43] I have discussed this domestication of Jesus the Jew elsewhere and we will now further explore the liberal and not-so-liberal similarities in the next chapter with particular focus on its significance for our postmodern, multicultural times. Before that, we might recall Bermejo Rubio's suggestion that one reason for Wright's dubious construction of the quests, especially the distinctive Third Quest, might have been an attempt to decaffeinate the challenge to orthodox Christian theology provided by Sanders's *Jesus and Judaism* (I would add Vermes's *Jesus the Jew*) by incorporating his own supersessionist work in a new scholarly tradition which has a rhetorically very positive view of Judaism.[44]

This might be the place to point out one of Wright's other three or four books for his desert island...'Sanders's *Jesus and Judaism*.'

Notes

1. J. Freedland, 'The Innocent Smoothies of Politics Are Still the Party of the Rich,' *Guardian* (9 March, 2010).
2. E. J. Hobsbawm, *The New Century* (London: Abacus, 2000), p. 123.
3. For far more useful interactions with issues concerning presuppositions, positivism, methodological self-consciousness, ideological frameworks and postmodernity, and notably at a time when such ideas were less of a cliché, see C. Marsh, 'Quests of the Historical Jesus in New Historicist Perspective,' *BibInt* 5 (1997), pp. 403–37.
4. See March, 'Quests,' pp. 408–409 for discussion and bibliography.
5. T. Eagleton's broadside is analogous to those constructing the newness of the so-called Third Quest: 'The West is now bulging at the seams with political radicals whose ignorance of socialist traditions, not least their own, is certainly among other things the effects of postmodernist amnesia' (*The Illusions of Postmodernism* [Oxford: Blackwell, 1996], p. 22).

6. M. A. Powell, *The Jesus Debate: Modern Historians Investigate the Life of Christ* (Oxford: Lion, 1998), pp. 95, 112, 142, 160.
7. N. T. Wright, *The Resurrection of the Son of God* (London: SPCK, 2003), p. 636.
8. S. Prothero, *American Jesus: How the Son of God Became a National Icon* (New York: Farrar, Straus and Giroux, 2003), p. 33. This is not to dispute Robert J. Miller's defence that the Jesus Seminar's voting system derives from biblical translation committees (R. J. Miller, *The Jesus Seminar and Its Critics* [Santa Rosa: Polebridge, 1999], pp. 65–66). Rather, the general cultural features of the Jesus Seminar are, just like its opponents and those professing indifference, reflective of cultural trends.
9. Powell, *Jesus Debate*, p. 76.
10. L. C. McGaughy, 'Robert W. Funk – A Profile', *Fourth R* 19.2 (March–April 2006), pp. 4–6.
11. Cf. Marsh, 'Quests', pp. 422–25.
12. His website (http://www.bartdehrman.com/) sells Ehrman as 'a leading authority on the New Testament and the history of early Christianity. His work has been featured in Time, the New Yorker, the Washington Post and other print media, and he has appeared on NBC's Dateline, The Daily Show with Jon Stewart, CNN, The History Channel, National Geographic, the Discovery Channel, the BBC, major NPR shows, and other top media outlets.'
13. R. W. Funk, 'The Watershed of the American Biblical Tradition: The Chicago School, First Phase, 1892–1920', *JBL* 95 (1976), pp. 4–22.
14. H. Avalos, 'The Ideology of the Society of Biblical Literature and the Demise of an Academic Profession', *SBL Forum* (April 2006), http://sbl-site.org/Article.aspx?ArticleID=520.
15. Eagleton, *Illusions of Postmodernism*, pp. 4–5. It does, though, seem as if there are degrees of shock, particularly in light of Roland Boer's 2010 'sausage-fest' paper at SBL. See R. Boer, 'SBL Censorship: "Sausage-fests" Are Unacceptable', Stalin's Moustache (23 October, 2010), http://stalinsmoustache.wordpress.com/2010/10/23/sbl-censorship-sausage-fests-are-unacceptable/; R. Boer, 'Why Does the SBL Not Like Sausages or Sausage-fests? Or, How to Deal with Censorship', Stalin's Moustache (23 October, 2010), http://stalinsmoustache.wordpress.com/2010/10/23/why-does-the-sbl-not-like-sausages-or-sausage-fests-or-how-to-deal-with-censorship/. Like the quest for the scholarly origins of the term 'New Perspective' in Pauline studies, the origins of 'sausage-fest' are not easy to establish. It seems one of the earliest uses of an approximate equivalent in biblical scholarship was used by R. J. Myles, 'Dandy Discipleship: A Queering of Mark's Male Disciples', *Journal of Men, Masculinities, and Spirituality* 4 (2010), pp. 66-81.
16. P. N. Anderson, F. Just and T. Thatcher (eds.), *John, Jesus, and History*. I. *Critical Appraisals of Critical Views* (Atlanta: SBL, 2007); idem (eds.), *John, Jesus, and History*. II. *Aspects of Historicity in the Fourth Gospel* (Atlanta: SBL, 2009). See also P. N. Anderson, *The Fourth Gospel and the Quest for Jesus: Modern Foundations Reconsidered* (London: T&T Clark, 2006). For a critical evaluation of the John, Jesus and History project see J. G. Crossley, 'Can John's Gospel Really Be Used to Reconstruct a Life of Jesus? An Assessment of Recent Trends and a Defence of a Traditional View', in T. L. Thompson and

T. S. Verenna (eds.), *'Is This Not the Carpenter?' The Question of the Historicity of the Figure of Jesus* (Sheffield and Oakville: Equinox, 2011, forthcoming).

17. P. N. Anderson, 'A Fourth Quest for Jesus...So What, and How So?', *Bible and Interpretation* (July 2010), http://www.bibleinterp.com/opeds/fourth357921.shtml#sdfootnote4sym.
18. P. N. Anderson, 'The John, Jesus, and History Project-New Glimpses of Jesus and a Bi-Optic Hypothesis', *Bible and Interpretation* (February 2010), http://www.bibleinterp.com/articles/john1357917.shtml; P. N. Anderson, 'Das "John-, Jesus-, and History"-Projekt. Neue Beobachtungen zu Jesus und eine Bi-optische Hypothese', *ZNT* 23 (2009), pp. 12–26.
19. The e-list discussion plus materials can be found at http://groups.yahoo.com/group/biblical-studies/message/23464, but require subscription to view. The discussion was announced by J. West, 'John, Jesus and History', Zwinglius Redivivus (1 November, 2009), http://zwingliusredivivus.wordpress.com/2011/01/09/john-jesus-and-history/.
20. P. N. Anderson, 'Why This Study Is Needed, and Why It Is Needed Now', in Anderson, Just and Thatcher (eds.), *John, Jesus, and History*, I, pp. 13–73 (57–58).
21. Anderson, *Fourth Gospel and the Quest for Jesus*, pp. 22, 45, 85, 154, 188.
22. Anderson, *Fourth Gospel and the Quest for Jesus*, p. 176.
23. Anderson, *Fourth Gospel and the Quest for Jesus*, p. 45.
24. Anderson, 'Why This Study Is Needed', pp. 63–65.
25. Eagleton, *Illusions of Postmodernism*, p. 25.
26. Compare, for instance, B. Witherington III, *Women in the Ministry of Jesus: A Study of Jesus' Attitudes to Women and Their Roles as Reflected in His Early Life* (Cambridge: Cambridge University Press, 1984); E. P. Sanders, *The Historical Figure of Jesus* (London: Penguin, 1993); E. S. Fiorenza, *In Memory of Her: A Feminist Theological Reconstruction of Christian Origins* (London: SCM, 2nd edn, 1994); N. T. Wright, *Jesus and the Victory of God* (London: SPCK, 1996), e.g. p. 52; H. Moxnes, *Putting Jesus in His Place: A Radical Vision of Household and Kingdom* (Louisville: Westminster John Knox, 2003); J. D. Crossan, *The Historical Jesus: The Life of a Mediterranean Jewish Peasant* (San Francisco: HarperCollins; Edinburgh: T&T Clark, 1991), pp. 298–302; R. Bauckham, *Gospel Women: Studies of the Named Women in the Gospels* (Edinburgh: T&T Clark, 2002); J. G. Crossley, 'Writing about the Historical Jesus: Historical Explanation and "the Big Why Questions", or Antiquarian Empiricism and Victorian Tomes?', *Journal for the Study of the Historical Jesus* 7 (2009), pp. 63–90.
27. G. O'Collins, 'The Resurrection: The State of the Question', in S. T. Davis, D. Kendall and G. O'Collins (eds.), *The Resurrection: An Interdisciplinary Symposium on the Resurrection of Jesus* (Oxford: Oxford University Press, 1997), pp. 5–28 (14).
28. A. Badiou, *Saint Paul: The Foundation of Universalism* (Stanford: Stanford University Press, 2003), p. 10.
29. C. Vander Stichele and T. Penner, *Contextualizing Gender in Early Christian Discourse: Thinking beyond Thecla* (London and New York: Continuum/T&T Clark, 2009), pp. 168–69.
30. Žižek, *Puppet and the Dwarf*, p. 96.

31. See also Žižek, *Desert*, e.g. p. 34.
32. M. F. Bird, 'Historical Jesus', in M. F. Bird and J. G. Crossley, *How Did Christianity Begin? A Believer and Non-believer Examine the Evidence* (London: SPCK, 2008), pp. 21–22.
33. D. C. Allison, *Resurrecting Jesus: The Earliest Christian Tradition and Its Interpreters* (London and New York: Continuum, 2005), pp. 111–48; idem, *The Historical Christ and the Theological Jesus* (Grand Rapids: Eerdmans, 2009). For further discussion see e.g. J. S. Kloppenborg with J. W. Marshall (eds.), *Apocalypticism, Anti-Semitism and the Historical Jesus: Subtexts in Criticism* (London and New York: T&T Clark/Continuum, 2005).
34. For an important example of confronting the eschatology head-on, as well as scholarly views, see now E. Adams, *The Stars Will Fall from Heaven: Cosmic Catastrophe and the World's End in the New Testament and Its World* (London: T&T Clark/Continuum, 2007).
35. In this sense, there is something significant about Allison's critique of secularizing Jesus. See Allison, *Resurrecting Jesus*, pp. 22–23.
36. D. Galbraith, 'Did Jesus Rise from the Dead? Casey on Jesus (5) – Did Jesus Consider Himself to Be "The Son of Man"?', Remnant of Giants (21 April, 2011), http://remnantofgiants.wordpress.com/2011/04/21/caseys-jesus-5-son-of-man/.
37. For examples see the discussion in P. M. Casey, *From Jewish Prophet to Gentile God: The Origins of New Testament Christology* (Louisville: Westminster John Knox, 1991), pp. 162–78.
38. N. T. Wright, *Jesus and the Victory of God* (London: SPCK, 1996), p. 97, italics original.
39. Anonymous, 'Author Interview: N.T. Wright', InterVarsity Press, http://www.ivpress.com/spotlight/2200.php.
40. Wright, *Victory*, pp. 95–96, n. 47.
41. Sanders, *Historical Figure of Jesus*, p. 174.
42. G. Vermes, *The Religion of Jesus the Jew* (London: SCM, 1993), pp. 208–15.
43. Wright, *Victory*, p. 93.
44. F. Bermejo Rubio, 'The Fiction of the "Three Quests": An Argument for Dismantling a Dubious Historiographical Paradigm', *JSHJ* 7 (2009), pp. 211–53 (238–53).

Part II

Jesus in an Age of Neoliberalism

At least in the United States, Jesus has been a classic other-directed personality. Ever eager to please, he has been all things to all people, adjusting his message and appearance in order to be loved by his peers...the American Jesus has been ever more attuned to shifts in the cultural winds.

– Stephen Prothero[1]

Chapter 6

A 'Fundamentally Unreliable Adoration': 'Jewishness' and the Multicultural Jesus

> Another of his disciples said to him, 'Lord, first let me go and bury my father.' But Jesus said to him, 'Follow me, and let the dead bury their own dead.' (Mt. 8:21–22//Lk. 9:59–60)

> There are times when racial thought shuns the vile rhetoric of the demagogue in favor of the dignified discourse of the poet and the intellectual... This form of racial thinking appears in discourse that is decidedly gentle and in rhetoric that can tend towards the inspirational... The aesthetic ideology is more than capable of prospering in the rarefied air of postmodern criticism.
>
> – Shawn Kelley[2]

> Tolerance arises at the dusk of Enlightenment Man not to relieve us of the problem of difference but to inscribe its power and permanence.
>
> –Wendy Brown[3]

Introduction

As we have just seen, one dangerous idea in historical Jesus studies is Jesus the Jew, or, rather, the 'problem' of Jesus being *as Jewish as the Judaism constructed by scholarship*, and how this is compensated in scholarship by what I would call a 'Jewish...but not *that* Jewish' Jesus.[4] Many historical Jesus scholars will now emphasize how Jewish their Jesus is, tell us what constituted Jewish identity in the first century, before having their Jesus transcend this Jewish identity, or at least do something new and unparalleled either generally or on some specific (and often crucial) issue, typically involving the Torah and/or Temple. Subtly or otherwise, this pattern is found from the more obscure Jesus scholarship through to the major works on the historical Jesus such as those by Sanders, Wright, Dunn, Meier, Theissen and Merz, Allison and so on.[5]

In the *Communist Manifesto*, Marx famously remarked that 'all that is solid melts into air'. Marx was arguing more generally about the bourgeois need for a constantly expanding and ever-changing market across the surface of the globe. Given an updating for our image-conscious age, this obviously tallies with, is analogous to, and often underlies, what we said about the expanding Jesus markets of our times. And what better example of meeting contemporary market needs than the 'Jewish...but not *that* Jewish' Jesus? This dominant Jesus, I argued, was a product of a post-1967 cultural shift, including the first widespread interest in the Holocaust[6] and a hugely favourable attitude towards Israel in Anglo-American political, educational and popular culture,[7] which nevertheless includes attitudes of cultural and religious superiority in relation to Jews, Judaism and Israel, and all as part of the general shift of the centre of biblical scholarship from Germany to North America.[8] As I repeatedly stress, a key aim of this present book is to complement ideas in *Jesus in an Age of Terror* by locating Jesus more specifically in a postmodern and neoliberal age, in this case, with the help of Žižek, how acceptance of the Other without the difficult Otherness is a key feature of contemporary liberal multiculturalism. This, I think, strongly enhances previous arguments concerning the Jewishness of Jesus as an excellent example of how all the key cultural issues come together and provide the specific context for Žižek's more theoretical analysis.[9] I will begin this analysis of what I have showed (as did Arnal in a different way) is a wide-ranging problem in historical Jesus studies with a perhaps more obscure example, but one which, I think, still works with commonly held assumptions of identity.

What Percentage of Alcohol Would Jesus Be?

'Very Jewish' (and the opposite 'not very Jewish') and 'Jewishness' are common phrases in contemporary historical Jesus studies, as I have documented elsewhere.[10] They are phrases that often go unexplained, at least in terms of identity, as if their meaning were obvious. An attempt at unpacking the meaning has come from Michael Bird who published an article on the Jewishness of Jesus, the peril of modernizing Jesus and the crisis of not contemporizing Christ.[11] On the peril of modernizing Jesus, and while noting points of continuity between Jesus and Cynic philosophers and some of Jesus' sayings (cf. Mk 2:17; 6:8–9; Mt. 10:9–10; Lk. 9:3; 10:4; 22:35–36), Bird sees a Cynic or Hellenized Jesus as an exercise in 'de-judaizing' Jesus. Such an exercise possesses

> some similarity with Walter Grundmann's *Jesus der Galiläer* which, written in Nazi Germany, advocated that Jesus was an ethnic Galilean and not a Jew. I am not accusing Mack and Crossan of anti-semitism, but it seems apparent that their works are analogous to older monographs that endeavoured to deny the Jewishness of Jesus. I have read a lot of kafuffle as to how Mel Gibson's *The Passion of the Christ* is blatantly anti-semitic and yet the de-judaizing of Jesus by the Jesus Seminar and others has met with little resistance from academia. Yet history shows that Christianity has done the most unforgiving violence to the Jewish people on those occasions when Jesus' Jewishness was denied or minimized.[12]

Heady stuff! This might raise the question, as it does for Bird, what is 'de-judaizing'? For Bird this does not mean 'anti-Jewish' or completely 'un-Jewish.' Instead, he adds the following ominous analogy: 'De-alcoholized wine still retains a small measure of alcohol, but not enough to impact the drinker. Thus by 'de-Judaizing [Bird uses lower and upper case for 'Judaizing'] I mean the act of moving Jesus' Jewishness to the periphery or else negating its effects by blanketing it with a Hellenistic overlay.'[13] This might raise the question, as it does for Bird, what is 'Jewishness'? Bird sees the Jewishness of Jesus as 'the fail safe' to stop modernizing Jesus yet then finds himself in difficulty when confronted with the problems of precisely what this might mean, concluding,

> a Jewish Jesus constrains modernization by seeing Jesus in conversation and confrontation with his times rather than ours. That means that intra-Jewish disputes about halakha, the status of Samaritans, paying imperial taxes, and maintenance of purity stipulations are more likely to feature as topics of Jesus' interest than feminism, globalization, or church growth strategies.[14]

I am not convinced that any of this provides an adequate way of understanding identity and Bird does not seem to have much interest in the masses of interdisciplinary research into identity. But Bird does spell out key underlying assumptions concerning 'very Jewish' and so on, namely that if we talk about something or someone being 'very Jewish' we are talking about measurements of identity: by this logic Jesus could be more or less Jewish than other people of his day, could he not? A few teasing questions and suggestions might help point out some of the problems with Bird's arguments and arguments assuming a measurement of identity more broadly (this critique is easily modified to incorporate most scholarly rhetoric about the Jewishness of Jesus). What if someone was identified as Jewish but could not care less about intra-Jewish disputes concerning halakhah, the status of Samaritans, paying imperial taxes and maintenance of purity stipulations? Rabbinic literature is perfectly aware of Jews uninterested in purity and halakhah (e.g. the 'people of the land'). We might surmise that plenty of Jews in the ancient world may never have met a Samaritan or cared less about Samaritans and plenty of Jews may have worried about payment of taxes but one master was as good or bad as another. Bird certainly uses these as examples and presumably this might mean more could be used and definitions could potentially be blurry. But then we get the wine/alcohol analogy which makes identity much more fixed and, to use the criticism of our times, essentialist. This can be highlighted better if we play around with his model.

So if we were to accept points of continuity what might this mean? That Jesus was 10% vol. Jew? Or are the points of continuity just general coincidence or ideas around in the Eastern Mediterranean? If so, does not the mixing up of ideas from different cultures say something problematic about Bird's model of identity? And what are we to do with the findings of Philip Harland who argues that identities and loyalties depend on context?[15] For instance, Harland points out that someone could be in a synagogue one moment, in a guild or trade association the next – do the alcohol levels of such individuals rise and fall according to context? Or again, if, say, someone claimed that they had a serious interest in Samaritans and maybe taxes but were utterly indifferent to issues of purity and halakhah, are they 'half-Jewish', or, rather, a 7% vol. Jew? What if a Jew thought Cynic or Hellenistic philosophy wonderful, even more wonderful than the Torah or apocalyptic thought, do they shift from being (say) a hearty 12% vol. to a mere 2% vol.? Ultimately, does someone become more or less an ancient Jew depending on what a scholar says?

Let us test out Bird's alcoholic analogy further by applying it to Jesus scholarship. N. T. Wright, a major influence on Bird, has his historical Jesus not simply involved with intra-Jewish halakhic issues but on issues involving Sabbath, food, purity family and so on; he has Jesus making them redundant and opening up the promises to Jews beyond Samaritans.[16] Could we not make the case that Wright's Jesus is, by developing Bird's methodology, a thoroughly non-alcoholic Jew, or at best a white-wine spritzer? Is Wright's Jesus only of use for underage drinkers in the park who have not yet acquired the taste for the strong stuff? Does not Wright's Jesus remove or de-alcoholize most of the symbols Wright constructs as central to Judaism, thereby making his Jesus effectively a Christian or proto-Christian?

Or, by engaging in questions about halakhah, purity and so on, is Wright's Jesus a good 14% vol.? Given that Bird cites Wright in favour of his argument that the Jesus Seminar has supposedly de-Judaized Jesus in a way not dissimilar to the Nazis (!), we would probably have to infer, yes. If this is the case, Wright's Jesus can transcend Judaism as much as he likes and yet Wright's Jesus patronizingly remains Jewish through and through and this is the trump card against any sufficiently threatening scholarly Jesus. If we assume that Wright (the Gentile former Bishop of Durham) and Bird (the Gentile evangelical) believe in what most of Wright's historical Jesus had to say, does that make Wright and Bird *Jewish*? The dark side of Bird's analogy also gets darker: it decides that the Jesus he does not like (the Cynic-like Jesus) cannot be 'very' Jewish, a non-alcoholic Jewish at best. But every contemporary advocate of a Cynic-like Jesus claims, to the best of my knowledge, that Jesus was Jewish!

Bird, however, tries to give evidence suggesting otherwise. He even goes as far as claiming that Mack '*purposely* dislodge[s] Jesus from being Jewish.'[17] I am, however, unaware of Mack ever making such a claim, yet Bird implies the following is an example of how the 'works of Mack… minimize the Jewishness of Jesus in favor of a Hellenistic framework': 'The Cynic analogy repositions the historical Jesus away from a specifically Jewish sectarian milieu and toward the Hellenistic ethos known to have prevailed in Galilee.'[18] All this tells us is that Mack's Jesus is removed from a certain kind of Jewish debate. Mack explicitly removes Jesus from a *sectarian* Jewish context and by Bird's logic *sectarian* Judaism would have to equal Judaism as a whole which, given the different types of people identifying as Jews in the ancient world, is problematic to say the least (and makes the term 'sectarian' redundant). Bird effectively does what Mack in fact did *not* do, that is, assume that being Jewish and endorsing or playing around with Hellenistic views must necessarily be two distinct entities. The works of Philo alone should tell us otherwise. And what if the majority of people who identified as Jewish in the ancient world did not care about sectarian disputes, would their 'Jewishness' not be eradicated by Bird's use of Mack? Mack may have been wrong to make such historical judgments about sectarian Judaism and a Hellenistic Galilee and there may be a range of modernizing factors which led him to make such judgments. But to claim that Mack was *purposely* dislodging Jesus from being Jewish is just plain wrong. If we follow Bird's logic, Philo, with his interest in Hellenistic philosophy and lack of sectarianism, could not be Jewish.

Bird's association of the work of Mack and the Jesus Seminar with Nazi scholarship and potential violence against Jewish people is disturbing. Nazi scholars tried to disprove Jesus' Jewish ethnic/racial identity in relation to Galilee with the obvious cultural ramifications this had in Nazi Germany. No member of the Jesus Seminar (including Mack) does this, at least as far as I am aware. Indeed, if we took self-identity as one way of establishing how someone thinks about themselves, then would not all contemporary historical Jesus scholars claim that their Jesus would have claimed to have been Jewish, and in notable contrast to Nazi historical Jesus scholars who would have claimed that their Jesus would not? Certainly, a case can be made for members of the Jesus Seminar producing a Jesus who stood over against aspects of certain Jewish religious practices in many ways, but this is no different from countless works on the historical Jesus, including Wright's work. To tie the Jesus Seminar in with some aspect of liberal America is one thing and probably accurate; to tie them in with the Nazis really is most unfortunate.[19]

There may well be good historical reasons for not believing Jesus was a Cynic philosopher. But to refute such claims on the basis of imposing Jewish identity so that the only way Jewishness works is through the imposition of ideas of a Gentile Christian (irrespective, it would seem, of how people identified themselves) seems as anachronistic as the modernized Jesuses Bird wishes to refute. And to do this by way of making some alarming and wholly inaccurate remarks about opponents' liberal Jesuses being like those produced by the Nazis no less would suggest something else is going on here. Ultimately, Bird's model of Jewishness is no safeguard against modernizing Jesus; on the contrary, it provides access to the 'postmodern' multicultural Jesus Bird requires, or at least a barrier to the very Jesus Bird does not require.

If the Right Doesn't Get You, the Left Will: Dissimilarity, Double Dissimilarity and Let the Dead Bury Their Own Dead

Bird's methodology is an excellent example of how contemporary multicultural approaches to Otherness function problematically in practice. Yet it would be unfair to single Bird out simply because he was prepared to explain the notion of 'Jewishness'. The idea of accepting the ancient Jewish Other without the Otherness is deeply embedded in mainstream historical Jesus methodology, even if not always as explicit as Bird's article. Paul Barnett, for instance, likes what he calls the 'criterion of similarity *and* dissimilarity' because it recognizes 'that as a Jew many of Jesus' words are "similar" to Jewish thought while also observing that Jesus' radicalism will often subvert or overturn Jewish thought'.[20] But who said Jesus was radical? What if he was not? What is 'radical' anyway? Is it proto-Christian? For this method to work, it has to be assumed that Jewish Jesus must *necessarily* be different from his Jewish context. By making bits of Jesus' teaching similar to Judaism, while retaining the all-important dissimilarity, is no real advance on the inbuilt demotion of Judaism now widely observed in the old 'criterion of dissimilarity', despite its facelift for a postmodern age.

What we can see with this sort of methodological approach is how an old anti-Jewish methodology gets updated with a liberal veneer of philo-Semitism while still, effectively, perpetuating the old differences. Barnett's twist on dissimilarity which still retains the assumption that Jesus must 'subvert' (read: be better than) Judaism is inspired in particular by Wright. Wright certainly entertains similarity, or 'double similarity', even if he cannot resist getting the difference maker in: 'when something can be seen to be credible (though perhaps deeply subversive) within first-century Judaism, and credible as the implied starting point (though not the exact replica) of something in later Christianity, there is a strong possibility of our being in touch with the genuine history of Jesus'. However, this is coupled with a watered-down version of the criterion of dissimilarity built into Wright's system. Thus, when discussing Jesus teaching, 'It is thus decisively *similar* to both the Jewish context and the early Christian world, and at the same time importantly *dissimilar*'.[21] Jesus the fully Other never had a chance.

While we are not really supposed to use the old criterion of dissimilarity anymore because it is too much in line with what the old generation of German scholars were doing to distance Jesus from Judaism, it is such liberalizing twists as this which maintain a similar kind of superiority and suggest that not everything has changed. If we were to give dissimilarity and its kindly relatives the benefit of the doubt, then should we not be finding as much Jewish evidence as possible to show that Jesus was different? This is precisely what Wright does not do. As I argued elsewhere, Wright and others regularly work with generalizations about Judaism without checking to see if this or that saying of Jesus can be paralleled in early Judaism. The driving assumption is that Jesus *must* be different. And nowhere else is this more evident in recent scholarship than in the saying 'let the dead bury their own dead' (Mt. 8:21–22//Lk. 9:59–60). Other than some broad generalizations that Judaism held family and ethnicity in high regard, Wright produces no evidence for the following assessment of Mt. 8:21–22//Lk. 9:59–60: 'This is, quite frankly, outrageous. Many scholars have pointed out that Jesus is here advocating behaviour that his contemporaries, both Jewish and non-Jewish, would have regarded as scandalous.'[22] The 'many scholars' reference is crucial because it is scholarship which supposedly backs up Wright's argument concerning difference from Judaism. And Wright cites two scholars in particular: E. P. Sanders and Martin Hengel.

E. P. Sanders has done as much as any scholar to illuminate Jesus' Jewish contexts, but in doing this there is clear evidence that he is an important example of the credible perpetuation of difference we discussed earlier. For instance, Sanders uses the criterion of dissimilarity in the case of Mt. 8:21–22//Lk. 9:59–60, claiming this saying is not comprehensible in 'any part of Judaism known to us', it would have been 'shocking' in a Jewish context, counters the Law as understood 'throughout Judaism' and is difficult to think of as coming from the early community.[23] This is a doubly surprising turn because Sanders has been critical of the criterion of dissimilarity, pointing out that we do not have a detailed enough knowledge of first-century Judaism and that the criterion is biased towards uniqueness.[24] Yet these points, as implied above, could equally be made to apply to Mt. 8:21–22//Lk. 9:59–60. Furthermore, in terms of the interpretation of Mt. 8:21–22//Lk. 9:59–60, we lack the literary support for the claim of uniqueness, at least in the sense that no one in Matthew and Luke is recorded as finding the saying shocking, not to mention the very fact that Matthew and Luke include the saying without any apparent reservations. Why, then, must this saying be unique or, as much scholarship would have it, shocking?[25]

Sanders's conclusions on 'let the dead bury their dead' are partly due to using one representative of the scholarship he so effectively undermined, which makes a Sanders endorsement of a Jesus deprived of Otherness all the more credible. In dealing with Mt. 8:21–22//Lk. 9:59–60, Sanders makes use, and many do, of none other than Martin Hengel. After noting a brief history of scholarship, Sanders claims that among recent scholars, 'it is primarily Martin Hengel who has seen the force of the saying, at least as far as its negative implications go', before adding that his own argument 'will be seen to be in close agreement with his position.'[26] Following Hengel, Sanders argues that the saying 'counters not only the Mosaic legislation as it was understood throughout Judaism, but also normal and common Graeco-Roman piety.' Indeed, 'one must follow Hengel: the attitude indicated is so shocking, not only in Judaism...'[27] For Hengel, the 'unique sharpness' of this saying is due to an apparent attack on the commandment to honour parents. Moreover, it flatly contradicts the core of Jewish piety where 'the last offices for the dead had gained primacy among all good works.'[28] Even exceptions to the burial of parents for high priests and Nazirites (Lev. 21:11–12; Num. 6:6) had, apparently, been softened by the Tannaitic period.[29]

Hengel's view has managed to be hugely influential, probably more so with important support from Sanders. The use of Hengel is, however, particularly problematic. Hengel's interpretation – like much, if not most, of his work – was dominated by what is often perceived to be an outdated 'Law versus Gospel' model, the driving myth behind the scholarship Sanders shattered in the 1970s and 1980s. In his discussion of Mt. 8:21–22//Lk. 9:59–60, Hengel has the typical pre-Sanders and highly Protestant-sounding claims such as 'any casuistic legal codification was repugnant' to Jesus and that the 'decisive thing is a faith that is put into practice.'[30] Or again, 'Jesus' answer, which in a unique way expresses his sovereign freedom in respect of the Law of Moses.'[31]

And, unsurprisingly, it may be that the dominance of the old-fashioned 'Law versus Gospel' model in Hengel's approach led to an overstating of the Jewish material. As Markus Bockmuehl has shown, and as Sanders had emphasized elsewhere,[32] there is a key distinction to be made between relaxation of biblical law and halakic priority. The texts used by Hengel actually show that we are dealing with the problem of a potentially unburied corpse with no family around to bury the dead relative. In such instances, the importance of burial will override the demands on the High Priest (cf. *Sifre Lev.* 21.11[211]; *b. Nazir* 47b) and on the Nazirite (*m. Nazir* 6.5; *Sifre Num.* 6.6[26]). As Bockmuehl notes, none of the sources cited by Hengel – nor indeed by Strack-Billerbeck – have the High Priest or Nazirite exempted to bury parents (cf. Philo, *Spec. Leg.* 1.113–15, 250). There is even evidence that there was some debate concerning the High Priest and/or the Nazirite coming into contact with an abandoned corpse (cf. Lk. 10:29–37; *Spec. Leg.* 1.113–15, 250; *m. Nazir* 7.1).[33] Is Jesus' saying *necessarily* so extreme in such contexts?

Hengel's use of such texts would suggest that 'the Jewish background' to the supposedly shocking nature of the saying attributed to Jesus has been amplified and it notably supports a view of Jesus in sharp distinction from Judaism (and indeed the ancient world). Sanders's use of Hengel, however, meant the 'Law versus Gospel' tradition could be continued in the use of this verse, notably, as ever, by Wright. Recall again that Wright claimed, with little more than a reference to Hengel and Sanders, that 'This is, quite frankly, outrageous. Many scholars have pointed out that

Jesus is here advocating behaviour that his contemporaries, both Jewish and non-Jewish, would have regarded as scandalous.'[34] We saw Hengel's use of anachronistic Protestant language, yet is this not the very type of language against which Wright, thanks in no small part to Sanders, so vigorously reacted? Given Wright's deep concern to avoid the language and arguments of Protestant anachronism, would he have been so enthusiastic about using Hengel without Sanders's endorsement?

It is also worth reminding ourselves, then, of one of the main reasons why Wright is so attracted to Sanders's work: Sanders's sympathetic approach to early Judaism. Wright consistently emphasizes that his Jesus is 'very Jewish' and that his approach will not be to explain the historical Jesus over against Judaism and Jewish groups in terms of a rejection of works, bad laws and cold legalism. Indeed, Wright mocks the very view which Hengel attempted to perpetuate, of 'events which showed the clash between false religion (here represented by sixteenth-century legalists or formalists thinly disguised as Pharisees) and the true one offered by Jesus.' Wright informs us that, 'It used to be thought that Jesus' clashes with the Pharisees...consisted of his standing up against the "petty legalism" of the Pharisees... There is no historical verisimilitude in the picture of the Pharisees as petty, and perhaps Pelegian, legalists.'[35]

However, Wright has only paid lip service to Sanders's concerns and Wright's rhetoric has a duplicitous and masking function. [36] We are told early on in his book that the 'most viable' argument concerning historical reconstructions of Jesus is 'a very Jewish Jesus who was nevertheless opposed to some high-profile features of first-century Judaism.'[37] Wright is a prime example of someone who has bought into the pro-Other rhetoric, denounced the ethically dubious scholarly arguments of the past, used arguably the most credible historical Jesus scholar of the past forty years, and by doing so perpetuates another form of de-othering the Other for our times. And a little genealogical research into the scholarship on 'let the dead bury their dead' on the Jewish foil for Wright's Jesus (and the Jesus of many scholars) shows the emptiness of the argumentation. It may not be quite what Marx was getting at, but in a different kind of way it goes to show that other things we thought were solid really do melt into air.

A Tale of Two Catholics: Ratzinger and Eagleton

> They [discussions in Ratzinger's *Jesus of Nazareth*] begin by acknowledging and voicing criticism of anti-Jewish readings of the passage at hand, but they end with a subtle, and, I believe, unintentional reinforcement of the stereotypes that underlie the anti-Jewish readings themselves.
>
> – Adele Reinhartz[38]

I want to develop the second half of this chapter to show the broader cultural links and how the Jewish Jesus deprived of his Jewish Otherness is part of one strand of cultural 'common sense' and, underlying this, why it has been such an important market for historical Jesus studies. I want to do this by using two different scholarly examples on the periphery of historical Jesus studies and having footholds in a range of cultural worlds the average New Testament scholar does not. In particular, I refer to the Pope's recent popularizing book on the historical Jesus and Terry Eagleton's popularizing use of historical Jesus scholarship.

It has been remarked that Ratzinger's *Jesus of Nazareth*[39] has some serious problems if read as a work of historical criticism, not least for being outdated and naive in its use of historical Jesus scholarship.[40] However, it is also clear that Ratzinger does set his book up, at least partly, as a work of historical Jesus scholarship and does acknowledge more historical Jesus works such as John Meier's multi-volume, *A Marginal Jew*. What I particularly want to do in this section is not so much to show how historically problematic Ratzinger's Jesus is (and it is) but more to show how Ratzinger's book shares dominant assumptions of recent historical Jesus scholarship, and of course the broader multicultural assumption of the acceptance of the Other deprived of Otherness with the construction of Jews and Judaism as a backdrop to make Jesus subtly – or, at times, not-so-subtly – better and more palatable.[41]

Ratzinger naturally has some perfectly complimentary things to say about Jews and Judaism. In reaction to Pierre Grelot's interpretation of Peter's confession at Caesarea Philippi, Ratzinger sharply points out that there is no Gospel repudiation of Peter's confession 'as completely "Jewish"', but rather Jesus forbade the disciples to speak openly in 'the public climate of Israel' for fear of being misunderstood.[42] The major contemporary Jewish scholar, Jacob Neusner, is famously described in glowing terms. Ratzinger openly admits that 'More than any other interpretations known to me', Neusner's analysis of the Sermon on the Mount in relation to Judaism 'has opened my eyes to the greatness of

Jesus' words.'[43] Praise indeed. In fact, Neusner was even given a private audience with the Pope.[44]

It also seems as if Ratzinger has positive things to say relating to Jews and the land of Israel. The Pharisees, he argues, 'refused conformity to the hegemony of Hellenistic-Roman culture, which naturally imposed itself throughout the Roman Empire, and was now threatening to force Israel's assimilation to the pagan peoples' way of life.'[45] Some of Ratzinger's rhetoric about the ideal function of the land for Jews may be positive sounding but is potentially worrying in terms of the contemporary issues surrounding the land of Israel. Galilee is not only, apparently, a 'half-paganized province', but 'Israel is living once more in the darkness of divine absence; God is silent, seemingly forgetful of the promises to Abraham and David… For that very reason, though, the land was full of unrest.'[46] Compare page 67 after the sentimental description of the landscape surrounding the traditional location for the Sermon of the Mount where 'the wonderful atmosphere of peace and the beauty of creation encountered' is contrasted with the 'land unfortunately lacking in peace'. While I stress that I am not accusing Ratzinger of views he may not personally hold, the implications of the discourse with the contemporary Israel–Palestine conflicts in mind is problematic when we remember his comments on the 'darkness of divine absence' in 'a half-paganized province' full of 'unrest'.[47] It is also not untypical of the pro-Land tendency in contemporary biblical scholarship.[48]

However, it is clear from the outset that Judaism will have to come second best. In the Foreword, where Ratzinger is quite explicit about the input of his faith-based perspective, we are told that Jesus is the hermeneutical key to the whole Bible. Furthermore, Ratzinger suggests that the rise of a 'high' Christology must derive from Jesus himself: 'Isn't it more logical', Ratzinger asks, and as John Milbank enthusiastically endorsed (see chapter 9), 'even historically speaking, to assume that the greatness came at the beginning, and that the figure of Jesus really did explode all existing categories and could only be understood in the light of the mystery of God?'[49] The answer, as we all know, is 'yes' for Ratzinger. But from the outset, this means that a Jesus the Jew as portrayed by, say, Geza Vermes and others would never stand a chance of being the result of Ratzinger's historical reconstruction of Jesus.

It is perhaps no surprise, then, that the rhetoric of superiority over against commonly constructed symbols of Judaism is common enough in Ratzinger's *Jesus of Nazareth*. But, like so many reconstructions of the historical Jesus, though a little less subtly perhaps, the tie-in with Judaism remains. Jesus was a 'true Israelite' and 'also...– in terms of the inner dynamic of the promises made to Israel – he transcended Judaism.'[50] The Sermon on the Mount is 'the new Torah brought by Jesus.'[51] Ratzinger does not like the idea of Christian ethics being deemed 'superior to the commands of the Old Testament' because this 'totally misconstrues these words [Beatitudes] of Jesus.' Yet Jesus still manages to give 'added depth to the commandments of the second tablet' even if he does not abolish them.[52] Physical descent no longer matters and Jesus 'spiritualizes' the Law and 'makes it the path to life for all,' opening up Israel 'in order to bring birth to a great new family of God drawn from Israel and the Gentiles.'[53] Ratzinger carefully points out that it would be 'a false interpretation' to read the parable of the prodigal son 'as a condemnation of the Jews.' While he points out that 'there is no support in the text' for this reading, he does claim that it is 'not illegitimate' to apply the text to Jews if we respect the form of the text 'as God's delicate attempt to talk Israel around.' There is no support for that either, it might be added, but let us remain, for now, at the level of rhetoric and discourse. Like much of contemporary historical Jesus scholarship, we have the clear impression of a Jewish Jesus deprived of his Jewish Otherness.

I do not want to get too heavily involved in debating Ratzinger's knowledge of the historical and cultural contexts of Jesus. Others have, and no doubt others will, done that and rightly so.[54] As it happens, I think his arguments simply would not work if he looked at the numerous Jewish parallels to Jesus' teaching. I will, then, touch upon the issue, but only in a way where I think Ratzinger's argument had a golden opportunity to use historical criticism in order to see Jesus as a Jew in roughly the sort of way which would not transcend a scholarly dominant construction of Judaism. On pages 324–25, Ratzinger discusses the son of man saying in Mk 2:27–28 which occurs at the end of the Sabbath dispute over plucking grain in 2:23–26. Verses 27–28 read, 'Then he said to them, "The Sabbath was made for humankind, and not humankind for the Sabbath; so the Son of Man is lord even of the Sabbath."' Ratzinger acknowledges that the term 'son of man' can simply mean 'man' in Hebrew and Aramaic, but with Jesus 'that simple word bends together with a mysterious allusion to a new consciousness of mission.' Moreover, according to Ratzinger, 'to say that the Sabbath is for man, and not man for the Sabbath, is simply not an expression of the sort of modern liberal position that we spontaneously read into these words.' The problem with Ratzinger's view is, however, that such a sentiment is actually biblical (e.g. Exod. 16:29), never mind the well-known parallels in early Judaism (e.g.

Jub. 2:17; *Mekhilta Exod.* 31.12–17). Furthermore, there is a significant nod in this direction in the use of this passage in the synoptic parallels: Matthew and Luke drop the generalizing Mk 2:27, presumably in the interests of tilting the saying towards the Christological *title* 'the Son of Man'. Ratzinger notices this and the only potential alternative to his own interpretation is (conveniently) that 'Perhaps the explanation is that Matthew and Luke omit the first sentence for fear that it will be abused.'[55] Presumably, then, Jesus as some kind of legal thinker simply cannot be an option for Ratzinger.

Excursus: 'Jewish Scholar Fetish'

We might add to this Ratzinger's lengthy interaction with Jacob Neusner's examination of Jesus where we find Jesus' attitude towards the Law, including the above Sabbath dispute, and including the Sermon on the Mount, further discussed. As mentioned, Ratzinger reserves high praise for Neusner's interpretation and it is not difficult to see why he is attracted to it. Perfection for Neusner is the state of being holy as God is holy and demanded by the Torah, but now comes through following Jesus, a view Neusner as a believing rabbi cannot accept.[56] But this, obviously, is a view Ratzinger has no problem in accepting. Yet, the choice of debating partner is interesting. Sometimes we find the idea of quoting a Jewish scholar who says something that affirms orthodox views of Scripture in historical Jesus studies. There seems to me a worrying element of tokenism about this approach – almost as if saying, 'well this Jewish person said it so it must be true!' – though I think Ratzinger's approach is sometimes more nuanced than that of some New Testament scholars. Anyway, let us turn this on its head and ask what would happen if another person were chosen. Put another way, would not Ratzinger's reconstruction have been more challenged if he had engaged in a dialogue with that other famous contemporary Jewish scholar, Geza Vermes, who has also discussed these important passages in detail but came to a very different conclusion by having Jesus' teaching located firmly *within* a dominant scholarly construction of early Judaism?

In fact this tokenism (or, let us be blunt, using a Jewish scholar to make a point about Christian superiority) is also found in more typical mainstream New Testament and historical Jesus studies. Todd Penner has controversially but accurately and entertainingly described this phenomenon as a 'Jewish scholar fetish' and, though Penner was referring to Pauline scholarship, his logic equally applies to Jesus scholarship.[57] This fetish justifies the perpetuation of implicitly anti-Jewish/

supersessionist categories because it always helps having an endorsement from a leading Jewish intellectual. This 'Jewish scholar fetish' is also present in discussions of the historical Jesus where issues of 'Jewishness' are perhaps most sensitive. Michael Bird, for instance, claims that Jesus' conflicts with his opponents best explain why Christianity emerged as a distinct religion from Judaism:

> The Jewish scholar Joseph Klausner maintains that, 'Jesus was a Jew and a Jew he remained till his last breath' but he also adds that: '*Ex nihilo nihil fit* [from nothing nothing comes]: had not Jesus' teaching contained a kernel of opposition to Judaism, Paul could never *in the name of Jesus* have set aside the ceremonial laws, and broken through the barriers of national Judaism... Similarly, another Jewish scholar Richard L. Rubenstein wrote (*My Brother Paul* [New York: Harper & Row, 1972], 121): 'In reality it was not Paul but Jesus who instituted the irreparable breach with established Judaism.'[58]

Again Bird makes clear the logic of certain scholarly assumptions and here we have a particularly clear example of Jewish scholars used in support of Bird's theology with a form of superiority over against Judaism maintained and the argument effectively hinging on the fact that the scholar is Jewish so it must be true. Let us look more closely at Bird's argument. Why not ask where Jesus got his views from if nothing comes from nothing? Even if we accept Klausner's argument that nothing comes from nothing, all this would mean is that we should investigate a variety of 'why questions,' not that Jesus was *necessarily* the origins of a split from Judaism. Alternatively, it could easily be argued – rightly or wrongly – that Paul could have set aside parts of the Law because, for instance, he had a vision after Jesus' death or that there were plenty of Gentiles associated with the Christian movement no longer interested in parts of the Law, so Paul attempts to deal with the problem by justifying non-observance. Clearly, this does not necessarily require Jesus to have said something so dramatic as to cause (effectively) a new religion. There is no logical reason why the split from Judaism must *necessarily* have come from Jesus' teaching. Bird's point is obviously light on argument, but its rhetoric of (attempted) persuasion comes through an emphasis on *Jewish* scholars with the apparent logic that if Jewish scholars say it must be true then this is not supersessionism for its own sake, and so on.

I did a radio debate with Bird and, like the Pope in his book on Jesus (which, interestingly, Bird had not at that point read), he favourably cited the Jewish scholar Neusner's argument that the Sermon on the Mount is so radical that Jesus must effectively be making hugely dramatic claims which might just be reserved for God.[59] But what happens if I choose another Jewish scholar, say Geza Vermes, who is not so impressed by Ratzinger's book,[60] but who also argues that Jesus' teaching in the Sermon on the Mount and his teaching on the Law are fairly typical pieces of Jewish teaching?[61] Do I score a point by getting another Jewish scholar? Should I see how many Jewish scholars I can line up on my side of the argument and try and get more than Bird? If I get 15 and he gets 12, do I win the argument?

Clearly, there is a perversity about this parlour game and it is a very good example of how this love for Judaism is superficial and, I think, providing the cover for the old myth of superiority in more benign dress. It is difficult to avoid the conclusion that Jewish scholars are being mentioned because (a) they say the right things and (b) because they add credibility to Gentile arguments by being token Jews. I think this move has an air of fraudulence about it and I am finding it difficult to think it is being done for love of Jews or Judaism. Jewish scholars just so happen to be useful. Ideally, an argument should stand or fall on its own merits and not because – this otherwise ought to be an obvious point – the arguer has a certain ethnic or religious background. This move to token Jewish scholars is a particularly good example of the ways in which cultural trends can dictate arguments and, in its own way, provide a liberal veneer of multicultural credibility.

Ratzinger's Critical Scholarship

Perhaps Ratzinger's Jesus in relation to Judaism was inevitable because of his model of critical biblical scholarship. Biblical scholarship, for Ratzinger, must have its limits and is often portrayed very negatively. A certain kind of scholarship is accused of imposing worldviews on the texts.[62] Furthermore, the 'highly scientific approach' can offer 'little protection' against 'fundamental mistakes'.[63] On the other hand, we find out in the Foreword and elsewhere (e.g. p. 78) that Ratzinger explicitly views the role of faith as absolutely crucial for interpretation. One way Ratzinger hits home his model of scholarship is by noting that even the devil, no less, is a biblical scholar of a certain variety.[64] Here Ratzinger notes Vladimir Soloviev's short story 'The Antichrist', arguing that this portrayal of the Antichrist,

> forcefully expresses his scepticism regarding a certain type of scholarly exegesis current at the time. This is not a rejection of scholarly biblical interpretation as such, but an eminently salutary and necessary warning against its possible aberrations... The alleged findings of

> scholarly exegesis have been used to put together the most dreadful books that destroy the figure of Jesus and dismantle the faith... And so the Bible no longer speaks of God, the living God; no, now *we* alone speak and decide what God can do and what we will and should do. And the Antichrist, with an air of scholarly excellence, tells us that any exegesis that reads the Bible from the perspective of faith in the living God, in order to listen to what God has to say, is fundamentalism...[65]

This might raise the question, where does this leave the idea of Jesus being a fairly ordinary Jewish figure of his time? Methodologically, this Jesus (and others) would seem to be impossible from the very beginning. Moreover, Ratzinger claims that the theological debate between Jesus and the devil (and thus a *certain kind* of biblical scholar) is not only a dispute over 'the correct interpretation of Scripture' but has the following hermeneutical question at the heart of exegesis: 'With what picture of God are we working?' For Ratzinger, this dispute is ultimately about the identity of God and is 'decided by the picture we form in Christ'.[66] This, of course, is not the way most Jews see God, as Ratzinger is aware in his dialogue with Neusner, and consequently rules out the possibility of Jesus the Jew fitting into a dominant scholarly construction of Judaism. If we are not careful, the implication of Ratzinger's logic is stark: anything other than a fully deified Jesus is scholarship of the devil, is it not? This of course would rule out a lot of things in historical Jesus studies, but for our present purposes method alone would appear to make sure Jesus transcends his Jewish context. Little surprise, then, that John's Gospel with its explicitly 'high' Christology is accepted as a legitimate document for understanding the life of the historical Jesus.[67]

The Protective Function of Judaism

While Ratzinger is favourably disposed towards the use of Greek philosophy, we do see Judaism having a kind of protective role, safeguarding Christianity against the dangers of paganism, while keeping the all-important link with the Hebrew Bible/Old Testament. As Todd Penner and J. Z. Smith in particular have shown, this is a common view in New Testament and Christian origins scholarship. For example, Ratzinger fires hard at Bultmann's view that Gnosticism was one of the main influences on John's Gospel.[68] Instead, Ratzinger turns to Martin Hengel's critique of Bultmann and to the positives of contemporary scholarship on John, such as the emphasis on the role of Scripture, 'how its whole way of arguing is deeply rooted in the Judaism of Jesus' time', and how, quoting Hengel, the Gospel is 'steeped in the language of Jewish piety'.[69] I am certainly not saying Bultmann was right and I am certainly not saying that John's Gospel did not have roots in Judaism. Rather, the pro-Jewish rhetoric in Ratzinger is double-edged. After all, John's Gospel for Ratzinger does ultimately construct itself over against Judaism. He may well have a point here, too, though whether this goes back to the historical Jesus seems stunningly unlikely to some of us. But in terms of rhetoric – and away from scholarly right and wrong – this remains an important ideological move and one shared with much of New Testament scholarship. It ultimately allows a Jesus to have his roots in Judaism, in line with Scripture, protected from idolatry, and yet ultimately constructed over against Judaism.

I would add to this a similar argument concerning Ratzinger's discussion of politics in *Jesus of Nazareth*, where 'Judaism' serves as a kind of protective barrier against that which could be deemed *politically* dangerous for the contemporary Vatican. Ratzinger has some very revealing things to say, no doubt with one eye on some old enemies, on issues relating to poverty and hunger. For Ratzinger, 'well meaning aid' offered by the West and 'the Marxist experiment' have failed because they have left God out of the picture and (somehow) this has contributed 'to the collapse of societies and brought about the "third world"'.[70]

Here again 'Judaism', or at least things Jewish, provides a protective function for Ratzinger (just as it does for problematic beliefs relating to eschatology[71]) when showing, implicitly, that Jesus and his followers would have been in line with Ratzinger's view of global politics. When discussing the 'poor in spirit' from the Matthean Beatitudes – and recall the problematic absence of 'in spirit' in Luke's version – he turns to Qumran, biblical literature and Israel in general. Ratzinger informs us that terms relating to 'poor' are the self-designation of the pious, showing awareness of being the 'true Israel'. Moreover, most Israelites/Jews were poor anyway and so 'Israel's faith' would recognize that poverty could bring closeness to God, unlike the rich 'who rely only on themselves'.[72] Yet things Jewish have their limits and the difference is eventually made clear with any bad Jewish bits filtered out. '[D]espite a great deal of spiritual affinity' with Qumran, there are 'contrasts': the New Testament story begins 'in full awareness of its perfect unity with the faith of Israel that has been maturing to ever greater purity... Silently evolving here was the attitude before God that Paul explored in his theology of justification...'[73]

Eagleton's Jesus

At this point we can turn to a different (lapsed/prodigal) Catholic vision of Jesus by the Marxist critic Terry Eagleton. Some of Eagleton's recent cultural prominence has been due to his responses to the hard anti-religious atheism of Richard Dawkins and others and in doing this Eagleton has turned to his Catholic past.[74] He is also part of a trend in Marxist and leftist philosophical/critical theoretical thought where there has been a turn to Paul and early Christianity. Whereas as figures such as Taubes, Badiou, Agamben and Žižek have largely turned to Paul, Eagleton has plenty to say on Jesus and has recently published a piece on Jesus as part of the Revolutions series for Verso.[75]

Eagleton's Jesus is a classic case of a counter-cultural Jesus and the downgrading of Judaism is crucial in establishing his Jesus. I might add as an aside that I have much sympathy with Eagleton's aims of critiquing some of the extremely hostile, unfair and inaccurate attacks on Christianity by certain atheists. My arguments, I stress, function as a qualification to his helpful response to certain atheist criticisms of Christianity because when it comes to Jesus, I think he repeats some of the unfortunate clichés of Christian superiority which are found repeatedly in works where Jesus is portrayed as some kind of revolutionary figure.[76]

As with Ratzinger, and many New Testament scholars, when Eagleton needs a positive *background*, Judaism becomes, as ever, useful. On the famous saying, 'Render unto Caesar...' Eagleton claims whatever it means it does not mean the separation of the world into religion and politics because 'Any devout Jew of Jesus's time would have known that the things that are God's include working for justice, welcoming the immigrants, and humbling the high-and-mighty.'[77] Yet, for Eagleton, it still follows that Jesus must have made a significant break from Judaism. Of course, it may (or may not) have historically been the case that Jesus behaved in such a revolutionary manner, but Eagleton can only show this by repeating scholarly generalizations and repeating the scholarly omissions of Jewish evidence. 'What is at stake here', Eagleton argues, 'is not a prudently reformist project of pouring new wine into old bottles, but an avant-gardist epiphany of the absolutely new – of a regime so revolutionary as to surpass all image and utterance.'[78]

Eagleton discusses what has become, as we have seen, the classic passage in which Jesus' difference from (and, implicitly, superiority over) Judaism is established: Mt. 8:21–22//Lk. 9:59–60. He argues, '"Let the dead bury their dead," Jesus brusquely informs his followers – a sentiment that the Jews of the time, for whom burial of the dead was a sacred duty and unburied corpses an unthinkable scandal, would have found outrageously offensive.'[79] While consistently recalling the intellectual history of the interpretation of this passage, we might begin by noting that in the context of Mt. 8:21–22//Lk. 9:59–60, no one appears shocked by what Jesus says, something we might expect if Eagleton's generalization 'the Jews of the time' was both accurate and applied to the specific case recorded in the Gospels (as we have seen above). We might also challenge Eagleton's generalization about 'the Jews' with evidence from the Gospels themselves. In the parable of the Good Samaritan, it seems as if the priest and Levite avoid the 'half-dead' man at the side of the road in case he might be an unburied corpse and thus they might contract corpse impurity (Lk. 10:30–32). Furthermore, and against Eagleton and much Gospel scholarship, it could easily be the case that the dead man will be left unburied because 'the dead' (presumably the 'spiritually dead' – cf. 1 Tim. 5:6) will bury the dead.

Jesus' saying 'Let the dead bury their dead' is typically found in relation to Jesus' general teaching on family in scholarship (hardly a surprise). Eagleton's view of Jesus is similar:

> Jesus's attitude to the family is one of implacable hostility. He has come to break up these cozy little conservative settlements so beloved of American advertisers in the name of his mission, settling members at each other's throats; and he seems to have precious little time for his own family in particular. In *The God Delusion*, Richard Dawkins greets this aspect of the Gospel with chilly suburban distaste. Such a cold-eyed view of the family can suggest to him only the kidnapping habits of religious cults. He does not see that movements for justice cut across traditional blood ties, as well as across, ethnic, social, and national divisions. Justice is thicker than blood.[80]

Perhaps. However, it might also be the case that Jesus' views on family stand in established Jewish traditions of getting priorities right: God first, family second. Josephus, for instance, can report the placement of observing the commandments over family ties without being hostile to the idea of family (*Ant.* 3.87). Jesus, we should never forget, is still recorded as saying,

> For Moses said, 'Honour your father and your mother'; and, 'Whoever speaks evil of father or mother must surely die.' But you say that if anyone tells father or mother, 'Whatever support you might have had from me is Corban' (that is, an offering to God) – then you no longer permit doing anything for a father or mother, thus making void the word of God through your tradition that you have handed on. (Mk 7:10–13)

Why not prioritize this aspect of the Gospel tradition, an aspect which cannot be classed as implacable hostility towards family or indeed one which attacks hostility towards family? Luke certainly records Jesus talking about 'hating' family (Lk. 14:26), but this could, alternatively, be hyperbole, not untypical of Jesus after all, and Matthew renders the sentiment in terms of 'love-less' (Mt. 10:37). Indeed, the English 'hate' might be too strong and the sentiment 'love-less' (cf. Gen. 29:31; Deut. 21:15–17) could underlie both Matthew and Luke.

What this might suggest is that Eagleton, like much contemporary scholarship, including those 'radicalizing' Jesus, could be overstating the case. Should not these alternative readings be entertained? Likewise, the selections made by Eagleton on ethnicity could be challenged. Is Jesus getting universalized a little too early by Eagleton because a case can be made (and regularly is) that the Jesus movement was very much an ethnically Jewish movement and that there is no serious indication that it initially cut across ethnic and national divisions? This is the Jesus recorded as saying, 'Go nowhere among the Gentiles, and enter no town of the Samaritans, but go rather to the lost sheep of the house of Israel' (Mt. 10:5–6). This is also the Jesus who, when he does come in contact with a Gentile, puts the woman in her ethnic place by effectively calling her a Gentile bitch and saying that Gentiles are permitted to eat the food under the table (Mk 7:26–27). Eagleton does not quite say that the Jesus' movement cuts across ethnic and national ties, but the application seems clear enough from the above quotation.

Unfortunately, we even get a consistent negative backdrop to Jesus which buys into, and develops, old clichés about Jesus' opponents:

> To the outrage of the Zealots, Pharisees, and right-wing rednecks of all ages, this body is dedicated in particular to all those losers, deadbeats, riffraff, and colonial collaborators who are not righteous but flamboyantly unrighteous – who either live in chronic transgression of the Mosaic law or, like the Gentiles, fall outside its sway altogether... These men and women are not being asked to bargain their way into God's favor by sacrificing beasts, fussing about their diet, or being impeccably well-behaved. Instead, the good news is that God loves them anyway, in all their moral squalor...despite their viciousness – that the source of inexhaustibly self-delighting life he calls his Father is neither judge, patriarch, accuser, nor superego, but lover, friend, fellow-accused, and counsel for the defense.[81]

There is a significant shift here from Pharisees and Zealots to 'right-wing rednecks of all ages', but one which is, strictly speaking, unfair because realistically what have the concerns of right-wing rednecks got to do with Zealots and Pharisees? Haven't plenty of right-wing rednecks happily been colonial collaborators? Moreover, by effectively paralleling the God who wants favour from sacrificial beasts, fussiness and moral behaviour with the God of love and justice, is Eagleton not simply repeating the old clichés of Christian superiority over against Judaism? We might also suggest that it is also possible to argue that Jesus, too, was interested in being impeccably well behaved. Given his call to repentance and the fruits by which a person would be known, we can see this in some of his teaching, most famously in the Sermon on the Mount.

What is noticeable about Eagleton's argument, as indeed with certain other Marxist discussions of Paul and Christianity in critical-theoretical circles, is that something about Christianity is worth preserving. Eagleton is certainly clear that his views of Jesus, Paul and Christianity may not be plausible and true in the sense that they are grounded in a very real divine, but he is equally clear that left-wing Christianity is something worthwhile. Such a form of Christianity is not, Eagleton adds, 'stupid, vicious, or absurd. And if it evokes no response from Ditchkins at all, then I think his life is the poorer...it may still serve as an allegory of our political and historical condition.'[82] I cannot help but add that I agree with much of this in the abstract and, to repeat, I share a lot of Eagleton's concerns. My problem, however, is that such arguments remain within the framework of Christian superiority, theological anti-Judaism and even (paradoxically?) an implicit liberalizing as much as that of the Pope.

Furthermore, as Roland Boer points out more broadly with reference to Eagleton's recent return to theology, 'it becomes easier to present theology as an autonomous discipline, concerned with itself and in some curious way immune from being implicated in the less than illustrious past of capitalism.'[83] We may update this and suggest that the rhetoric of Eagleton's revolutionary Jesus, alongside his Jesus who is immersed in Judaism and is yet above Judaism, rhetorically makes this Jesus immune from multicultural aspects of contemporary capitalism. However, the Jewish Jesus deprived of his Jewish Otherness, like the contemporary multicultural Other without the Otherness, is clearly part of a broader 'common sense' whether we are talking about mainstream historical Jesus scholars, such as Wright or even Sanders, or whether we are talking about figures more culturally prominent, such as Ratzinger. Some may emphasize difference more starkly than others, but the pattern of Jesus as ultimately different from Judaism remains.

Concluding Remarks

Ratzinger's language is much stronger and starker than that of most contemporary historical Jesus scholarship. The reasons for this are obvious enough. While many New Testament scholars have the broad constraints of the Church, few could legitimately claim to have the constraints of the Pope! Moreover, many New Testament scholars work in universities where other perspectives are ever present, no matter how isolated, and at least their presence may try and keep check on one specific faith getting carried away. Consequently, it is hardly a great revelation that for Ratzinger, and for all the positive rhetoric about Judaism, Christianity is rooted in the historical Jesus and has to come out best and fully orthodox.

And we ought to repeat this: the scholarly love, or the broader cultural love, for Jews is limited. In *Jesus in an Age of Terror,* I pointed this out, in detail, in terms of contemporary political and religious alliances. Now we can add that this Jewish Jesus deprived of his Jewish Otherness is only something which has a broad market appeal at present. Jesus the Jew is only useful while contemporary multiculturalism remains part of the dominant liberal consensus. Once Jesus the Jew loses his usefulness, he will, presumably, be ditched in favour of the next flavour of the month. Who knows? One day ethnicity might not be deemed as important as gender in Jesus studies and in forty years from now we might all be talking about the cliché of Jesus the gender transgressor or traditional family man.

We ought also to end on a slightly more positive note. In his analysis of different types of present-day anti-Semites, Adorno finished with a seemingly contradictory category: 'The Jew-lover.'[84] In this curious sounding category, Adorno pointed out that 'There are people, however, who stress the differences between Jews and Christians in a way friendly to the Jews. This type of thinking contains an anti-Semitic nucleus which has its origin in racial discrimination.' What we find, Adorno suggests, is an apologetic for secret discrimination and this overcompensation is a 'fundamentally unreliable adoration.' We need not necessarily be as strong as Adorno in using the language of anti-Semitism for our times. Adorno's discussion of anti-Semitism was written in the dark shadow of the Holocaust, which ought to shame certain historical Jesus scholars who use issues surrounding anti-Semitism to denounce their contemporary opponents. What we are dealing with in the case of the contemporary 'Jew-lover' in scholarship is actually not any real love for Jews, but one where being superficially nice to Judaism only perpetuates their own contemporizing underlying agendas. We saw earlier how Michael Bird claims that 'history shows that Christianity has done the most unforgiving violence to the Jewish people on those occasions when Jesus' Jewishness was denied or minimized'. Indeed; but superficial concern for Jewishness has kept the negative difference ticking over until times of serious conflict when difference gets exploited in horrific ways. Perhaps it is time we ought to think seriously, and critically, about another suggestion from Adorno (and by now it should be clear that this is more broadly culturally applicable than to Jews alone): 'Those persons are really free of anti-Semitism to whom the distinction makes no difference, to whom the so-called racial traits appear unessential.'[85]

Notes

1. S. Prothero, *American Jesus: How the Son of God Became a National Icon* (New York: Farrar, Straus and Giroux, 2003), p. 294.
2. S. Kelley, 'Race, Aesthetics, and Gospel Scholarship: Embracing and Subverting the Aesthetic Ideology', in L. Nasrallah and E. S. Fiorenza (eds.), *Prejudice and Christian Beginnings: Investigating Race, Gender, and Ethnicity in Early Christian Studies* (Fortress: Minneapolis, 2009), pp. 191–209 (192, 208).
3. W. Brown, *Regulating Aversion: Tolerance in the Age of Identity and Empire* (Princeton and Oxford: Princeton University Press, 2006), p. 90.
4. See also W. Arnal, *The Symbolic Jesus: Historical Scholarship, Judaism and the Construction of Contemporary Identity* (London and Oakville: Equinox, 2005).
5. See e.g. E. P. Sanders, *Jesus and Judaism* (London: SCM, 1985), e.g. pp. 204–208, 252–55; J. D. G. Dunn, *Jesus Remembered* (Grand Rapids: Eerdmans, 2003); N. T. Wright, *Jesus and the Victory of God* (London: SPCK, 1996), almost everywhere; G. Theissen and A. Merz, *The Historical Jesus: A Comprehensive Guide* (London: SCM, 1998), e.g. pp. 366–67; D. C. Allison, *Resurrecting Jesus: The Earliest Christian Tradition and Its Interpreters* (London: T&T Clark, 2005), pp. 149–97; J. P. Meier, 'Did the Historical Jesus Prohibit All Oaths? Part 1', *JSHJ* 5 (2007), pp. 175–204; J. P. Meier, 'Did the Historical Jesus Prohibit All Oaths? Part 2', *JSHJ* 6 (2008), pp. 3–24.
6. The common idea that the emphasis on the Jewishness of Jesus was a reaction to the Holocaust itself is simply wrong (see chapter 1) unless we can explain a scholarly delay of at least 25 years given that it took until the 1970s for this widespread scholarly emphasis to become popular. A reaction to new or renewed interest in the Holocaust post-1967 is a more accurate contributing explanation.
7. Cf. also Brown, *Regulating Aversion*, pp. 107–48.
8. J. G. Crossley, *Jesus in an Age of Terror: Scholarly Projects for a New American Century* (London and Oakville: Equinox, 2008), pp. 143–94.

9. Again, Wendy Brown's work on tolerance, identity, terror, and empire further show the connections. On 'Jewishness' and 'tolerance', see Brown, *Regulating Aversion*, pp. 48–58, 60–67. On connections and histories of the links between liberalism, war, and terror see e.g., R. Seymour, *The Liberal Defence of Murder* (London and New York: Verso, 2008); M. Dillon and J. Reid, *The Liberal Way of War: Killing to Make Life Live* (New York and London: Routledge, 2009). For an important example of how all the key cultural issues come together in Gospel and parable studies can be found in the work of Shawn Kelley. Kelley shows how emerging scholarship of the 1970s, with liberal and Jewish-friendly scholars leading the way, was not only in part a product of emerging postmodern thinking of the time, but was able to maintain the structure of Jewish inferiority. See e.g. S. Kelley, *Racializing Jesus: Race, Ideology and the Formation of Modern Biblical Scholarship* (London and New York: Routledge, 2002); S. Kelley, 'Race, Aesthetics, and Gospel Scholarship'.
10. Crossley, *Jesus in an Age of Terror*, pp. 173–94.
11. M. F. Bird, 'The Peril of Modernizing Jesus and the Crisis of Not Contemporizing the Christ', *Evangelical Quarterly* 78 (2006), pp. 291–312.
12. Bird, 'The Peril of Modernizing Jesus', p. 296.
13. Bird, 'The Peril of Modernizing Jesus', p. 297, n. 29.
14. Bird, 'The Peril of Modernizing Jesus', p. 310.
15. E.g. P. A. Harland, *Associations, Synagogues, and Congregations: Claiming a Place in Ancient Mediterranean Society* (Minneapolis: Fortress, 2003), pp. 33–36, 177–264; idem, 'Spheres of Contention, Claims of Pre-eminence: Rivalries among Associations in Sardis and Smyrna', in R. S. Ascough (ed.), *Religious Rivalries and the Struggle for Success in Sardis and Smyrna* (Waterloo: Wilfrid Laurier University Press, 2005), pp. 53–63, 259–62; idem, *The Dynamics of Identity in the World of the Early Christians* (London and New York: T&T Clark/Continuum, 2009).
16. Wright, *Victory*.
17. Bird, 'The Peril of Modernizing Jesus', p. 310; my italics.
18. Bird, 'Peril', p. 297, quoting B. L. Mack, *A Myth of Innocence: Mark and Christian Origins* (Philadelphia: Fortress, 1988), p. 73. See also Bird's comments on J. G. Crossley, 'Once Again on the Historical Jesus, Who Is Deciding Jewish Identity?', Earliest Christian History (21 December, 2008) http://earliestchristianhistory.blogspot.com/2008/12/once-again-on-historical-jesus-who-is.html, where Bird ties the above Mack reference in with Mack's supposed removal of Jesus from 'Jewishness'.
19. On the unfortunate use of 'Nazi' and 'anti-Semitism' labelling and insinuations in historical Jesus scholarship see Arnal, *Symbolic Jesus*, p. 17; J. S. Kloppenborg, 'As One Unknown, without a Name? Co-opting the Apocalyptic Jesus', in J. S. Kloppenborg with J. W. Marshall (eds.), *Apocalypticism, Anti-Semitism and the Historical Jesus: Subtexts in Criticism* (London and New York: T&T Clark/Continuum, 2005), pp. 19–21 (2, n. 3); Crossley, *Jesus in an Age of Terror*, pp. 132–33, 174–76.
20. P. Barnett, *Finding the Historical Christ: After Jesus, Volume Three* (Grand Rapids: Eerdmans, 2009), pp. 223–24.
21. Wright, *Victory*, p. 132.
22. Wright, *Victory*, p. 401.

23. Sanders, *Jesus and Judaism*, pp. 252, 254.
24. Sanders, *Jesus and Judaism*, p. 17. Cf. E. P. Sanders and M. Davies, *Studying the Synoptic Gospels* (London: SCM; Philadelphia: Trinity, 1989), p. 317. For further discussion see J. G. Crossley, 'Jesus and the Law: Taking E.P. Sanders to Some Logical Conclusions', in R. L. Webb and M. S. Goodacre (eds.), *Jesus as Restoration Prophet: Engaging the Work of E. P. Sanders* (London and New York: Continuum/T&T Clark, forthcoming).
25. For an example of issues relating to dissimilarity in action and with Jesus being placed above and beyond Judaism see Wright, *Victory*, pp. 132–33.
26. Sanders, *Jesus and Judaism*, p. 252.
27. Sanders, *Jesus and Judaism*, pp. 252, 254; M. Hengel, *The Charismatic Leader and His Followers* (Edinburgh: T&T Clark, 1981), p. 12. Cf. Sanders and Davies, *Studying*, p. 317.
28. Hengel, *Charismatic*, p. 8.
29. Hengel, *Charismatic*, p. 9.
30. Hengel, *Charismatic*, p. 9, n. 21.
31. Hengel, *Charismatic*, p. 14. See further the comments in M. Bockmuehl, *Jewish Law in Gentile Churches: Halakhah and the Beginning of Christian Public Ethics* (Edinburgh: T&T Clark, 2000), p. 25.
32. Sanders, *Jesus and Judaism*, pp. 256–60.
33. Bockmuehl, *Jewish Law*, pp. 23–48.
34. Wright, *Victory*, p. 401.
35. Wright, *Victory*, pp. 13, 93, 107, 108.
36. On the history of this duplicitous use of Judaism in New Testament and Christian origins scholarship see e.g. Crossley, *Jesus in an Age of Terror*, pp. 143–94. Cf. J. Z. Smith, *Drudgery Divine: On the Comparison of Early Christianities and the Religions of Late Antiquity* (Chicago: University of Chicago Press, 1990), p. 83; Kelley, *Racializing Jesus*; Arnal, *Symbolic Jesus*; T. Penner, '*Die Judenfrage* and the Construction of Ancient Judaism: Toward a Foregrounding of the Backgrounds Approach to Early Christianity', in P. Gray and G. O'Day (eds.), *Scripture and Traditions: Essays on Early Judaism and Christianity* (Leiden: Brill, 2008), pp. 429–55.
37. Wright, *Victory*, p. 93.
38. A. Reinhartz, 'The Gospel according to Benedict: Jesus of Nazareth and Jews and Judaism', in A. Pabst and A. Paddison (eds.), *The Pope and Jesus of Nazareth: Christ, Scripture and the Church* (London: SCM in association with The Centre of Theology and Philosophy, University of Nottingham, 2010), pp. 233–46 (238).
39. J. Ratzinger, *Jesus of Nazareth: From the Baptism in the Jordan to the Transfiguration* (London: Bloomsbury, 2007).
40. See especially G. Vermes, 'Review of Ratzinger, *Jesus of Nazareth*', *The Times* (19 May, 2007); G. Lüdemann, *Eyes That See Not: The Pope Looks at Jesus* (Santa Rosa: Polebridge Press, 2008).
41. For a critique of the supersessionism and Judaism in Ratzinger's book see Reinhartz, 'The Gospel according to Benedict'.
42. Ratzinger, *Jesus of Nazareth*, p. 297; cf. p. 294.
43. Ratzinger, *Jesus of Nazareth*, p. 69.

44. For Neusner's recollections see J. Neusner, 'Visiting the Vatican', *Bible and Interpretation* (February 2010), http://www.bibleinterp.com/articles/pope357908.shtml.
45. Ratzinger, *Jesus of Nazareth*, p. 13.
46. Ratzinger, *Jesus of Nazareth*, p. 12.
47. Cf. Ratzinger, *Jesus of Nazareth*, pp. 82–84.
48. See e.g. K. W. Whitelam, *The Invention of Ancient Israel: The Silencing of Palestinian History* (London and New York: Routledge, 1996); N. Abu el-Haj, *Facts on the Ground: Archaeological Practice and Territorial Self-Fashioning in Israeli Society* (Chicago and London: University of Chicago Press, 2001); N. Masalha, *The Bible and Zionism: Invented Traditions, Archaeology and Post-colonialism in Israel-Palestine* (London: Zed, 2007); Crossley, *Jesus in an Age of Terror*, pp. 143–94.
49. Ratzinger, *Jesus of Nazareth*, p. xxiii; cf. p. 6.
50. Ratzinger, *Jesus of Nazareth*, p. 57.
51. Ratzinger, *Jesus of Nazareth*, p. 68.
52. Ratzinger, *Jesus of Nazareth*, p. 70.
53. Ratzinger, *Jesus of Nazareth*, p. 101.
54. Vermes, 'Review of Ratzinger'; Lüdemann, *Eyes That See Not*; M. Casey, *Jesus of Nazareth: An Independent Historian's Account of His Life and Teachings* (London and New York: T&T Clark, 2010), pp. 28–30.
55. Ratzinger, *Jesus of Nazareth*, pp. 324–25.
56. Ratzinger, *Jesus of Nazareth*, p. 105.
57. T. Penner, '"Home Is Where the Heart Is" – A Concluding Methodological Prescript', unpublished paper delivered to the 'Holy Land as Homeland?' seminar, University of Oslo, 6–8 March, 2009.
58. M. F. Bird, 'Earliest Christianity', in M. F. Bird and J. G. Crossley, *How Did Christianity Begin? A Believer and Non-believer Examine the Evidence* (London: SPCK, 2008), pp. 155–56.
59. Available at http://www.premierradio.org.uk/listen/ondemand.aspx?mediaid={FE6B5E54-449B-48D0-A438-A37DD1C8EB9F} and http://www.premier-radio.org.uk/listen/ondemand.aspx?mediaid={10A2C09A-824B-4580-B00D-BC674D928A88}.
60. See also Vermes, 'Review of Ratzinger'.
61. G. Vermes, *The Religion of Jesus the Jew* (London: SCM, 1993), pp. 30–37.
62. Ratzinger, *Jesus of Nazareth*, pp. 34, 52.
63. Ratzinger, *Jesus of Nazareth*, p. 220.
64. Ratzinger, *Jesus of Nazareth*, pp. 34–36.
65. Ratzinger, *Jesus of Nazareth*, pp. 35–36.
66. Ratzinger, *Jesus of Nazareth*, p. 36.
67. Cf. Ratzinger, *Jesus of Nazareth*, pp. 110–11.
68. Ratzinger, *Jesus of Nazareth*, pp. 219–21.
69. Ratzinger, *Jesus of Nazareth*, p. 221.
70. Ratzinger, *Jesus of Nazareth*, p. 33; cf. p. 198.
71. Ratzinger, *Jesus of Nazareth*, pp. 56–59.
72. Ratzinger, *Jesus of Nazareth*, p. 75.
73. Ratzinger, *Jesus of Nazareth*, pp. 75–76.

74. T. Eagleton, 'Lunging, Flailing, Mispunching', *London Review of Books* 28.20 (October, 2006); idem, *Reason, Faith, and Revolution: Reflections on the God Debate* (New Haven and London: Yale University Press, 2009), pp. 3–6.
75. T. Eagleton, *Terry Eagleton Presents Jesus Christ: The Gospels* (London: Verso, 2007) and available at idem, 'Was Jesus Christ a Revolutionary?', *New Internationalist* 411 (1 May, 2008).
76. On implicit anti-Jewish tendencies sometimes found in constructions of a revolutionary Jesus see e.g. A. -J. Levine, *The Misunderstood Jew: The Church and the Scandal of the Jewish Jesus* (San Francisco: HarperCollins, 2006).
77. Eagleton, *Reason, Faith and Revolution*, pp. 19–20.
78. Eagleton, *Reason, Faith and Revolution*, p. 23.
79. Eagleton, *Reason, Faith and Revolution*, p. 28.
80. Eagleton, *Reason, Faith and Revolution*, p. 31.
81. Eagleton, *Reason, Faith and Revolution*, p. 20.
82. Eagleton, *Reason, Faith and Revolution*, p. 33.
83. R. Boer, 'An Intrinsic Eagleton?', *JCRT* 9.1 (2008), pp. 1–17 (15).
84. T. W. Adorno, *The Stars Down to Earth and Other Essays* (London: Routledge, 2001), p. 204.
85. Adorno, *Stars Down to Earth*, p. 204.

Chapter 7

The Jesus Who Wasn't There? Conservative Christianity, Atheism and Other Religious Influences

> ...you will not always have me. (Mk 14:7)

> the ever-expanding discourse of religion-and-the-secular continues to develop hand in hand with Western notions of governance, concepts of human rights, and market interests...
>
> – Ward Blanton[1]

Introduction: Redrawing the Battle-lines

More than any other group of scholars, the Jesus Seminar courted historical Jesus controversy in both academic and popular culture in the 1980s and 1990s. Liberal, sage-like and shocking to certain wings of Christianity this Jesus may have been, the Jesus Seminar still had Jesus at, and perhaps in, its heart and it was essentially a Christian project. While Jesus may have been deemed a 'secular sage', and while some critics may have seen this Jesus as a product of secularization, it remained tied in with Christianity. John Dominic Crossan, like other major fellows such as Marcus Borg, is a well-known Christian of a liberal stripe. Crossan openly sees his historical Jesus work as a critique of the present, even to the extent of performing 'open-heart surgery on Christianity itself'.[2] Robert Funk's rhetoric remained religious and Protestant of a very liberal variety, a Christianity shorn of its dogma and miraculous stories.[3] He may have come to challenge the worlds of traditional Christianity and right-wing Christianity, but he would do so by bringing a new Reformation and a new gospel, not least by posting 'Twenty-one Theses' on his website, a very modern spin on Luther's famous '95 Theses' on the door of the Wittenberg church.[4]

But that was so last century; in the first decade of this century, the seemingly direct replacement as the centre of controversy in historical

Jesus studies, The Jesus Project, has upped the ante and has instead toyed with resurrecting an old controversy: the idea of all Jesus' sayings, and indeed Jesus himself, being invented. Furthermore, a significant number of the people telling us such things, as we will see, are not simply from the liberal end of liberal Christianity, but atheists or 'secularists'. This is part of a more general pattern in biblical studies. For instance, a number of scholars have now been defined, by themselves or others, as 'secular', 'atheist' or 'agnostic' in work which has received a notable degree of scholarly and public attention. We might think of: Jacques Berlinerblau's *The Secular Bible*; Hector Avalos's *The End of Biblical Studies*; the high-profile evangelical-cum-agnostic Bart Ehrman's hugely popular *Misquoting Jesus* and *Jesus, Interrupted*; William Arnal's article on dividing confessional-driven biblical studies and the academic study of religion; my own suggestion that New Testament/Christian origins studies has historically missed out on different scholarly approaches due to the numerical dominance of Christians; SBL/AAR sessions dedicated to 'secular' approaches; the debates sparked by a Michael Fox article on scholarship and faith for the *SBL Forum*; Ronald Hendel's SBL broadside published in *Biblical Archaeology Review*; Maurice Casey's major book on the historical Jesus from a scholar who self-identifies as someone who does 'not belong to any religious or anti-religious group'; and Roland Boer's edited volume on secularism and biblical studies which picks up key debates from the past decade.[5]

The very idea of Jesus not existing was not even entertained seriously on the fringes of *contemporary* academic New Testament study but this intellectual context helps us partly understand why there have been some voices suggesting such a thing, including some of the voices present in the ill-fated Jesus Project (e.g. Thomas Thompson, Robert Price, Richard Carrier, Frank Zindler).[6] In fact, all the above views are not new but collectively this is distinctive and there ought to be little doubt that the 'secular' trend has been as prominent as it has been in living memory. I will analyse the ideological, cultural and historical reasons for such developments in due course. Before that, a more detailed overview of more specific movements in historical Jesus studies is required.

An Atheist Jesus? The Rise and Fall of The Jesus Project

The Jesus Project effectively began life in 2007 and, after invitations, became a scholarly gathering which met for the first time in 2008 in Amherst, New York. Scholars listed as its fellows included those who have published in areas relating to Jesus, the Gospels and Christian origins, such as: Bruce Chilton, Robert Eisenman, Joseph Hoffmann, Gerd Lüdemann, Dennis MacDonald, James McGrath, Justin Meggitt, James M. Robinson and this author. The Project's potential contribution to historical Jesus scholarship is described as follows in its website statement:

> It is 'new' in advocating a faith-free approach to the sources and greater attention to method than previous inquiries...its scholar associates represent not only professionals in New Testament Studies, but specialists in the social sciences, including archaeology, legal history, intertestamental Judaism, educational studies, Near Eastern studies, philosophy and classics.[7]

The Project was due to meet approximately every nine months in North America and Europe over a five-year period, but came to an abrupt end in 2009 due to a combination of politics, debates over the time dedicated to the question of Jesus' existence, and funding running dry.[8] Yet, despite its short life-span (pending any resurrection) the Project managed to generate a great deal of publicity, both academic and popular (see below).

While the fellows of the Project came from a range of academic and ideological perspectives, there was an influential atheistic/secular tendency underlying it, as its website statement already implies. The Project was backed by the explicitly secular/atheistic Committee for the Scientific Examination of Religion (CSER), which in turn is a research division of the Center for Inquiry in Amherst. The Center for Inquiry has been driven by Paul Kurtz, Professor Emeritus of Philosophy at the State University of New York at Buffalo.[9] Kurtz has been a leading figure and chair of different secular humanist organizations such as the Committee for Skeptical Inquiry, the Council for Secular Humanism, Prometheus Books and editor-in-chief of *Free Inquiry*. The Center for Inquiry is quite explicit about its vision in relation to certain religious texts and world views. In addition to its statement on 'religion, ethics and society', where the Center for Inquiry claims to be a 'leader in the struggle for a more rational, secular world',[10] it makes the following bold claims about replacement:

> If the naturalistic outlook is to supplant the ancient mythological narratives of the past, it needs a new institution devoted to its articulation and dramatization to the public. The Center for Inquiry is that institution... We are also interested in providing rational ethical

> alternatives to the reigning paranormal and religious systems of belief...[11]

Clearly, then, the Center for Inquiry fits neatly into the very public debates on science versus religion and non-belief versus belief. So too, naturally enough, does the CSER. The CSER claims it has 'worked to encourage humanistic, critical and non-parochial approaches to the study of religious traditions and institutions'. Figures consulted by CSER include a range of those from secular and religious perspectives, though it makes claims to a 'broadly humanistic' perspective.[12] This is reflected in CSER's Executive Committee and Fellows of the Committee which includes well-known radical religious thinkers, atheists and secular humanists (e.g. Hector Avalos, Paul Kurtz, Jacques Berlinerblau, Don Cupitt, Hermann Detering, John Dominic Crossan, Daniel Dennett, Michael Goulder, Gerd Lüdemann, Steven Pinker, Robert M. Price, Philip Pullman and Ibn Warraq).[13]

Furthermore, The Jesus Project claimed to be an outworking of the 'non-confessional' study of religion, a 'core activity' of the Center for Inquiry and CSER. This is also reflected in the leading figures in the Project. According to the driving force behind The Jesus Project, Joseph Hoffmann, 'it's my impression that all of those so far associated with the project take "scholarship" very seriously indeed and want this to be, at the very least, a faith-free process'.[14] One of Hoffmann's co-chairs was Gerd Lüdemann, a controversial New Testament scholar in relation to faith and belief, particularly as his non-confessional views barred him from being able to teach in the Theology Department at the University of Göttingen, and which also led to collective support for Lüdemann by Project members.[15] The final co-chair was Robert Price. Price's ideological position on religion may not be quite the same as those of Hoffmann and Lüdemann, but he is probably the closest mainstream New Testament scholarship has come in recent times to denying that the historical Jesus existed, though, as Price is aware, this position is typically regarded as being on the extreme fringes and is rarely taken seriously in mainstream scholarly books on the historical Jesus.[16] Yet, with The Jesus Project and his position as co-chair, Price's kind of argument has been pushed closer to the mainstream than ever before in the last hundred years of New Testament scholarship. Finally, we should add that the publication of Jesus Project material was to be through Prometheus Press, a well-known secular humanist publisher which has published controversial and radical biblical studies books, such as Hector Avalos,

The End of Biblical Studies, and numerous books by, or which have the involvement of, Price, Lüdemann and Hoffmann. Indeed, the one significant publication from the Project, *Sources of the Jesus Tradition*, was published by Prometheus in 2010.[17]

The Jesus Project has also provided a platform for scholars of a more secular humanist or overtly atheistic persuasion hardly typical of mainstream Jesus scholarship. Fellows of the Project again included a notable number of radical Christians (in terms of the existence of God), atheists and secular humanists and, keeping to its promise, fellows included those outside the traditional bounds of biblical studies, including classicists, ancient historians, legal studies scholars, religious studies scholars, scientists and philosophers (e.g. Richard Carrier, Dorothy King, Stephen Law, Solomon Schimmel, Frank Zindler and the ubiquitous Paul Kurtz). There are also notable developments. Fellows (active or otherwise) included leading 'minimalist' scholars known for strenuously questioning the historicity of much of the Hebrew Bible/Old Testament narratives (e.g. Philip Davies, Niels Peter Lemche and Thomas Thompson, Thompson writing a recent book heavy with scepticism towards the historical usefulness of material on the life and teaching of Jesus[18]). The Jesus Project had strong secular humanist sympathies from top to bottom, even if we allow for the contributions of prominent Christians (e.g. Chilton), and clearly had the potential for secular humanist and atheist/agnostic agendas to make waves in historical Jesus studies.

The perception that the Project might be all about showing Jesus did not exist became the biggest point of controversy, at least in the reporting of the Project in the press. These are some of the headlines:

> 'For Scholars, a Combustible Question: Was Christ real?', *Toronto Star* (27 December, 2008)
>
> 'Scholars to Debate if Jesus Existed', *Ottawa Citizen* (10 January, 2007 [sic?])
>
> 'Scholars to Explore Existence of Jesus', *Buffalo News* (30 November, 2008)
>
> 'New Quest for Historical Jesus Draws Skeptics, Scholars', *Christian Post* (10 December, 2008)

The media reporting itself did little to downplay the perception of denying the existence of Jesus, even if some knew the situation was more nuanced. Despite noting the claim of the organizers that 'they're not out to disprove the existence of Jesus', Jay Tokasz for *Buffalo News* still opened with classic journalistic sensationalism:

> Billions of Christians around the world believe that a man named Jesus roamed the earth 2,000 years ago, performing miracles and delivering salvation to his followers. But as Christians prepare to celebrate Jesus' birth later this month, a group of skeptical scholars, historians and biblical experts will meet in Amherst to examine more closely whether he existed.[19]

The *Toronto Star* opened dramatically and unambiguously on the issue of the Project and Jesus' existence: 'Earlier this month, just before most Christians would mark the birth of their saviour, a group of scholars gathered in Amherst, NY to begin pondering a simple yet combustible question: Did Jesus exist?'[20] In no less dramatic terms, Jennifer Green, for the *Ottawa Citizen*, opens her article with the questions, 'A hardy gang of scholars is again trying to ask the question: did Jesus really exist? And can my career survive if I even bring up the topic?'[21] In a later article on The Jesus Project, which acknowledges that there is no goal to disprove Jesus' existence, she opens in similar terms saying, 'Internationally recognized biblical scholars are set to launch The Jesus Project, a new endeavour to examine the historical existence of Christ.'[22]

But the issue of the non-existence of Jesus and The Jesus Project was not about the media getting another topic in biblical studies badly wrong. In fact, I think the media hype generated by the Project itself (intentionally or unintentionally) goes to the very heart of its aims, as the inclusion of Price as one of the three co-chairs might suggest. Moreover, the idea of debating the very existence of Jesus is grounded in the words of the Project itself. Hoffmann still acknowledged the relevance of the existence, or not, of the historical Jesus whilst trying to downplay the media hype. In his words,

> I was not the inventor of the preposterous slogan 'What if the Most Influential Man in Human History Never Lived?' but I should have been its destroyer. I was, however, the 'creator' of the suggestion that the non-historicity of Jesus is a testable hypothesis and can no longer be ignored, and I still believe it.[23]

The hard rhetoric of entertaining the non-existence of Jesus is certainly present in the output of the Project and I think this can be established beyond any reasonable doubt. Price has articles published on The Jesus Project's webpage.[24] In one of these, Price recalls his 'gravitating to that crazy view, that Jesus hadn't existed, that he was mythic all the way down, like Hercules', speaks of the 'wholly fictive Jesus story' and ends as follows:

> I have not tried to amass every argument I could think of to destroy the historicity of Jesus. Rather, I have summarized the series of realizations about methodology and evidence that eventually led me to embrace the Christ Myth Theory. There may once have been an historical Jesus, but for us there is one no longer. If he existed, he is forever lost behind the stained glass curtain of holy myth. At least that's the current state of the evidence as I see it.[25]

Similarly, other 'mythicists' have a presence on the website, and the Project has allowed this 'group' to come as close to mainstream academic historical Jesus studies as they have done for a century. Put simply, and inevitably covering over the diversity of opinions, 'mythicism' is a movement, historically outside and largely ignored by mainstream scholarship, which believes Jesus did not exist and was instead a product of the Christian imagination or myth-making, perhaps in line with other mythic figures in the ancient world or woven out of a range of stories readily available from different traditions. As well as Price and Thompson, the more popular recent proponents of this old argument have included G. A. Wells, Alvar Ellegård and Earl J. Doherty. In addition to the appointment of Price as co-chair, a 'mythicist' presence is found in the Project's administration, namely Thomas Verenna, a biblioblogger whose blog, The Musings of Thomas Verenna, regularly discusses 'mythicist' issues, and who has co-edited a volume on the historicity of Jesus with Thomas Thompson which includes contributions from both mainstream biblical scholars and 'mythicists'.[26]

The Project's website also provides a link to the Mythicists' Forum, an online discussion group where membership 'is open only to those who deny the historicity of Jesus of Nazareth'.[27] There is also a link to the little less drastic Jesus Mysteries, an online discussion group which asks, 'Was Jesus an historical person, a mythical figure, a fictional character, a theological construction, or some combination of these?'[28] These links are doubly significant because there were no online links given to more mainstream debating arenas on issues relating to the historical Jesus, the most notable absence being the Cross-Talk discussion group. I do not think it is going too far to suggest that this nod in the direction of 'mythicism' somewhere close to mainstream New Testament studies was unthinkable even a decade ago, and it is notable that James McGrath has had extensive discussions of 'mythicism' on his popular blog, Exploring Our Matrix, and that Maurice Casey felt the need to debunk 'mythicist' positions in his major recent book on the historical Jesus.[29] The recent re-emergence of a typically off-the-radar obscure group with clear atheistic sympathies will need to be explained (see below).

Some of the difficulty in assessing the results of The Jesus Project has now been eased: some of the conference papers have been published in *Sources of the Jesus Tradition*, edited by Hoffmann and including a mixture of 'mythicists' and established New Testament scholars of different persuasions (e.g. Lüdemann, MacDonald, Meggitt, Chilton, David Trobisch, Eisenman). But not all papers; it is, however, possible to do also a little detective work by turning to alternative sources and eyewitnesses. Unable as I was to attend the opening meeting, it is most fortunate that we have a detailed eyewitness source. Classicist Richard Carrier blogged extensively about the Project's first meeting and, most importantly for present purposes, it is clear from his reporting that the non-existence of Jesus, and related theses, was firmly on the agenda.

An important example is the paper of the established scholar of Christian origins, Arthur Droge, who presented on "Jesus and Ned Lud[d]: What's in a Name?" According to Carrier's report, 'Droge confessed he was an agnostic about the historicity of Jesus and might even be leaning to the conclusion that Jesus was apocryphal.' Droge is further reported to have argued that 'just as Ned Ludd...is likely ahistorical, and even if not, unrecoverable (and therefore, either way, only the mythical Ned Ludd can be studied now, so that's all we should study...)... so, too, for Jesus...since it's silly to try and find the "historical" Ned Ludd (whether he existed or not), it's just as silly to try and find the "historical" Jesus (ditto).'[30] Carrier also added that this was more-or-less the conclusion maintained by another established scholar of Christian origins, Dennis MacDonald.[31] While I have no reason to doubt the accuracy of Carrier's reports (and I stress this), the emphasis in MacDonald's article in *Sources of the Jesus Tradition* seems a little different, though a radical edge (in relation to historicity) remains:

> I see no compelling reason to doubt the existence of Jesus of Nazareth, but I also see no compelling reason to attribute any individual saying to him, including the Golden Rule or the Lord's Prayer. At stake is not the recovery of Jesus' words but of his distinctive voice... Not only did an earthly Jesus exist, he provided his followers a coherent moral vision in his teaching on the kingdom of God, a moral vision that apparently shaped his conduct and that of his first followers.[32]

Perhaps we might add that even if Carrier unintentionally misrepresented these scholars it remains significant that Carrier could still report such ideas in such terms.

Furthermore, there were even more explicit 'mythicist' agendas and positions registered in *Sources of the Jesus Tradition*. Robert Price ends his contribution with the following challenge:

> prejudice makes it falsely obvious to conservatives that the canonical Gospels could not be the result of wholesale fabrication by well-meaning Christians. There is just no reason Christian writers could not have composed the Sermon on the Mount if they created the Dialogue of the Savior. If they could have fabricated Pistis Sophia, they could much more easily have fabricated the Gospel of John. Whether they did is another matter, the discussion of which starts here, not stops.[33]

Related concerns are taken up by Frank Zindler where the non-existence of Jesus is explicit:

> there is no compelling or convincing evidence to support the proposition that a man – carrying out all the bodily functions common to human beings generally – identifiable as Jesus of Nazareth was living in Palestine at the turn of the era...there is irrefutable evidence against the proposition – even though it is not beholden upon me to prove the negative... I must tell you that I find absolutely no good reason to suppose he was any more historical than Mithra, Dionysus, Zeus, or Thor.[34]

Hoffman also plays around with concepts of non-existence and historicity, even if he is more concerned with critiquing ideas concerning the generation of traditions. The following is from his introductory essay:

> the 'nonhistoricity of Jesus' [is] still considered risible or taboo...no similar imperative exists to corroborate the existence (or sayings) of the 'historical' Adam, the historical Abraham, or Moses, or David – or indeed the prophets... We are prone to think that the Jesus we excavate with literary tools is more historical than the religious icons Michelangelo released through his sculpting... As a Christian origins scholar by training, I am not even sure how one would go about the task, if it is a necessary task, of 'proving' that Jesus existed.[35]

More examples could be added, but by now it should be clear that we should be under no illusions: the non-existence of the historical Jesus was one of the most notable, or at least prominent, concerns of the Project's flagship publication.

There is further evidence of a significant concern with questions of the non-existence of Jesus being prominent within the Project. Writing as a

Project insider and an eyewitness to the opening meeting of the Project, Bruce Chilton rebukes the Project for focusing on 'an incoherent set of some of the least important questions in scholarship', adding, 'it keeps asking "Did Jesus exist?" as if that issue had not been raised repeatedly during the past two centuries'. Quite what Chilton means by 'as if that issue had not been raised repeatedly during the past two centuries'[36] I am not entirely sure, but it certainly has not been a question raised in more contemporary historical Jesus studies (as Chilton perhaps also implies). Still, this is a further insider perception of the question of Jesus' existence being raised. When added to the publications (online and edited volume), the inclusion of 'mythicists' among the fellows, and the various comments made by Hoffmann and others, we must conclude that the significance of the non-existence (or non-historicity) of Jesus was a serious part of the overall agenda of the Project, no matter how much the media may have sensationalized the story.

A development in the Project's fellows was also significant in relation to the issue of the non-existence of Jesus: 'outside' scholarly perception. After two years of reflecting, April DeConick decided against participating in the Project. Her reasons are significant for present purposes because she thought the goal of the Project was vague and 'the goal to prove Jesus' existence or not is methodologically a black hole from my perspective'. The possible connection with the presentation of the results in the media was a further problem for DeConick. 'The media', she suggested, 'will have a heyday – "now scholars prove that Jesus didn't exist" or "scholars say that we can know nothing about Jesus"'. Intriguingly, Mark Goodacre commented that he made the same decision about the Project 'for similar reasons' as DeConick's.[37]

There should, therefore, be no doubt that the non-existence of Jesus is present as a serious option, or 'testable hypothesis', for the Project, both in perception and reality – and perhaps somewhere in between – and that this is certainly tied in with, as might be expected, the significant presence of atheists, secular humanists and a certain type of radical Christian.

This is further enhanced by the Project's deliberate distancing from that other project with the not dissimilar name, the Jesus Seminar. It is no surprise that parts of the media picked up on the similarities. For instance: 'The Jesus Project...is the descendent of the ill-fated Jesus Seminar, a similar academic inquiry that collapsed amidst cheesy techniques and internecine quarrels in the 1980s' (*Ottawa Citizen*, 6 December, 2008).[38]

The Project has made clear, and unambiguously attempted to distance itself from, the obvious point of comparison. Hoffmann is emphatic:

> TJP was never construed as a sequel to the Jesus Seminar. (I have now written that sentence eight times in different places.)... It did not begin as a corrective or a replacement to the Jesus Seminar. There is overlap only insofar as it is impossible to create a brand-new scholarly conversation without involving some of the same personalities and dealing with some of the same questions. Consider the Obama White House and the Clinton White House in terms of recidivist personnel and "issues." I have said, recently and rather forcefully I hope, that the Seminar asked some of the wrong questions in the wrong order, skated past others, and that to accept any critique of TJP methodology, as it evolves, from a seminar whose own methods were often seen as risible would be – risible. Hence, without being dismissive of the Seminar Jeremiahs who've been there, done that, TJP cannot proceed without an evaluation of what the Seminar accomplished, failed to accomplish, and the reasons for its performance.[39]

This distancing is sometimes framed in terms of faith, at least implicitly ('It is "new" in advocating a faith-free approach to the sources'[40]). These general sentiments were picked up by the media. So in the media reception we get statements such as, 'organizers of The Jesus Project say their effort is different from The Jesus Seminar as it is not largely theologically driven' (*Christian Post,* 10 December, 2008) and 'one key difference [from the Jesus Seminar]: These scholars regard the belief that Jesus of Nazareth was a historical figure to be a "testable hypothesis." The seminar continues through the Westar Institute in California, but the Center for Inquiry is seeking a new investigation of Jesus' life that is free of any theological constraints' (*Buffalo News,* 30 November, 2008).[41]

The contrast with the Jesus Seminar is significant in two respects. First, the Jesus Seminar is the most obvious point of contrast and The Jesus Project would just as obviously have to be doing something different to justify its existence. Second, the Jesus Seminar previously represented the most radical end of mainstream historical Jesus scholarship and the more overtly secular humanist persuasion of The Jesus Project meant it has to supplant its nearest 'rival' (so to speak) and show that the liberal Jesus Seminar never really represented secular humanism unlike its successor.

What if Richard Bauckham is Right...?

An opposite movement of equal prominence has also gathered pace in recent times and needs outlining before we move on to analysis. A number of what might be labelled 'evangelical' or 'conservative' Christian positions have now entered into the heart of the mainstream in ways which would have been unlikely in the heyday of Bultmann-influenced scholarship (though I stress as an aside that I make no exegetical judgment on either 'evangelical'/'conservative' or Bultmann-influenced scholarship). Indeed, certain conservative books have now found themselves among the most influential and widely discussed books in contemporary New Testament studies. In addition to Richard Bauckham's *Jesus and the Eyewitnesses* (2006) and James Dunn's *Jesus Remembered* (2003), both of which develop this millennium's penchant for memory studies, we have also seen books such as Larry Hurtado's *Lord Jesus Christ* (2003), arguing for an extremely early date for Christ devotion, and N. T. Wright's other massive book, *The Resurrection of the Son of God* (2003), the latter arguing that a supernatural explanation for the resurrection of Jesus is the key to explaining the evidence for the emergence of the Christian movement. Wright's book is perhaps most surprising of all and, with its emphasis on apparently proving the role of the divine in history, might be described as being what Intelligent Design is to the scientific study of evolution, if it were not for the obvious point that Intelligent Design is not part of the scientific mainstream. Confirming their mainstream status, all the above books were reviewed at article length in major New Testament journals.[42] And in the world of biblioblogging, bibliobloggers were asked (by each other) to name their top five books. From over seventy responses, the most popular author was Wright (with Dunn also doing well).[43]

Arguably, the work with the most impact on historical Jesus studies for this conservative revival has been that of Richard Bauckham on eyewitnesses. What I want to do with Bauckham is to follow his arguments through to their logical conclusions and see what happens if we assume that Richard Bauckham is right in that there were eyewitnesses to the extent he claims. We can then see that he is making some dramatic claims in terms of conventional understandings of history.

One area where the sceptic might see invention and rewriting of history is in the miraculous, stories that were undeniably circulating in the earliest years of Christian origins when eyewitnesses to the life and teaching of Jesus were still around. Here I would omit healings and exorcisms from the miraculous, which Bauckham does not do,[44] because these are the kinds of things that are known cross-culturally and do not necessarily require a supernatural explanation. Even so, the supernaturally miraculous (so to speak) is clearly attested across the synoptic tradition, is early, is undeniably present in the Gospel tradition when eyewitnesses were alive and, if we follow Bauckham some way, perhaps even recounted by eyewitnesses to Jesus. We are dealing with 'uniquely unique events' of the sort that might well be thought by conventional historians (at least of the variety to be found outside biblical studies) to involve invention and fiction.

However, Bauckham implies that stories surrounding the miraculous may well have been grounded in basic historical facts. According to Bauckham, Mk 4:36 and the mention of 'other boats' *may* be part of an eyewitness memory, referencing scholars who think it may well be.[45] Bauckham does not push hard for such a case, but if he did we would have to go one step further and ask, is the rest of the story – a story where Jesus calms a storm – part of eyewitness memory? Furthermore, in the context of his discussion of Mk 4:36, Bauckham tentatively suggests, 'It is true that Gospel scholars have a deep-rooted desire to explain all detail as significant, and so it may be that on occasions where their explanations are disputed or implausible we should more willingly accept that some details are irrelevant survivals of eyewitness memory.'[46] Elsewhere on the stilling of the storm, and in comparison with Holocaust memories, Bauckham writes of allusions made by the retelling, how 'concrete experience and mythic resonance…converge naturally' and how 'the interpretation does not come in between us and the realistic character of the story.'[47] But we can push Bauckham a little further here and point out that human beings miraculously stilling storms would be a remarkable discovery for historians. What would happen if Bauckham were to discuss – and not simply in terms of artistic license – the notable ramifications of such historical reconstruction? Are we dealing with an eyewitness reporting of an *actual* miraculous event? Bauckham's approach would seem to suggest just that.

Again, Bauckham is very close to answering in the affirmative when dealing with other events concerning the miraculous. Writing on the 'gist' and 'details' of the story through memory, Bauckham refers to the miracles of the feeding of the five and four thousand respectively. Numerical details are important and memorable and 'would have been essential to the story as it was formulated and transmitted by the eyewitnesses.'[48] In this context, Bauckham can write about 'the realistic extent to which memory can be relied upon, in the case both of the memory of the eyewitness and the memory of the performer of oral tradition.'[49] Does this include the miraculous core of the feeding stories? Did eyewitnesses really see such things?

Of John, the Gospel traditionally thought to contain the least valuable information about the historical Jesus, Bauckham says that 'the finished Gospel has a high degree of highly reflective interpretation.'[50] If we assume Bauckham's views of eyewitness, to what extent can we say this in terms of historical accuracy? If I understand Bauckham correctly, it would seem that for all the Johannine elaboration, Bauckham is again making the case for eyewitness reports of the miraculous, even in the case of John's Gospel. Bauckham argues that the Beloved Disciple – an eyewitness according to Bauckham – is claiming that the thrust of the sword in to Jesus' side produced flows of blood and water, that the resurrected Jesus prepares breakfast, and that there was a huge catch of fish. Bauckham claims that 'these details do help to give readers the impression that the Gospel portrays the Beloved Disciple as an observant witness of what happened.'[51] There is also some suggestion about eyewitnesses to the wedding at Cana where, according to John, Jesus famously turned water into wine.[52] Again, these arguments made by Bauckham seem to come close to the implication that these miraculous events really did happen. If not, are the central details made up? It is difficult to read the latter into Bauckham's argument.

In fact, there are some further indications in Bauckham's methodology which imply that eyewitnesses are close to preserving basic historical facts. In his interdisciplinary study of memory, Bauckham can write about 'the "gist" of an event that is remembered even when details are inaccurate' and about 'Those who recall the past really do intend to recall the past, not to create it to suit present needs and purposes.'[53] He also adds that 'We must beware of a historical methodology that prejudices inquiry against exceptionality and is biased towards the levelling down of the extraordinary to the ordinary.'[54] Though certainly not without qualification, much of Bauckham's methodology seems to be geared toward general historical accuracy and, more specifically, the Gospels as recalling unique, unusual, memorable and salient *historical* events.

Furthermore, Bauckham writes about historical practice throughout his book. He also appears to have some concern about a lack of knowledge of the way historians go about their task. For example, he writes, 'Most scholars in this field have little or no experience of working as historians in other areas of history' and Gospel scholarship's own attempts at historical methodology do 'not necessarily correspond well to the way evidence is treated in other historical fields.' Bauckham stresses: 'It has to be said over and over again, that historical rigor does not consist in fundamental scepticism toward historical testimony but in fundamental trust along with testing by critical questioning... Testimony should be treated as reliable until proved otherwise.'[55] If I read Bauckham fairly, this would seem to edge away from a view of the Gospel tradition that would include creative fiction because the default mode is one of general historical accuracy.

While Bauckham is undoubtedly right about the lack of knowledge among New Testament scholars concerning how historians go about their task, it is also important to note that if Bauckham is correct then this actually means going well beyond conventional historical practice outside historical Jesus studies. This is because the miraculous, rightly or wrongly, is not even close to being on the agenda for conventional historians. In the 1960s, E. H. Carr, in his famous introduction to the study of history, emphatically rejected the idea of the miraculous or supernatural in historical explanation ('history is a game played, so to speak, without a joker in the pack').[56] Indeed, for other, more recent, primers on history, the miraculous is not even deemed worthy of serious discussion.[57] I was involved in a project on historians, historiography and religious studies, including biblical studies. The issue of the miraculous *really happening* was never discussed and was never on the agenda. With Bauckham's work in mind, were we wrong in such an omission?[58]

If I read Bauckham fairly, this would mean that his results would imply, like Wright's results on the resurrection, that we are dealing with something remarkably different (in terms of the practising historian) and coming close to showing that the miraculous really did happen. If we have eyewitnesses to a human being miraculously feeding people, miraculously calming the elements, miraculously turning water into wine, and miraculously raised from the dead and preparing breakfast, we have to decide how reliable we think these reports are. If these things really happened, this means the discipline of history will have to be completely revolutionized, something akin to Intelligent Design replacing evolution in Biology.

The alternative to this would be that, if Bauckham is right, people, including eyewitnesses, sometimes invented fictional or theologized stories about Jesus, at times with only the emotional impact of the historical Jesus and the fact that he lived being the historical foundation. Should we, then, be thinking more along the lines of the way Bauckham summarizes Josephus' self-involvement in events alongside eyewitnesses: 'Of course, this does not guarantee that Josephus' account is always accurate, let alone objective'?[59] If Gospel stories are theologized, fictional or have been invented (intentionally or not) by eyewitnesses, or are not always accurate, then we are in a situation not too dissimilar from the one in which we were in the pre-*Jesus and the Eyewitnesses* era. This would therefore mean that in terms of the historical Jesus, we would remain in a chaotic situation. Put crudely, some material reflects the historical Jesus, some does not, and all the shades in-between. Yet, Bauckham claims, 'To insist, with some Gospel critics, that the historicity of each and every Gospel pericope must be established, one by one, with arguments for each, is not to recognize testimony for what it necessarily is.'[60] If the more sceptical views are anywhere near correct, then would this critiqued principle still hold more weight than Bauckham allows? Or are the Gospel accounts unlike Bauckham's portrayal of Josephus and they push the miraculous harder still? It would seem Bauckham's logic goes with the latter.[61]

New Atheism, Religion, Conservative Christianity

In 2008, the evangelical Michael Bird and I published, *How Did Christianity Begin? A Believer and Non-Believer Examine the Evidence*, a project deliberately echoing Borg and Wright's liberal Christian and traditionalist/evangelical dialogue a decade earlier (with the latter duo notably making mention of praying together). Clearly, there was a different dividing line, no doubt a sign of the times: believer versus non-believer rather and liberal Christian versus evangelical (or: 'traditionalist') Christian.[62] How did it come to this? The popularity of two apparent 'extremes' we have seen in this chapter – eyewitness testimony of the life and teaching of Jesus (not to mention supernatural resurrection) and the entertaining of the idea that Jesus did not exist – alongside the popular scholarly debates over faith and scholarship, neatly replicates debates in contemporary American culture, in particular the rising prominence of atheistic or secular liberalism, which is partly a reaction to conservative evangelical Christianity, which itself has been growing in political and cultural prominence since the 1970s.[63]

In fact, these notable trends are a part of the explanatory approach underlying my overall arguments, particularly in the works of David Harvey and Noam Chomsky. According to Harvey, the 'progress of fundamentalist evangelical Christianity in the US has some connection with proliferating job insecurities, the loss of other forms of social solidarity, and the hollowness of capitalist consumer culture.'[64] In response to Gilbert Achcar's expert comments on the political, social and economic reasons underlying the rise of Islamic 'fundamentalism', Chomsky points out the general (and no more) similarities with Christian 'fundamentalism' in America and the emergence of neoliberalism and neoconservatism, in particular the politicization of Christian 'fundamentalism' in recent decades. The mobilization of 'fundamentalist' Christian voters away from their economic interests to 'religious' issues such as gay rights, abortion, evolution in schools and so on has been most beneficial for those wanting to destroy traditional working-class opposition and a system further benefiting the most powerful (see chapter 2). In recent decades, as we have seen, wages have stagnated or declined for the majority over a lengthy period (over 20 years) with working hours increasing and indebtedness rising rapidly while social benefits decreased. By mobilizing Christian 'fundamentalism' into a political force, the discourse and focus was shifted towards those 'fundamentalist' issues.[65]

In America at least, the prominence of, and interest in, 'New Atheism' is, as noted above, partly a reaction to the evangelical revival and the Christian right and, as we will see below, part of a hard secularizing tendency in the 'war on terror'. But the roots of the popularity of New Atheism could also be seen as a symptom of neoliberalism. The social dislocations associated with neoliberalism led to alternative forms of institutions and networks to express collective ideas, including, among many things, the rise of religious sects and what David Harvey might at a push call 'secular cults'.[66] The recurring rock solid confidence across the well-organized online atheist and related 'secular' groups, particularly in attitudes to religion, bear this out only too well. Readers might want to go online and view the particularly well-organized and popular website, Internet Infidels, which also has plenty of discussion on Christian origins and the historical Jesus (or not), or the popular 'mythicist' blogs often manufacturing controversy relating to historical Jesus and biblical studies and in attempted dialogue with mainstream biblical scholars, or even any number of 'mythicist' comments left on mainstream biblical scholars' blogs.[67] It is worth noting that others have argued that there is a tendency among certain 'mythicist' writers, including bloggers, to avoid the details of an argument and, typically despite rhetoric to the contrary, a general closed-mindedness that, it is argued, allows the label 'fundamentalism' to be easily applied. Indeed, as Maurice Casey has discovered, there are a significant number of 'mythicists' who are converts from Christian 'fundamentalist' groups, effectively swapping one 'fundamentalism' for another.[68]

It should be no surprise that a general neoliberal context has a tendency to produce fertile ground for any number of conspiracy theories. As Chomsky claims after applying such an approach to September 11 conspiracy theories, as well as obvious broader application, 'It's easy for that to happen in an atomized, depoliticized society.'[69] As we also saw in chapter 2, the past forty years have, at least in the UK and North America, led to a sharp decline in the power of unions and traditional parties of the working class have become much closer to big business and distanced themselves from organized opposition on the left. This has meant a major traditional base for popular opposition has gone, with the Church one of the few areas left for organized activism (and there is lots of ambiguity among the churches concerning that).[70] When distrust of government rises, not least in harsher economic times, where else is there to turn? Certainly one place in this more atomized and depoliticized society is the internet and conspiracy theories. The internet provides the means of perpetuating and multiplying with ease a whole host of unsubstantiated, but overtly oppositional, claims. Blogs and websites can gain popularity, with more hits and links, and thus greater group reinforcement, irrespective of expertise in the area. An analogous process can be found on hard atheist blogs and some of the amateur blogs which advocate that Jesus did not exist, the latter being strong on the rhetoric of professional historical Jesus scholars not really knowing how to undertake proper history. There are also notable politicized claims that the 'mythic Jesus', so to speak, can help fight right-wing evangelicals in America or that politically engaged scholarship on issues relating to the stereotyping of Jews, Muslims and Palestinians by analogy should be turning its fire on scholarship advocating the existence of Jesus, along with further peculiar examples of victim mentality and comparisons between the treatment of mythicist (or related bloggers) and racism.[71]

This sort of context actually means we should partly be seeing the two seemingly polarizing movements in scholarship and popular culture as related symptoms of neoliberalism. Indeed, the world of conspiracy theories, conservative evangelicals, aliens and communist and/or Islamic plots to take over America are, to some extent, interlinked. Timothy LaHaye, co-author of the *Left Behind* series and a major figure of the politicized American Christian Right, also believes that secret societies, such as the Illuminati, and a variety of liberal and humanist groups are plotting against Christianity and working towards turning America into a Soviet-style state.[72] A dramatic example of this sort of crossover is Peter Ruckman, the controversial proponent of the King James Bible as the final revelation of God. His brand of KJV-onlyism brings him in line with a certain brand of American 'fundamentalism', but he is equally famous for his *apparent* belief in, among other things, UFOs and their role in human history, brain transmitters implanted in African Americans (among others), different types of aliens with different coloured blood, CIA dealings with aliens, CIA kidnapping of children, a race with webbed feet and so on.[73] Is it not telling that in the run up to the 2010 Mid-Term Elections in America, Christine O'Donnell – the Tea Party candidate and conservative Christian with a distinctive take on masturbation – can open a potentially counter-productive political advert on television by denying she is a witch as well as claiming on Fox News that American scientific companies are cross-breeding humans and animals and coming up with mice with fully functioning human brains?[74]

There is also a certain irrationality at play in some of the above which can be linked with certain strands of postmodernity, most forcefully put in Eagelton's critique of Lyotard and postmodern trends (e.g. 'junked history, refused argumentation, aestheticized politics'),[75] as seen in cases where scholars such as N. T. Wright and Scot McKnight have avoided, or alarmingly misrepresented, argumentation and effectively used the force of their personalities to drive home their position, irrespective of detail.[76] We might also mention some hair-raising suggestions, such as Ben Witherington's claim that the once dead Lazarus wrote John's Gospel ('If our author...had been raised by Jesus...from being well and truly dead, this was bound to change his worldview!'),[77] and Wright's infamous semi-defence of the historicity of the resurrected dead saints of Mt. 27:52–53 ('Some stories are so odd that they may just have happened').[78]

On the other hand, as with the rise of Intelligent Design, there has been a tendency actually to invoke the power of science and reason in order to show the existence of that which might be deemed to be beyond science and reason: the supernatural. After all, Wright wants to show, with all the powers of reason and debate, that supernatural intervention in history (the bodily resurrection), is the most plausible way to explain the emergence of Christian origins, a view not uncommon among conservative scholars.[79] But on the virgin birth and resurrection,

Michael Bird is as explicit as anyone on the use of science in relation to the supernatural:

> in early 2007 it was reported in the news that a female Komodo dragon named Flora conceived through parthenogenesis (i.e. reproduction without the aid of a male). I cannot help but think that if a Komodo dragon can do it, why not God?... When British botanists arrived in Australia they reported the existence of a mammal that laid eggs, had fur like a rabbit, a bill like a duck, and webbed feet. When the report reached Britain it was ridiculed as a hoax... My point is that evidence does not always conform to scientific expectations, so I am reticent to let anyone place limits on what is possible in a space-time universe which might co-exist with a divine being.[80]

We can see how the rhetoric of science and reason masks a conservative and a not conventionally rational agenda in certain uses of the scholarly criteria for finding the historical Jesus. We should not now be surprised to learn that a criterion for finding the words of Jesus has been developed to include anything that is in the Gospels. Paul Barnett has championed the 'criterion of inclusion' which 'points to the likelihood of authenticity based on the simple reality that a saying included in the canonical gospel is more likely than not to be authentic'.[81] There is a potentially interesting logic to this somewhat convenient criterion if pushed to its extreme conclusion: if the canonical Gospels only included authentic sayings, what is the point of having other criteria? Barnett lists the 'criterion of inclusion' alongside other criteria which have found 'wider acceptance' than others. It is not entirely clear that such a criterion has found wider acceptance but, given the conservative revival in recent years, it is significant that Barnett can make such a dramatic claim. Interestingly, like other conservative scholars, he likes the 'criterion of embarrassment'. Superficially, this might suggest that Jesus did something, well, embarrassing and that this might seem at odds with a conservative agenda. But look closely at Barnett's language:

> Examples within the Gospel of Mark include Jesus' association with people of ill repute (2.14–16); the accusation of demon possession (3.22–27); the appearance of failure in his hometown, Nazareth (6.4), that his healing was not always immediate (8.22–26); and his apparent petulance towards the fruitless fig tree (11.12–14).[82]

There is much we could say about this criterion, but focusing on the question at hand we can say that Jesus' association with people of ill repute and the accusation of demon possession would not necessarily be embarrassing for conservative Christians. However, notice that the failure in his hometown was the 'appearance of failure' and that the petulance towards the fig-tree is an 'apparent petulance'. Now we might want to ask Barnett the following: was Jesus petulant or not and did Jesus fail in his healings in his hometown or not? If Jesus was both petulant and a failure, this is a problem, is it not, for certain conservative Christians? Barnett's argument is sufficiently ambiguous for him to have his cake and eat it, to keep a historical criterion without offending Jesus.

And yet is there not also an unintentional undermining of his argument on embarrassment? If Jesus did not *really* do something embarrassing, if we read 'appearance' and 'apparent' as get out clauses, can the passages in question really be shown to come from Jesus thanks to the criterion of embarrassment? Perhaps we need not worry though: the criterion of inclusion will presumably rescue sayings for the historical Jesus.

Given the connections and cultural location of The Jesus Project (not least its rise to prominence at the same time as Dawkins and New Atheism), it is unsurprising that the rhetoric of 'science' comes through. Some of the uses of science are relatively uncontroversial. Hoffmann accepts the term 'scientific' as it is used by the CSER and in the Germanic sense of 'scholarly'.[83] Still, the harder rhetoric is present. Compare the *language* used by Hoffmann in his description of the Project's potential contribution to scholarship:

> Again, the analogy is the sciences. There is nothing about the world of the twentieth century (save global warming) that is physically different from the world of Thomas Aquinas' day. Our mode of describing the same things *about* that world has changed dramatically, however, and with it our understanding of how life evolved and human beings assumed their place on the planet. There is nothing in the nature of old evidence that cannot provide better understanding if the right methods of description are developed. TJP, if it is new, will be new to that extent.[84]

Hoffmann is consistently nuanced in his presentation of the Project and we must respect the emphasis on *analogy*. Other Project members are more generous with the rhetoric of science. While aware that he is dealing with the necessarily rough estimates inevitably involved with ancient history, Carrier provides an introduction to Bayes's Theorem for the study of the historical (or non-historical) Jesus.[85] This article must be in a very small minority of things written in historical Jesus (and New Testament) studies which include formal logic and extended mathematical equations. Zindler, another 'mythicist' member of the Project, is a trained scientist, and presented a paper to the initial meeting on

'Prolegomena to a Science of Christian Origins' which was then published in *Sources of the Jesus Tradition*. A key argument in the article was for a detailed and wide-ranging 'database of facts' and scholarly literature as has been carried out in the sciences, such as is found in *Chemical Abstracts*.[86] The rhetoric and methodology of science is laid on thick with examples given from experiments in the laboratory, astronomy, neuroscience ('one of my areas of expertise'), geology, spectroscopic analysis, and molecular and evolutionary genetics ('another one of my areas of expertise'). And so, when applied to studying the historical Jesus, Zindler claimed the following: 'for all claims of existence, science presumes the negative. For us that means that the burden of proof lies not with those who deny the historicity of "Jesus of Nazareth", but rather with those who hold the traditional view that even if he might not have been a god, he was at the very least a man.'[87]

Politics of Interpretation and By-products of the War on Terror

There is, of course, a hard politicizing edge to all this, another thing certain hardened secularists and certain conservative evangelicals share in common. I have argued elsewhere that the rhetoric and argument of Wright's discussion of the bodily raised Jesus explicitly buys into the discourse of imperialism and empire by producing an alternative empire headed by the raised Jesus, and all this despite Wright's own well-known hostilities to American-backed activities in the Middle East.[88] But we should not make the mistake of believing that this sort of imperialistic rhetoric is typically 'Christian' or belongs to the realm of right-wing presidents alone. For a start, one of the most famous New Atheists, Christopher Hitchens, became a fully paid up neoconservative and admirer of the apparently 'bleeding heart' Paul Wolfowitz.[89] Richard Dawkins may well have wanted regime change in Washington in the Bush era, but, in line with part III, the ideological underpinnings of his form of New Atheism is hardly alien to certain trends in the 'war on terror'. Indeed, as we saw in chapter 3, Dawkins provided an analysis of the 'religious motivations' of the attacks on the Twin Towers four days after September 11, 2001. Getting people to kill themselves in order to take out a target is extremely difficult in itself, so Dawkins suggests the following:

> Offer them a fast track to a Great Oasis in the Sky, cooled by everlasting fountains. Harps and wings wouldn't appeal to the sort of young men we need, so tell them there's a special martyr's reward of 72 virgin

> brides, guaranteed eager and exclusive... It's a tall story, but worth a try. You'd have to get them young, though. Feed them a complete and self-consistent background mythology to make the big lie sound plausible when it comes. Give them a holy book and make them learn it by heart. Do you know, I really think it might work. As luck would have it, we have just the thing to hand: a ready-made system of mind-control which has been honed over centuries, handed down through generations. Millions of people have been brought up in it. It is called religion and, for reasons which one day we may understand, most people fall for it...[90]

For Dawkins, religion and religion's devaluing effect on the life of others is the elephant in the room nobody is prepared to acknowledge. By Dawkins' rationale, if we could accept that death is the end, the rational agent would not be so keen to risk their life and the world is made a safer place. The 'insane courage' comes from religion and, according to Dawkins, 'Religion is also the underlying source of the divisiveness in the Middle East which motivated the use of this deadly weapon in the first place.'

Dawkins is, of course, talking about a particular religion, Islam. Dawkins adds that 'To fill a world with religion, or religions of the Abrahamic kind, is like littering the streets with loaded guns. Do not be surprised if they are used.' However, the immediate target is clear. Interestingly, the terms 'Islam' and 'Muslim' are never mentioned in his response to September 11, yet the references to the Middle East and 72 virgin brides, not to mention the obvious context of the Twin Towers mass murder, make it all too clear which religion is especially in mind, even if a broader 'religion' is responsible. 'Religion,' and especially Islamic 'religion,' as the root of evil gets even more special treatment in the work of other prominent atheists that have emerged as part of this cultural movement of the past decade: Martin Amis, Sam Harris and Christopher Hitchens, Hitchens being particularly fond of the phrase 'Islamofascism.' For Amis, it seems as if the mysterious religion-as-the-cause-of-evil blurs into Islam:

> Since it is no longer permissible to disparage any single faith or creed, let us start disparaging all of them. To be clear: an ideology is a belief system with an inadequate basis in reality; a religion is a belief system with no basis in reality whatever. Religious belief is without reason and without dignity, and its record is near-universally dreadful. It is straightforward – and never mind, for now, about plagues and famines: if God existed, and if He cared for humankind, He would never have given us religion.[91]

The rest of the article is largely taken up with Islam, as was his piece commissioned for the *Observer* on the fifth anniversary of September 11,[92] but here the general 'religion' becomes a code for Islam.[93] Despite his dislike of things religious, Sam Harris makes vague distinctions between religious believers and he openly places Islam as the worst, claiming, 'There is a reason why we must now confront Muslim, rather than Jain terrorists, in every corner of the world', because Islam has a far too high percentage of 'bad beliefs'.[94]

The flip side of the reason that 'religion' is the primary cause of wars and violence in the world is that socio-economic reasons for the rise of violence in the name of Islam are not deemed helpful. Dawkins was vague on the issue of socio-economic problems in his article:

> if a significant number of people convince themselves, or are convinced by their priests, that a martyr's death is equivalent to pressing the hyperspace button and zooming through a wormhole to another universe, it can make the world a very dangerous place. *Especially if they also believe that that other universe is a paradisical escape from the tribulations of the real world...*[95]

Sam Harris is certainly aware of socio-economic problems in parts of the Middle East, but these can be ignored as a factor underlying Islamic violence because much of the world is unpleasant and yet lots of non-Muslims do not resort to terrorism. So only if Muslims are prepared to abandon most of their Scripture and tradition will the world be a better place.[96]

So what, precisely, is this 'religion thing' that causes all sorts of violence? Why have plenty of other Muslims not engaged in violence? Why was this not so much of a widespread problem (say) 50 years ago? Why has facial covering for women become far more popular from Palestine to Cairo to Bradford in the past 50 years? Why did the seemingly inevitable violence and fundamentalism of this 'religion thing' not kick in then? And what of Muslims who still do not foreground their religious identity? Those of us taught history and who practise history usually go for (say) the social, political, economic and religious reasons, did we, and do we, not? Indeed, some of the standard reasons given by scholars of revolutionary Islam for the rise of this sort of 'fundamentalism' are from a complex range of issues, as keeps needing to be stressed. To keep repeating, among many others these include: the decline of secular nationalism in North Africa and the Middle East; the specific context of the key American ally, Saudi Arabia, the homeland of the majority of the September 11 killers; the destructive sanctions on Iraq; Palestine; the petro-crash; the rise of slums and population growth; and US support for various dictators.[97] None of these factors are properly discussed among prominent New Atheists, an alarming oversight given their own emphasis on reason, scholarship and logic. Perhaps more remarkable still is that we are now incredibly close to the world of Radical Orthodoxy and Red Tories and their handling of Islam (see chapter 9).

This mysterious 'religion' is simply inadequate in explaining violence. In fact, this approach to 'religion' is more than reminiscent of a dominant approach to 'religion' in our multicultural and liberal capitalist era, and has a long a long history in liberalism.[98] As Russell McCutcheon argues, 'religion' is typically constructed as an internal private decision and maintained both explicitly and implicitly, in the latter case in scholarly attempts to repackage credibly the overtly personalizing of 'religion' with some emphasis on its corporate and external aspects. The influence of Žižek is clear: 'the same old story is being told. In short, the true function of these displacements and subversions is precisely to make the traditional story relevant to our "postmodern" age – and thus to prevent us from replacing it with a new narrative.'[99] The ideological function of the privatization of inner religion 'is firmly entrenched in the well-established liberal tradition of distinguishing the relatively apolitical freedom "to believe" from the obviously political freedom to behave, organize, and oppose. It is none other than the rhetorical distinction between private and public...that makes possible both the internalization of dissent and conformity of practice.'[100]

'Religion' is therefore constructed in such vague ways that it can be used to justify almost anything. In some ways this is what New Atheism does, but with a twist. 'Religion' justifies explanations of things that are bad in the world. Moreover, New Atheism, clearly buying into contemporary liberal capitalist discourses,[101] also fits into McCutcheon's reading of the construction of 'religion', but again with a twist. What it does instead is to react against something which has not been kept in its private place and has externalized itself in dramatic ways. The sort of 'religion' associated with Islamic 'fundamentalism' has not obeyed the 'rules' of liberal democratic capitalism, has not obeyed the 'rules' of US-led imperialism and it has not obeyed the 'rules' of multiculturalism by not behaving as an Other without its Otherness.[102] 'Religion' in New Atheism circles becomes another way of masking all those difficult social, economic and geopolitical problems and any unpalatable Otherness in general. I would argue, then, that in New Atheism circles 'religion' remains (to twist McCutcheon) 'that versatile little problem solver.'[103]

The timing of New Atheism is also crucial. Dawkins has been writing about or against religion for years, but his rise to cultural prominence, alongside his famous book *The God Delusion*, and the rise of the movement known as New Atheism, has emerged at the same time as the war on terror. Indeed, the whole phenomenon of New Atheism has spawned masses of books in favour, against or even, very occasionally, somewhere in-between, though most of these tend to discuss whether Dawkins has disproved God or not, with the issue of Islam, conveniently, left relatively untouched.[104] Again, this New Atheist development is a clear by-product of US-led culture wars and the rise in prominence of New Atheism in the past decade. Whether they like it or not, the rise of New Atheism and its take on Islam also places the practitioners in the role of the 'useful idiots' and in a long tradition of liberal justification of imperialism and state-endorsed brutality, as recently documented by, among others, Richard Seymour, Michael Dillon and Julian Reid.[105] Indeed, Sam Harris takes his logic to the nakedly brutal conclusion, 'were democracy to suddenly come to these countries, it would be little more than a gangplank to theocracy…the only thing that currently stands between us and the rolling ocean of Muslim unreason is a wall of tyranny and human rights abuses that we have helped to create'.[106] The advantage of the New Atheism from the perspective of power is that there is, of course, nothing like a liberal, rationalist discourse to justify murder, or at least to lay the blame for some of the world's ills conveniently at the door of this mysterious category 'religion'.

Here we might compare the recent output of the well-known non-confessional scholar, Gerd Lüdemann, famous for, among other things, some of the most important work on Jesus' resurrection, particularly his attempts to show it is a Christian fiction and the product of grief visions.[107] There is also, though, an implicit politicizing angle to his arguments. In a 2007 article for the prominent atheist journal, *Free Inquiry*, Lüdemann provided a general overview of the key themes and events of earliest Christianity between 30 and 70 CE, with some focusing on Jesus' resurrection.[108] But the final sections bring out what Lüdemann sees as the massive problems with Christianity. The claims of the earliest Christians, according to Lüdemann, 'become dangerous when, after two millennia, they are still advocated by the Christian churches, and even by academic theologians'. One example raised by Lüdemann is the claim that 'the resurrection of Jesus is of objective, historical significance' and 'the turning point of world history and thereby an event of cosmic importance'.[109] Reminiscent of New Atheism, 'the religious zeal of its representatives remains suspiciously close to a fanaticism that, since it found an ally in political power, cost the lives of at least a million people per century for the last two millennia. Unfortunately, as history shows, conflict inevitably turns that kind of commitment against the wellbeing of mere mortal men and women.'[110]

The issue of intolerance – and here we may again recall the arguments of Wendy Brown – explicitly tied in with the resurrection of Jesus was the topic of another *Free Inquiry* article by Lüdemann in 2006 (though originally published in German in *Die Welt am Sonntag* at the end of 2004).[111] His reading of the New Testament evidence suggests that the other side of Christian peace is an aggressive side of the Christian faith and, by modern standards 'indefensible':

> Jesus Christ himself will return to carry out God's will and by force, empowered by the authority of his resurrection, will establish his father's kingdom of peace on earth. On the basis of this promise, believers in Jesus Christ have at all times claimed access to that power and used it with a good conscience against those they perceive to be enemies of the Gospel.

These reasons underlie the importance for Lüdemann of a hard historical-critical reading of the resurrection accounts because Christian authority is based on this historical claim. Yet, if the resurrection claim is not historically accurate, and if we are dealing with deluded or self-deceived visions of those who claim to have seen the resurrected Jesus, then, Lüdemann argues, no reasonable person could call themselves Christian.

It is notable that Lüdemann's argument on the irrational and violent ramifications of the resurrection and earliest Christian claims has found such fertile ground this past decade when such claims go hand-in-hand with the post-September 11 rise of New Atheism, and its emphasis on ideas or 'religion' over socio-economic issues. As with Dawkins and like-minded thinkers, the argument, which effectively amounts to the old cliché 'religion causes all wars,' covers over the complexities of power, politics and economics, but we can see why Lüdemann's work can reach a level of prominence, even notoriety, and how the logical conclusions buy into a very contemporary and 'credible' narrative of power.

Concluding Remarks

Once again we have seen how an understanding of the broader neoliberal context of the past forty or so years has a powerful explanatory force in terms of why certain debates are happening in scholarship at present. The more immediate influences on the polarizing debates in historical Jesus studies, and biblical studies more generally, which can be loosely labelled 'secular' and 'confessional', have been reactions to September 11 and the war on terror, where such debates are replicated more broadly, particularly in America. However, there are longer-term influences which have helped such polarizing debates gain momentum and so be in a position to become more prominent in both scholarship and popular culture. Neoliberalism has, in part, given rise to the politicized Christian Right and even the parallel 'secular cults' (so Harvey) and conspiracy theories. The decline in organized union power and its oppositional potential has meant a more atomized and fragmented society has had to turn elsewhere in its opposition, if not to the Church then to a range of conspiracy theories or even 'secular cults'.

While these trends were hardly deeply hidden, they well and truly came to the fore after September 11, aided massively by the internet. The more intensified demonization of Islam, or at least parts of Islam not deemed 'moderate' or 'true', meant certain types of Christians (including those like John Milbank – see chapter 9) could start to reinforce their type of Christianity. This perceived double religious threat also propelled New Atheism to the fore and a decade of Dawkins, Hitchens, Amis, Harris and so on. In historical Jesus studies, and biblical studies more generally, this past decade has thus seen the high profile work of Bauckham, Wright, Hurtado, Avalos, Berlinerblau and others (including my own) which explicitly relates to 'secular' versus 'confessional' issues. Admittedly, with the benefit of hindsight, is it any real surprise that this past decade has seen mainstream historical Jesus scholarship produce eyewitnesses to Jesus' life and teaching and arguments in favour of the bodily resurrection really happening as well as a return of an overt secularism, atheism and agnosticism and the re-emergence of the possibility of a Jesus who was never really there?

Notes

1. W. Blanton, 'Neither Religious nor Secular: On Saving the Critic in Biblical-Criticism', in R. Boer (ed.), *Secularism and Biblical Studies* (London and Oakville: Equinox, 2010), pp. 141–61 (143).
2. J. D. Crossan, *A Long Way from Tipperary* (San Francisco: HarperSanFrancisco, 2000), p. 175.
3. R. W. Funk, *Honest to Jesus: Jesus for a New Millennium* (San Francisco: HarperSanFrancisco, 1996).

4. S. Prothero, *American Jesus: How the Son of God Became a National Icon* (New York: Farrar, Straus and Giroux, 2003), pp. 32–41.
5. H. Avalos, *The End of Biblical Studies* (Amherst, NY: Prometheus Books, 2007); J. Berlinerblau, *The Secular Bible: Why Nonbelievers Must Take Religion Seriously* (Cambridge: Cambridge University Press, 2005); B. D. Ehrman, *Misquoting Jesus: The Story behind Who Changed the Bible and Why* (New York: HarperOne, 2005); idem, *Jesus, Interrupted: Revealing the Hidden Contradictions in the Bible (and Why We Don't Know about Them)* (New York: HarperOne, 2009); W. Arnal, 'A Parting of the Ways? Scholarly Identities and a Peculiar Species of Ancient Mediterranean Religion', in Z. A. Crook and P. A. Harland (eds.), *Identity and Interaction in the Ancient Mediterranean: Jews, Christians and Others: Essays in Honour of Stephen G. Wilson* (Sheffield: Sheffield Phoenix Press, 2007), pp. 253–75; J. G. Crossley, *Why Christianity Happened: A Sociohistorical Account of Christian Origins* (Louisville: Westminster John Knox, 2006); M. V. Fox, 'Bible Scholarship and Faith-Based Study: My View', *SBL Forum* , http://sbl-site.org/Article.aspx?ArticleID=490; R. Hendel, 'Farewell to SBL: Faith and Reason in Biblical Studies', *BAR* 36 (July/August, 2010), http://www.bib-arch.org/bar/article.asp?PubID=BSBA&Volume=36&Issue=4&ArticleID=9; M. Casey, *Jesus of Nazareth: An Independent Historian's Account of His Life and Teachings* (London and New York: T&T Clark, 2010), p. 2; R. Boer (ed.), *Secularism and Biblical Studies* (London and Oakville: Equinox, 2010).
6. Cf. R. M. Price, *The Incredible Shrinking Son of Man: How Reliable Is the Gospel Tradition?* (Amherst, NY: Prometheus Books, 2003); T. L. Thompson, *The Messiah Myth: The Near Eastern Roots of Jesus and David* (New York: Basic Books, 2005).
7. http://www.centerforinquiry.net/jesusproject.
8. R. J. Hoffmann, 'Threnody: Rethinking the Thinking behind The Jesus Project', *Bible and Interpretation* (October, 2009), http://www.bibleinterp.com/opeds/hoffman1044.shtml.
9. http://www.secularhumanism.org/index.php?section=main&page=kurtz.
10. http://www.centerforinquiry.net/advocacy/.
11. http://www.centerforinquiry.net/about.
12. http://www.centerforinquiry.net/cser/about.
13. http://www.centerforinquiry.net/cser/about/fellows/.
14. Cf. R. J. Hoffmann, 'A Discourse on Method: The Jesus Project', *Bible and Interpretation* (January 2009), http://www.bibleinterp.com/hoffman1/hoffman1.shtml.
15. R. J. Hoffmann et al., 'Gerd Lüdemann: A Declaration of Solidarity', *Bible and Interpretation* (24 February, 2009), http://www.bibleinterp.com/articles/ludeman_case/solidarity.shtml.
16. R. M. Price, 'The Quest of the Mythical Jesus', http://www.centerforinquiry.net/jesusproject/articles/the_quest_of_the_mythical_jesus.
17. R. J. Hoffmann (ed.), *Sources of the Jesus Tradition: Separating History from Myth* (Amherst, NY: Prometheus, 2010).
18. Thompson, *Messiah Myth*.

19. J. Tokasz, 'Scholars to Explore Existence of Jesus', *Buffalo News* (30 November, 2008), http://www.buffalonews.com/cityregion/northernsuburbs/story/508858.html.
20. R. Csillag, 'For Scholars, a Combustible Question: Was Christ Real?', *Toronto Star* (27 December, 2008), http://www.thestar.com/News/Ideas/article/55754.
21. J. Green, 'Why Can't We Ask if Jesus Existed?', *Ottawa Citizen* (6 December, 2008), http://communities.canada.com/ottawacitizen/blogs/meaning/archive/2008/12/06/why-can-t-we-ask-if-jesus-existed.aspx.
22. J. Green, 'Scholars to Debate if Jesus Existed', *Ottawa Citizen* (January 10, 2007 [sic?]), http://www2.canada.com/ottawacitizen/news/story.html?id=f659e6b0-913b-4032-9264-52f1831d345f&k=92094.
23. Hoffmann, 'Discourse on Method'.
24. Price, 'Mythical Jesus'; R. M. Price, 'The Jesus Mirage', http://www.centerforinquiry.net/jesusproject/articles/the_jesus_mirage.
25. Price, 'Mythical Jesus'.
26. T. Verenna, The Musings of Thomas Verenna, http://tomverenna.wordpress.com/; T. L. Thompson and T. S. Verenna (eds.), *'Is This Not the Carpenter?' The Question of the Historicity of the Figure of Jesus* (Sheffield and Oakville: Equinox, 2011 forthcoming).
27. http://groups.yahoo.com/group/mythicists_forum/.
28. http://groups.yahoo.com/group/JesusMysteries/.
29. J. F. McGrath, Exploring Our Matrix, http://exploringourmatrix.blogspot.com; Casey, *Jesus of Nazareth*, pp. 33–43.
30. R. Carrier, 'Amherst Conference', Richard Carrier Blogs (January 10, 2009), http://richardcarrier.blogspot.com/2009/01/amherst-conference.html.
31. Carrier, 'Amherst Conference'.
32. D. R. MacDonald, 'An Alternative Q and the Quest of the Earthly Jesus', in Hoffmann (ed.), *Sources of the Jesus Tradition*, pp. 17–44 (18, 44).
33. R. M. Price, 'The Abhorrent Void: The Rapid Attribution of Fictive Sayings and Stories to a Mythic Jesus', in Hoffmann (ed.), *Sources of the Jesus Tradition*, pp. 109–17 (117).
34. F. R. Zindler, 'Prolegomenon to a Science of Christian Origins', in Hoffmann (ed.), *Sources of the Jesus Tradition*, pp. 140–56 (143).
35. R. J. Hoffmann, 'Of Rocks, Hard Places and Jesus Fatigue', in Hoffmann (ed.), *Sources of the Jesus Tradition*, pp. 9–16 (12, 15).
36. B. Chilton, 'Plus ça change... "The Jesus Seminar" and "The Jesus Project"', *Bible and Interpretation*, (January 2009), http://www.bibleinterp.com/articles/chilton1.shtml.
37. A. DeConick, 'My Decision about the Jesus Project', The Forbidden Gospels Blog (February 5, 2009), http://forbiddengospels.blogspot.com/2009/02/my-decision-about-jesus-project.html.
38. Green, 'Jesus'. Cf. Csillag, 'Combustible Question?'.
39. Hoffmann, 'A Discourse on Method'.
40. http://www.centerforinquiry.net/jesusproject.
41. A. J. Leichman, 'New Quest for Historical Jesus Draws Skeptics, Scholars', *Christian Post* (10 December, 2008); Tokasz, 'Jesus'.

42. Major space and several articles are devoted to the works of Dunn, Hurtado, Wright and Bauckham in e.g. *JSNT* 26 (2004); *JSNT* 27 (2004); *JSHJ* 3 (2005); *JSHJ* 6 (2008); and *JSNT* 31 (2008).
43. K. Brown, 'Biblioblog Top 10 Most Influential Authors and Books,' C. Orthodoxy (20 June, 2009), http://corthodoxy.wordpress.com/2009/06/20/biblioblog-top-10-most-influential-authors-and-books/.
44. R. Bauckham, *Jesus and the Eyewitnesses: The Gospels as Eyewitness Testimony* (Grand Rapids: Eerdmans, 2006), e.g. pp. 345, 353; cf. 346, 351, 353–54, 355.
45. Bauckham, *Eyewitnesses*, p. 343.
46. Bauckham, *Eyewitnesses*, p. 343.
47. Bauckham, *Eyewitnesses*, p. 504.
48. Bauckham, *Eyewitnesses*, p. 344.
49. Bauckham, *Eyewitnesses*, p. 345.
50. Bauckham, *Eyewitnesses*, p. 411.
51. Bauckham, *Eyewitnesses*, p. 399.
52. Bauckham, *Eyewitnesses*, p. 405.
53. Bauckham, *Eyewitnesses*, p. 399–400.
54. Bauckham, *Eyewitnesses*, p. 506.
55. Bauckham, *Eyewitnesses*, p. 486.
56. E. H. Carr, *What Is History?* (London: Penguin, 2nd edn, 1987), pp. 74–75.
57. See e.g. the popular R. J. Evans, *In Defence of History* (London: Granta, 2nd edn, 2000).
58. J. G. Crossley and C. Karner (eds.), *Writing History, Constructing Religion* (Aldershot: Ashgate, 2005).
59. Bauckham, *Eyewitnesses*, p. 385.
60. Bauckham, *Eyewitnesses*, p. 502.
61. This discussion can be applied to Bauckham's arguments on the theology of John's Gospel, its dramatic claims concerning Jesus and eyewitness testimony. See R. Bauckham, *The Testimony of the Beloved Disciple: Narrative, History and Theology in the Gospel of John* (Grand Rapids: Baker, 2007); J. G. Crossley, 'Can John's Gospel Really Be Used to Reconstruct a Life of Jesus? An Assessment of Recent Trends and a Defence of a Traditional View,' in Thompson and Verenna (eds.), *'Is This Not the Carpenter?'* (forthcoming).
62. N. T. Wright and M. J. Borg, *The Meaning of Jesus: Two Visions* (London: SPCK, 2008); M. F. Bird and J. G. Crossley, *How Did Christianity Begin? A Believer and Non-Believer Examine the Evidence* (London, SPCK, 2008). It might be worth comparing the contemporary mini-industry of conservative Christian books refuting non-conservative claims about Jesus, e.g. C. A. Evans, *Fabricating Jesus: How Modern Scholars Distort the Gospels* (Nottingham: IVP, 2007), and D. L. Bock and D. B. Wallace, *Dethroning Jesus: Exposing Popular Culture's Quest to Unseat the Biblical Christ* (Nashville: Thomas Nelson, 2007), the latter attacking 'Jesusanity,' and with Ehrman as one of its primary targets.
63. Anyone who thinks that Americans as opposed to Brits are obsessed with religion and secularism, and inventing all sorts of things about the latter, should read the wild allegations concerning secularism in British culture as collected and analysed by O. Burkeman, 'Mulled Whine,' *Guardian* (12 December, 2006).

64. D. Harvey, *A Brief History of Neoliberalism* (Oxford: Oxford University Press, 2005), pp. 171–72.
65. N. Chomsky and G. Achcar, *Perilous Power: The Middle East and U.S. Foreign Policy* (Boulder and London: Paradigm Publishers, 2007), pp. 30–34.
66. Harvey, *Neoliberalism*, p. 171. There are also resonances here with Alberto Toscano's comment on certain cultic reactions to capitalism: 'fanaticism comes into view at the frontier of political groupings, as both product and agent of conflict'. See A. Toscano, *Fanaticism: On Uses of an Idea* (London and New York: Verso, 2010), p. 59.
67. E.g. Secular Web, http://www.infidels.org; The Musings of Thomas Verenna, http://tomverenna.wordpress.com/; Acupuncture Coyote, http://michael-turton2.blogspot.com/; Vridar, http://vridar.wordpress.com/. Perennial comment-makers with 'mythicist' sympathies and holders of some highly unusual views (in scholarly terms) on Christian origins are Steven Carr and Geoff Hudson, the latter openly expressing that much of the New Testament and Josephus is an ancient conspiracy.
68. On 'fundamentalism' and 'mythicism', see the debate on Deane Galbraith's blog, 'Did Jesus Rise from the Dead? Casey on Jesus (7) – Visionary Experiences of Jesus' Resurrection', *Remnant of Giants* (23 April, 2011), http://remnantofgiants.wordpress.com/2011/04/23/caseys-jesus-7-visions-of-jesus-resurrection/. In a forthcoming book on 'mythicism' and the historical Jesus, Maurice Casey shows the clear parallels, at least in attitudes towards argument and evidence, between Christian 'fundamentalists' and the 'fundamentalism' associated with 'mythicism'. Casey also provides detailed biographical information of various 'mythicists'. I am grateful to Maurice Casey for showing me this research in advance of publication.
69. N. Chomsky, *What We Say Goes: Conversations on U.S. Power in a Changing World* (New York: Metropolitan, 2007), p. 38.
70. Chomsky, *What We Say Goes*, p. 39.
71. An excellent example of this attempt at politicizing the 'mythical Jesus' can be found in the bitter exchange between Jim West and the 'mythicist' Michael Turton over Turton's review of James Tabor's work. See also the numerous discussions on the blog with heavy 'mythicist' content, Vridar, http://vridar.wordpress.com/. This blog suggested that there was an analogy between an argument dedicated to critiquing of implicit and explicit scholarly stereotyping of Jews, Muslims and Palestinians and the ways in which the discipline apparently refuses to challenge its assumptions of historical methodology, or at least a level of betrayal that scholars do not extend such critiques to questions of the historicity of Jesus. See e.g. N. Godfrey, 'Chomsky, Crossley and the betrayal of an independent approach to historical Jesus studies', Vridar (21 April, 2010), http://vridar.wordpress.com/2010/04/21/chomsky-crossley-and-the-betrayal-of-an-independent-approach-to-historical-jesus-studies/. In a different way, the author of a blog dedicated to some sensationalist and conspiratorial explanations of Christian origins, Stephan Huller, complains: 'The racist folks at Biblioblog Top 50 will not acknowledge one simple fact – this blog was ranked 41st among Biblioblogs this month. I know it is dangerous to throw around accusations of racism but how else do you explain this?' See S. Huller, 'This Site is Now a Top 50 Biblioblog (Even if the Bastards at Biblioblog

Top 50 Site Refuses to Acknowledge it)', Stephan Huller's Observations (31 May, 2011), http://bibliobloglibrary.com/archives/stephan-hullers-observations-biblioblog-top-50.html.

72. T. LaHaye, *Rapture (under Attack)* (Sisters, OR: Multnomah Press, 1998), pp. 137–48.
73. Based on the out-of-print P. Ruckman, *Black Is Beautiful* (Pensacola: Bible Believers Press, 1996) and discussed on many anti-Ruckman websites, most damningly, http://www.wayoflife.org/database/ruckman.html. I have not been able to obtain a copy of this book and have only seen scanned online copies. Given the bizarre nature of the content, I still remain somewhat sceptical.
74. These can be viewed at http://www.youtube.com/watch?v=uxJyPsmEask&feature=related and http://www.youtube.com/watch?v=ZXvV11-Xwpw.
75. T. Eagleton, 'Awakening from Modernity', *Times Literary Supplement* (20 February, 1987), in D. Harvey, *The Condition of Postmodernity* (Oxford: Blackwell, 1989), p. 210.
76. I have firsthand experience of this frustrating scholarly procedure. For discussion see e.g. http://earliestchristianhistory.blogspot.com/2007/07/resurrection-and-scholarly-rhetoric.htmlandhttp://earliestchristianhistory.blogspot.com/2008/09/mcknight-in-battered-armour.html.
77. B. Witherington III, 'What's in a Name? Rethinking the Historical Figure of the Beloved Disciple in the Fourth Gospel', in Anderson, Just and Thatcher (eds.), *John, Jesus, and History*, II, pp. 209–12.
78. N. T. Wright, *Resurrection of the Son of God* (London: SPCK, 2003), p. 636.
79. Cf. B. Witherington III, *New Testament History: A Narrative Account* (Carlisle: Paternoster; Grand Rapids: Baker, 2001), p. 170.
80. M. F. Bird in Bird and Crossley, *How Did Christianity Begin?*, pp. 21, 65.
81. P. Barnett, *Finding the Historical Christ: After Jesus, Volume Three* (Grand Rapids: Eerdmans, 2009), p. 223.
82. Barnett, *Finding*, p. 223.
83. Hoffmann, 'A Discourse on Method'.
84. Hoffmann, 'A Discourse on Method'.
85. R. C. Carrier, 'Bayes's Theorem for Beginners: Formal Logic and Its Relevance to Historical Method', in Hoffmann (ed.), *Sources of the Jesus Tradition*, pp. 81–107.
86. Zindler, 'Prolegomenon'. See Carrier, 'Amherst Conference', for a summary of the oral presentation.
87. Zindler, 'Prolegomenon', pp. 140–43.
88. J. G. Crossley, 'Manufacturing Resurrection: Locating Contemporary Scholarly Arguments', *Neot.* (forthcoming).
89. C. Hitchens, 'That Bleeding Heart Wolfowitz', *Slate* (22 March, 2005), http://www.slate.com/id/2115170/.
90. R. Dawkins, 'Religion's Misguided Missiles', *Guardian* (15 September, 2001).
91. M. Amis, 'The Voice of the Lonely Crowd', *Guardian* (1 June, 2002).
92. M. Amis, 'The Age of Horrorism', *Observer* (10 September, 2006); italics mine.
93. Amis, 'Lonely'.
94. S. Harris, *The End of Faith: Religion, Terror, and the Future of Reason* (London: Simon & Schuster, 2004), pp. 105–52.
95. Dawkins, 'Religion's Misguided Missiles'.

96. Harris, *End of Faith*, p. 132.
97. For a full discussion see J. G. Crossley, *Jesus in an Age of Terror: Scholarly Projects for a New American Century* (London and Oakville, 2008), pp. 58–99.
98. For a full recent discussion with particular reference to secular constructions of 'religion' and 'violence' see W. T. Cavanaugh, *The Myth of Religious Violence: Secular Ideology and the Roots of Modern Conflict* (Oxford: Oxford University Press, 2009). On 'religion', liberalism and the state see now C. Martin, *Masking Hegemony: A Genealogy of Liberalism, Religion and the Private Sphere* (London and Oakville: Equinox, 2010).
99. R. T. McCutcheon, *Religion and the Domestication of Dissent: or, How to Live in a Less Than Perfect Nation* (London & Oakville: Equinox, 2005), p. 10, citing S. Žižek, *Welcome to the Desert of the Real! Five Essays on September 11 and Related Dates* (London and New York: Verso, 2002), p. 70.
100. McCutcheon, *Religion*, p. 62.
101. T. Eagleton, *Reason, Faith, and Revolution: Reflections on the God Debate* (New Haven and London: Yale University Press, 2009).
102. This is particularly clear in Harris, *End of Faith*, pp. 109–11.
103. McCutcheon, *Religion*, pp. 82–95. On charges and uses of abstraction in relation to the construction of 'fanaticism' see e.g. Toscano, *Fanaticism*, pp. xi–xii, 172–202, 249–50.
104. We should, however, note that work on the problematizing of the secular versus religion dichotomy has hardly stopped and is now present in biblical studies, particularly in the theoretical publications of Ward Blanton. See e.g. W. Blanton, *Displacing Christian Origins: Philosophy, Secularity, and the New Testament* (Chicago: University of Chicago Press, 2007); idem, 'Neither Religious nor Secular: On Saving the Critic in Biblical-Criticism', in Boer (ed.), *Secularism and Biblical Studies*, pp. 141–61.
105. R. Seymour, *The Liberal Defence of Murder* (London: Verso, 2008); M. Dillon and J. Reid, *The Liberal Way of War: Killing to Make Life Live* (New York and London: Routledge, 2009). In this general context, the critique of the New Atheists by T. Beattie, *The New Atheists: The Twilight of Reason and the War on Religion* (London: Darton Longman and Todd, 2007), ought to be read by anyone interested in New Atheism.
106. Harris, *End of Faith*, p. 132.
107. E.g. G. Lüdemann, *The Resurrection of Jesus: History, Experience, Theology* (London: SCM Press, 1994).
108. G. Lüdemann, 'What Really Happened? The Rise of Primitive Christianity, 30–70 C.E.', *Free Inquiry* (April/May, 2007), pp. 24–31. For further discussion see Crossley, 'Manufacturing Resurrection'.
109. Lüdemann, 'What Really Happened?', p. 31.
110. Lüdemann, 'What Really Happened?', p. 31.
111. G. Lüdemann, 'The Intolerant Gospel', *Free Inquiry* (February/March, 2006), http://www.secularhumanism.org/index.php?section=library&page=luedemann_26_2.

Part III

Contradictions

Andrew Marr: What I don't get is that all of this suggests – I'm a journalist – people like me are self-censoring.

Noam Chomsky: I don't say you're self-censoring. I'm sure you believe everything you're saying. But what I'm saying is, if you believed something different you wouldn't be sitting where you're sitting.[1]

Chapter 8

'Forgive Them; for They Do Not Know What They Are Doing!' Other Problems, Extremes and the Social World of Jesus

It is important, of course, not to de-emphasize the roles of personal politics and scholarly rhetoric completely. For instance, it is no surprise that certain historical Jesus scholars are pro-Israeli in the sense that they will tow dominant media and party-political lines on issues relating to the state of Israel and the Palestinians, and perhaps unsurprisingly reflect such concerns and narratives in their work on the historical Jesus.[2] But what I want to do here is look at the less predictable examples and how the seemingly contradictory figures end up buying into, or helping explain, dominant political discourses once their work enters the scholarly arena, with ultimate reference to the social world constructed around Jesus. One feature of Herman and Chomsky's approach to propaganda I want to develop here is the role of the individual as discussed briefly in the Introduction. Herman and Chomsky are both clear that individuals may hold different views from the dominant ideological positions but ultimately they will, intentionally or otherwise, buy into such trends. I want to push this tension to its extreme in this chapter by looking at the influential work of Bruce Malina and his personal politics, and how they work out (or not) in relation to Jesus and 'the Land' and how his scholarly output buys into dominant American media and party-political views on the Middle East, all of which run clean contrary to his political intentions.

Extremes

Before turning to Malina, it is worth looking at some of the functions of extremes in scholarship. On one level, extremes can function in something like the ways in which we have described the function of the far right, that is, the construction of an extreme can maintain the validity and credibility of the centre or a broad consensus. But where the concerns of the far right, or their equivalents, are dismissed easily enough, some of those ideas which seriously challenge dominant views in terms of, for instance, major political issues, are not. We need only think of the ways in which Norman Finkelstein, Keith Whitelam and Nadia Abu el-Haj have been treated in scholarship when the issues they raised concerning Palestinians were a little too close to the bone of what is 'permitted' in academic discourse in America and the United Kingdom at least. Yet the vicious polemic, slurs (e.g. of anti-Semitism), and at times outright lies, have a similar effect of marginalizing such scholarship as little better than the far right and maintaining the intellectual and ethical purity of the liberal centre while pushing to one side any of the more uncomfortable questions about scholarly complicity and politically dominant views.[3]

Another way of looking at extremes could be to use the work of the historian of eighteenth-century French culture, Robert Darnton, but with a twist. In *The Great Cat Massacre*, Darnton advocates a more anthropological approach to history and the importance of a perception of distance from the culture under investigation. For Darnton, the best starting point in attempting to penetrate an alien culture is 'where it seems to be most opaque'. By 'getting' the joke, proverb, riddle, ceremony or whatever it is possible to start grasping a 'foreign system of meaning'.[4] While one of my overall arguments it to look at the function of normative aspects of contemporary culture, it is worth turning Darnton's suggestion on our own general cultural contexts in looking at parts of our culture that seem alien to the investigator and how they help us understand our own systems of meaning.

As I have argued elsewhere,[5] there are few better examples of this approach to Darnton than the late British politician and classicist, Enoch Powell (1912–1998). Powell can be labelled an 'extremist' on more than one level. Enoch Powell was one of the most notorious politicians in twentieth-century British politics.[6] In the UK he is probably now best known for his controversial anti-immigration 'Rivers of Blood' speech, delivered to the Conservative Political Centre in Birmingham on 20 April, 1968. Powell, alluding to the *Aeneid*, famously said: 'As I look ahead, I am filled with foreboding. Like the Roman, I seem to see "the River Tiber foaming with much blood."'[7] The Rivers of Blood speech was the moment when Powell would cease to be a direct influence on front-bench party politics while at the same time becoming one of the most popular British politicians of the past one-hundred years. To this day, he remains a potent symbol – whether based on a misunderstanding or not – for English nationalists and far-right groups in the UK. Put another way, and referring back to the Introduction, he is another figure of the popularist right the centre still loves to hate.

Powell was also an academic and, like his politics, he could function both as part of the establishment and on the extreme fringes of scholarship, particularly New Testament scholarship. Powell excelled in classics and in 1937, aged just 25, he became Professor of Classics at Sydney University. He published major work in Classics including: *A Lexicon to Herodotus* (Cambridge: Cambridge University Press, 1938), *The History of Herodotus* (Cambridge: Cambridge University Press, 1939) and *Herodotus: A Translation* (Oxford: Clarendon, 1949). Powell also published studies on the Bible and Christianity, with a combination of academic, confessional and popularist interests.[8] It was, however, towards the end of his life that Powell seriously started to promote his academic study of the Bible, particularly his detailed work on studies of the Gospel tradition. These publications were with reputable publishers. Powell published a Yale University Press book, *The Evolution of the Gospel*, in 1994 and a *Journal for the Study of the New Testament* article in 1991, both on the origins of the Gospel tradition with particular focus on the Gospel of Matthew.[9] *Evolution of the Gospel* further contained Powell's translation of Matthew and his own accompanying commentary. As his classical background would already suggest, Powell was deeply immersed in the world of the New Testament – indeed, as a schoolboy he had already memorized the entirety of Galatians in Greek.[10] The Acknowledgments in *Evolution of the Gospel* show that Powell had consulted with the highly distinguished scholars of early Christian history, Henry Chadwick and William Horbury. Powell also consulted – as he did for his other work on the Gospel tradition – with Semitic and Ethiopic expert, and Fellow of the British Academy, Edward Ullendorff. In 1991 Powell gave the eighth annual *Journal for the Study of the Old Testament* lecture at the University of Sheffield on the 'Genesis of the Gospel' which was the basis of his 1991 *Journal for the Study of the New Testament* article.[11]

Clearly, then, we are not dealing with someone who can be dismissed as one of Jim West's dilettantes: Powell earned his stripes by any normative scholarly standards. That said, Powell had some very peculiar views on the origins of Matthew and the Gospel tradition, none more so than his view that Jesus was not crucified. Instead, Powell argues, the earliest Gospel tradition (which he believed was behind Matthew's Gospel) has

Jesus stoned to death and convicted by the 'Jewish establishment' for 'the blasphemy of allowing himself to be called "the son of God"'.[12] Not only was this the earliest tradition, it was a view which Powell believed reflected historical reality. Equally clearly, then, Powell is a prime candidate to be constructed on the extremes of scholarship.

And indeed he was. There were some hostile critical reactions to Powell's book in the British press and linked with established scholars. While critics acknowledged Powell's learning, and thereby his place at the table perhaps, there was also a dose of ridicule. N. T. Wright's evaluation was reported as follows:

> This is clearly a work of great erudition, which seems to have lost touch with the distinction between that which is possible and that which is plausible... There is something to be said for starting again from scratch, but the catty answer is that he has chosen to ignore everyone else, so he can't grumble if they return the compliment.[13]

We might recall Wright's views on the resurrection of dead saints possibly rising and how in massive books on Jesus and the resurrection he does not seem to think the Gospel writers invented anything, but it would hardly be going too far to suggest that Wright can also reasonably place himself at the centre in contrast to the extreme, despite his conservatism. More serious criticisms involved potential anti-Semitism, especially Powell's argument that Jesus was stoned to death.[14] Hyam Maccoby was reported as saying,

> It could undoubtedly have anti-Semitic repercussions. The gospels do that already: they say that Pilate was reluctant to carry out the execution. If it is now said that the Romans did not do the executions, the Jews did, this intensifies the blame against the Jews even more.[15]

Anti-Semitism, perhaps more than any other allegation, can function as a way of dismissing an opponent extremely effectively (while constructing the personal credibility of the critic), whether accurate or not, and historical Jesus scholarship is no exception.[16] It should be noted, however, that Maccoby is not reported as levelling claims of anti-Semitism at Powell personally and so it is probably worth further emphasizing that Powell's work is, at least partly, at the mercy of broader social and intellectual trends. While Powell may have had disturbing views on immigration and, contrary to many revisionists, some of his views expressed in the Rivers of Blood speech were little more than old-fashioned racist language and scaremongering,[17] he was no anti-Semite. Indeed, Powell had once remarked that the Second World War was not against the Nazi party but against a development among the German people because the Nazi party shared what Powell believed were some of the strongest negative traits of the German people, such as hero-worship, love of power and force for their own sake and, most significantly for present purposes, anti-Semitism.[18] This, Powell argued, was most unlike the English mindset. People may well want to debate whether that in itself is a fair assessment, and whether the use of English and German 'mindsets' is helpful, but the point for now is that anti-Semitism was something which Powell saw as completely alien to himself and the English.

I note this not because I particularly want to excuse Powell's work from the charges of potential anti-Semitism or the like, but because I think it is more fruitful to see the downgrading of Judaism as part of broader social and intellectual trends and in ways which equally affect some of his critics (see chapter 4). In other words, the importance of cultural context in analysis of scholarship is heightened because the results of scholarship can be seen to contradict personal beliefs. It certainly *is* clear that Judaism comes out a very poor second in Powell's work on the Gospel tradition and elsewhere.[19] This is more or less in line with the general pattern concerning the construction and tolerance of Judaism in the previous chapter. What this also does is to show how, in line with our spin on Darnton, Powell's 'extremist' reconstruction of the historical Jesus is an entrée to understanding cultural trends. As I have argued in detail, this sort of approach is also shown throughout Powell's work on the Gospel tradition, particularly in his nostalgic views of empires (British and Roman) and nation which dictate the ways in which Matthew's Gospel is believed to be the Roman gospel of ecclesiastical and political consensus, as much a part of the *Pax Romana* as Augustus himself.

Powell's views of empire may have been extremely old fashioned (at least rhetorically) by the time he wrote his major work on the Gospel tradition, but it is certainly one way to understand scholarship, and Jesus scholarship in particular. If postcolonial studies have shown us anything, it is that the role of empire runs deep in intellectual thought and biblical studies more generally, and Gospel studies more specifically. And it is not difficult to show how many academic studies clearly reflect a coming to terms with shifting imperial powers. The Nazi Jesuses are a glaring example of imperialism and nationalism combined.[20] In post-war Germany, Günther Bornkamm devoted some space to what may seem an unusual debate for a book on the historical Jesus – namely, an attack on Bolshevism – illustrating obvious Cold War concerns (see chapter 1).[21] From the UK, a different type of engagement with empire from Powell's (and one, no doubt, Powell would have deeply disliked) was Brandon's nationalistic, anti-Roman revolutionary Jesus where Brandon's publications tie in with some of the feelings of de-colonialization in the 1960s, with such a view almost immediately prompting a reaction in mainstream historical Jesus studies.[22]

Even more recently, concerns with empire are present. It is perhaps no surprise that the anti-imperialistic Jesus (and Paul) really came to the forefront of New Testament scholarship, led by American scholarship in particular. Most significantly, while American cultural and physical imperialism was taking off, a streak of self-denial has been common, from politics through to the superficial anti-imperialism of films about the ancient world coming from that bastion of cultural imperialism, Hollywood.[23] In a different way, and with the culturally prominent rise of the not-always-loved American Empire, it is perhaps no surprise that prominent British scholars such as N. T. Wright have willingly taken up an anti-imperial Jesus (and Paul).

Again (largely) in North America, the extensive work of Bruce Malina and some members of the Context Group have repeatedly given us constructions and tabulations of supposed individualist US culture over against the ancient and contemporary Mediterranean and Arab world (see below).[24] The intention may be to show the alien nature of the New Testament documents, but regularly such descriptions replicate the clash-of-civilizations rhetoric so prominent in US intellectual and popular culture. Indeed, the often static 'Mediterranean world' of certain imaginations is an increasingly popular backdrop in historical Jesus and Christian origins scholarship, though some scholars are much more careful and avoid some of the highly dubious stereotyping of contemporary Mediterreneans and Arabs. John Dominic Crossan is a good example of this and his work is tied in with goals of liberation. Yet, for all the anti-imperial rhetoric of scholars such as Crossan, including anti-British Empire rhetoric, it is noticeable that Crossan's Jesus stands over against the alien Mediterranean world as a noticeably liberal figure.[25] Many have criticized Crossan's Jesus for being too liberal and, though this is often for the polemical reason to prove historically a more Christianized conservative Jesus rather than establish the political locations of scholarship, the general criticism can be taken up: I do not think it is going too far to see that Crossan's liberal Jesus is a representation of liberal America and constructed over against the Other civilization represented by the grand 'Mediterranean'.[26] Crossan's Jesus is as much a product of the new American Empire as it is a critique of it.

Bruce Malina and the Social World of Jesus

Clearly, then, dominant views do not give up their dominance easily and have even claimed the most noble as their victims. It is also clear, obviously, that we are not dealing with one overall Big Brother-like narrative which controls all but, in line with a legitimate development of the Propaganda Model and with some Gramsci more to the fore, we are dealing with a number of competing but dominant narratives reflecting key interests of power. In the cases of the construction of 'extremes' above, I know of no better example for discussion of their impact on mainstream scholarship than Bruce Malina.

More than any other New Testament scholar, Bruce Malina is responsible for bringing cultural/social anthropology into the study of Christian origins. His famous 1981 book, *The New Testament World: Insights from Cultural Anthropology*, has proven to be hugely influential on New Testament scholarship and is often cited as one of the authoritative places to look for understanding the social world of the earliest Christians.[27] In the 1980s, Malina was instrumental in establishing the Context Group, a group of scholars dedicated to using the social-sciences in New Testament interpretation. In addition to their own meetings, Context Group members have become dominant figures in the social-scientific interpretation sessions at the annual Society of Biblical Literature meetings and can boast some major names in New Testament scholarship, such as Philip Esler and John Elliott. It is largely through Malina's work, and those of his followers, associates and colleagues that New Testament scholars use the language of 'honour and shame', 'dyadic personality' and 'the Mediterranean' as a fixed 'culture area'.

Even critics acknowledge that Malina and the related work of the Context Group have made a contribution to New Testament scholarship. David Horrell, for instance, suggests that 'the results of their studies have served to illuminate the strikingly different social dynamics at work in the biblical texts and thus to guard against any hermeneutic which elides the distinction between ancient and modern contexts'.[28] This particular piece of common praise can, however, also be seen as a distinctive problem. As others have pointed out, in the work of Malina (and certain other Context Group members), and for all the emphasis on heuristic use, 'the Mediterranean' reads like an Orientalist construct, essentially a fixed entity largely unchanging over millennia.[29] Furthermore, as I have shown in more detail elsewhere, 'the Mediterranean' blurs into 'the Arab world' or 'Middle East' (including the contemporary Arab world and Middle East) in the work of Malina and certain other members of the Context Group, with some alarming generalizations about 'the Arab', 'the Mediterranean' and 'the Middle East'.[30] It is striking that the work of Malina emerged just after the 1970s, the decade when 'the Arab', 'the Middle East', 'the Persian' and 'Islam' became the intense focus of the American cultural and political gaze.[31] Malina's work, the emergence of the Context Group, and the popularity of both, are partly explained by this cultural shift. I have also argued that the stereotyping of 'the Arab world' in the work of Malina and certain other Context Group members has consistently bought into dominant elite positions on 'the Middle East' in Anglo-American media and political discourse, right up to and including the 'war on terror'.

Malina and Politics

With this background in mind, it becomes easy to see why Bruce Malina is a dramatic example of how personal beliefs are liable to surrender to broader cultural trends. Malina, along with his wife, Diane Jacobs-Malina, are known for their highly distinctive political views, particularly their widely circulated emails on politics and scholarship, including a series of emails sent to 88 biblical scholars in 2006 and widely circulated since, which take us into the world of Ernst Zundel, Germar Rudolf, David Irving and Michael James.[32] These emails make the nature of Malina's personal politics absolutely explicit. We also have further accessible examples of the personal politics of Bruce Malina and Diane Jacobs-Malina, even if they are much watered down. In a letter to *Asia Times Online*, Jacobs-Malina wrote,

> You must have a special interest in promoting the Anglo-American-Zionist's propaganda regarding Muslims, al-Qaeda, and terrorism. You should be embarrassed for pushing such blatant propaganda… Perhaps you could scare the oil-producing nations into just lying down and letting the Anglo-American-Zionist predator take whatever it wants… What was Germany's chief problem from the beginning of the 20th century onwards? It threatened the British Empire's No 1 status.[33]

In 2004, Bruce Malina and Diane Jacobs-Malina signed an International Response to the Bush Declaration on the Palestinian Right to Return.[34] Malina signed a petition against the appointment of General Dan Halutz, former chief of staff of the Israeli army, as director general of Kamor, the official BMW dealer in Israel.[35] Malina also signed a counter-petition in favour of granting the Palestinian American scholar, Nadia Abu el-Haj, tenure (as did I).[36] From all this, it is clear that the Malinas have a strong concern for the well-being of Palestinians, are hostile to things perceived to be Zionist ('the Anglo-American-Zionist predator'), and have more sympathy for Germany in the first half of the twentieth century than is conventional ('Germany's chief problem from the beginning of the 20th century onwards? It threatened the British Empire's No 1 status'). It is also clear from all this that Malina's idiosyncratic personal politics thrust in the political arena are seemingly at odds with the dominant trends we have seen in contemporary scholarship. However, as we will see, while these political perspectives do manifest themselves in Malina's scholarship, they are simultaneously absorbed and transformed into the more conventional trends we have come to expect from the scholarship associated with Malina and those influenced by him.

Analysing Malina's Scholarship: Jews, Judeans and Israelites

At first sight it might seem that Malina's scholarly output has resisted the dominant pro-Jewish rhetoric of contemporary scholarship. We can see this, for instance, in one crucial area where Malina has been influential: the high-profile debates in contemporary historical Jesus studies (and beyond) on the term 'Jew'. In particular, Malina has been influential in advocating the translations of Ἰουδαῖος as 'Judean' and the removal from scholarship of the standard translation, 'Jew'. John Elliott's article in *Journal for the Study of the Historical Jesus*, pushing for Jesus to be variously labelled as 'Galilean' or 'Israelite' – not Jesus 'the Jew' – has provoked a lot of discussion, and a largely positive response.[37] As long-time Context Group colleagues, it is no surprise that Malina's influence is regularly noted, though it should be stated emphatically from the outset that Elliott's concerns are overtly linguistic and that Elliott was and is explicitly hostile towards, and sensitive about, any hint of anti-Semitism, a point worth highlighting in what can be such a sensitive issue.

Malina's printed work on these crucial social and linguistic contexts for our understanding of Jesus and his world is found in his co-authored commentaries on the Gospel of John and the Synoptic Gospels. On the translation of 'Jews' in John's Gospel:

> modern readers will think John makes reference to those persons whom readers today know from their experience to be Jews. The fact is, from a religious point of view, all modern Jews belong to traditions

> developed largely after the time of Jesus and compiled in the Babylonian Talmud (sixth century C.E.). As for ethnic origin, Central European Jews (called Ashkenazi Jews) largely trace their origin to Turkic and Iranian ancestors who comprised the Khazar empire and converted to Judaism in the eighth century C.E. (*Encyclopaedia Britannica*, 15th ed. Micropaedia, 5:788; on the Internet: www.khazaria.com). Thus, given the sixth-century C.E. origin of all forms of contemporary Jewish religion, and given the U.S. experience of Jews based largely on Central European Jews, themselves originating from eighth-century C.E. converts, it would be quite anachronistic to identify any modern Jews with the 'Judeans' mentioned in John's Gospel or the rest of the New Testament...in all of the sixty-nine other instances in John where the term *Judeans* (Greek *Ioudaioi*) appears, there is nothing of the modern connotations of 'Jew' or 'Jewishness'...[38]

Notice here the shift from modern Jews, at least from a religious perspective, belonging to traditions developed 'largely after the time of Jesus' to the 'sixth-century C.E. origin of all forms of contemporary Jewish religion' and 'there is nothing of the modern connotations of "Jew" or "Jewishness"'. This is deeply misleading. For a start, vast amounts of rabbinic literature are concerned with biblical interpretation and so there is, obviously, some continuity between rabbinic Judaism and the 'religion' that came before it. The argument that the Jews or Judeans in John's Gospel have 'nothing of the modern connotations of "Jew" or "Jewishness"' depends on modern definitions of 'Jew' and 'Jewishness'. While never forgetting the differences between now and then, we might note that John's Gospel uses the term in the context of, for instance, Passover (Jn 2) and it is fair to say that this is a festival associated by many with modern Judaism, modern Jews and manifestations of Jewishness.[39] In the hands of Malina and Rohrbaugh, Judaism prior to the rabbis at the time of Jesus gets more-or-less removed.

This downplaying of Judaism as an important context for understanding Jesus and the New Testament texts is found more generally in Malina's work. Markus Bockmuehl has pointed out, with plenty of supportive evidence, that 'In terms of culture and above all religion, it is at best misleading to characterize Galilee's peasants and artisans in terms of a generically "Mediterranean" social anthropology. (Cultural-studies approaches typically ignore the role of religion for the definition of identity, whether Jewish or otherwise.)'[40] Bockmuehl, who knows as much about early Judaism as any contemporary New Testament scholar, also made the following criticisms of Malina's book, *The New Testament World*:

> And it is Jews, after all, whose role in the 'New Testament world' arguably matters more than most. Both in their own eyes and in those of their pagan critics, they were culturally unique. Little of that distinctness, however, comes into the fore in this book. Malina refers to ancient Jews and their literature in curiously arm-waving and unspecific terms ('Semites', 'Semitic subculture', 'Ben Zakaiists', 'late Israelites'), citing the Mishnah only twice and the Dead Sea Scrolls not at all, and virtually ignoring the first-century role of the Pharisees, who (rather than the priests) were in Josephus's view the *real* 'bearers of the Great Tradition'.[41]

Malina-style anthropology would seem to give little scope to understanding specifically Jewish contexts of Jesus' teaching. This seems to be the case in Malina's entry on social-scientific criticism in the recent *Encyclopaedia of the Historical Jesus* where he does not write about much (opposing) non-Context Group social-scientific and anthropological interpretation (not even John Dominic Crossan's work on the historical Jesus!):

> Malina introduced the label 'social sciences' rather than 'sociology' in a 1981 task group at the Catholic Biblical Association that he has convened annually since then. That same year his cultural anthropological introduction to the New Testament appeared. Malina also introduced members to the work of Carney... The label 'social scientific criticism' was coined by Malina and Elliott after Malina pointed out the inadequacy of labelling what Elliott sought to do as 'sociological exegesis'. Elliott adopted the new label as the title of his book... To make such a historical judgement [about the cultural world of the Eastern Mediterranean], the interpreter must remove the filters deriving from the historical developments called Technologism and Scientism...the Industrial Revolution, Sense of History, the Enlightenment, the Renaissance and Reformation...Islam, Christendom, Jewishness (Rabbinic and Talmudic)... [T]he social scientific interpretative enterprise has produced works...of such superb quality...(see Malina, 2002)... By and large, the main contributors to original research employing social scientific methods are members of the Context Group...[42]

However, on issues relating to Judaism it seems that we may also be dealing with the influence of slightly different, but certainly complementary, cultural trends when it comes to the work of Malina and certain work influenced by Malina. Moreover, the afterlife of Malina's work on the use of terms such as 'Israelite' or 'Judean', and the downplaying of terms such as 'Jew', makes for contrasting reading with Malina's personal politics and coheres, albeit slightly differently, with politicized views of Judaism and Israel in New Testament scholarship over the past forty years.

In fact, Malina-influenced scholarship not only complements such trends but goes one step further, as we can see with the issue of 'the land'. Scholars such as John Elliott who, as we have previously observed, brought such debates to the forefront of historical Jesus studies, has the centre of Jesus' Jewish, or, if we follow Elliott, 'Israelite', identity become something close to the *physical* land of Israel no less:

> his Israelite ingroup, identified him, also...more broadly as a member of the people of Israel, the House of Israel, not of 'Judaism'... 'Jew' is still a misleading identifier of Jesus and 'Israelite' should be preferred... Let us refer to Jesus and his earliest followers as 'Israelites' or members of the 'House of Israel'... Let us stress their roots in Israel, not in 'Judaism'... My point is that calling Jesus an Israelite rather than a Jew is consistent with Israelite usage in Jesus' time and more accurately indicates his identity and that of his earliest followers.[43]

The ease with which the shift from Jewishness moves to the land of Israel is further emphasized by Elliott's views on teaching the historical Jesus: 'After having taught a course at the University of San Francisco for over twenty years on "Jesus the Jew" with my colleague Rabbi David Davis in which we stressed the thorough-going "Jewishness" of Jesus, I would now rename that course "Jesus the Israelite".'[44]

Elliott along with Philip Esler, who has been prominent in pushing for dropping the term 'Jew' in Pauline studies, have made it crystal clear (as noted above) that their historical analysis has nothing to do with anti-Semitism and that such work even helps combat anti-Semitism. While I certainly would not challenge the moral concerns of scholarship, nor indeed their motivations, it remains significant that for all the talk of tying identity to the land of Israel and the contemporary moral implications, Elliott does not mention any concern for contemporary Palestinians, an otherwise obvious issue if contemporary ramifications of the use of the land of Israel are to be discussed.[45] This should be no surprise as it is hardly breaking news that a pro-Israel and anti-Palestinian agenda is dominant in key parts of US culture. In contemporary scholarship and American higher education, Palestinian concerns are a sensitive issue, with groups such as Campus Watch breathing down the necks of any scholars deemed pro-Palestinian. As we have seen, in and around biblical studies, Keith Whitelam and Nadia Abu el-Haj have both shown in detail that there is a strong anti-Palestinian bias in scholarship and both have been the recipients of vitriolic campaigns against them.[46] What is particularly significant for our present purposes is how far the 'Jesus the Israelite' debate has settled into the concerns of American culture in relation to Israel and Palestine and how far removed it has now got from Malina's personal politics on Israel. There cannot be many better examples of how cultural context can dictate the results of scholarship even when they run clean contrary to personal intentions.

This pattern is clear in Malina's co-handling of the issue of 'the land.' Above, we saw that Malina and Rohrbaugh's assessment of the term Ἰουδαῖος in John's Gospel was partly developed through inaccurate views on Jewish history. What is all the more striking is how, in the sentences immediately following the above quotation, the argument put forward by Malina and Rohrbaugh slots neatly into dominant views on 'the land' (which would be most unlikely to entertain the distorted views of Jewish history): whoever these people most of us would define as Jewish are, they must be tied in with the land. Notice just how strong the language of tying a people in with the land is ('organically,' 'rooted'):

> Rather, Judean meant a person belonging to a group called Judeans, situated geographically and forming a territory taking its name from its inhabitants, Judea. Judea is precisely a group of people, Judeans, organically related to and rooted in a place, with its distinctive environs, air, and water. Judean thus designates a person from one segment of a larger related group, Israel (John 1:47, 49), who comes from the place after which the segment is named, Judea (*Ioudaia*). The correlatives of Judean in John are 'Galilean' and 'Perean,' and together they make up Israel.[47]

Jewish 'religious' identity may well have been overlooked by Malina and Rohrbaugh but it is remarkable how, for all Malina's explicit personal concerns for the problems in Palestine and Israel, he manages to co-write this up in effectively Zionist language.

This contradictory pattern is also evident in the ways in which Malina handles 'the Arab.' For all Malina's well-known opposition to stereotyping Arabs and support for Palestinians (Malina has also made this known publically at SBL presentations), we have an equally remarkable example of how cultural context can dictate results of scholarship even when running clean contrary to personal politics, because it is difficult to avoid the conclusion that Malina's scholarship has bought into the dominant (negative) cultural portrayals of 'the Arab' of the sort Malina would personally abhor. As mentioned above, perhaps more than anything else in Malina's work, it is the way in which the Mediterranean has become a fixed 'Other' that had wide-ranging influence and the reason why it is part of the very ideological construction of 'the Arab' Malina seeks to reject personally. The contemporary political implications of treating the Middle East and 'the Arab world', for all their sheer size and population, as a fixed entity, I hope do not need spelling out any further. However, it may be that Malina is constructing the Middle East as a positive entity. But what he believes personally about the positive nature of his constructions of the Arab world and the Mediterranean is now another issue, because it is clear that Malina produces some distinctive comments which are instantly recognizable for their contemporary politicized rhetoric. Among the many quotable passages where Malina makes generalizations about 'the Arab world' and 'the Mediterranean', which I have collected elsewhere,[48] the following (which apparently holds for 'village Mediterraneans' in general) is particularly notable, not least because it comes by way of Raphael Patai's *The Arab Mind*:

> personalization of problems goes so far in the Arab countries that even material, technical difficulties accompanying the adoption of elements of Western civilization are considered as resulting from human malevolence and felt to be a *humiliation*... Where the Arab encounters an obstacle he imagines that an enemy is hidden. Proud peoples with a weak 'ego structure' tend to interpret difficulties on their life path as personal humiliations and get entangled in *endless lawsuits* or throw themselves into the arms of *extremist political movements. A defeat in elections*, a risk that every politician must face in a democracy, appears to be such a humiliation that an Arab can thereby be induced without further ceremony to take up arms against the victor and the legal government...[49]

Clearly, the sentiments of Malina's argument fit neatly into the neo-Orientalism of the contemporary clash-of-civilizations rhetoric and Western ideas of how Iraq and the Middle East are not inherently 'suited' to democracy, or at least not without 'our' help. Likewise, the idea of Arab or Muslim 'humiliation' is a common category with which the problems with the strange Arab and Muslim natives in Iraq and Palestine are conveniently explained.[50] Indeed, Patai's work on 'the Arab mind' has been used in governmental and military circles as a means to understand Iraq and was the thinking partly behind the acts carried out by the US military in Abu Ghraib, despite contemporary anthropologists spurning such old-fashioned approaches to the study of the Middle East.[51]

We should, however, also point out that one of the great ironies here is that Patai was a notable Zionist of the mid-twentieth century and many of his ideas concerning Arabs were formulated at the very creation of the state of Israel, where Patai was then based, as is clear enough from Patai's letters and notes.[52] Patai was a son of a prominent Zionist and 'followed his own Zionist impulses' in studying for a doctoral degree (awarded in 1936) at the Hebrew University in Jerusalem.[53] Among Patai's many publications were his editing of an encyclopaedia of Zionism and a collection of essays on Zionist thought, both published by none other than Herzl Press.[54] Herzl Press is described as follows on its website:

> In wake of the Holocaust, in the wake of the establishment of the State of Israel and of the profound changes in Jewish communities in the Diaspora, it is vital to broaden understanding of the issues that govern the lives of Jews everywhere. The Herzl Press was founded to do just that. Through its publications, which deal with Zionism, with Israel, and with Jewish subjects in general, the Herzl Press aims to strengthen the ties between Jews everywhere and in Israel.[55]

Collectively and individually, these are hardly the most expected influences on someone claiming to be on 'the Arab side', so to speak, and so sealing the argument, I think, that Malina is an excellent example of how personal politics can be dramatically reversed when inserted into the world of politics, culture and higher education.

Concluding Remarks

Ordinarily it might be pointed out that scholars use works of scholars of different perspectives as a matter of routine and, theoretically, going where the evidence led him may have been central to Malina's attempt to bring his form of anthropological approaches to the New Testament to the fore. But some of the results of Malina's scholarship are not backed up by serious evidence and so instead we have a prime example of the power of dominant cultural influences on scholarship. Of course, his presentation, and often lack of presentation, of Judaism and Jews seems to go against major cultural and scholarly trends. Yet in doing so, it is striking that it is another dominant cultural trend which takes over. His use (and he is not alone in this) of outdated Orientalist scholarship and approaches, with seemingly no concern for the famous criticisms made by Edward Said, and with a staggering lack of supportive evidence, have produced an approach which owes much more to contemporary politicized constructions of the Other that is 'the Arab world' than to basic fidelity to ancient sources.[56]

While deep problems with Malina's work may seem obvious to some of us, it would be wrong to dismiss Malina, and perhaps also his strictest followers, because the influence of Malina-inspired anthropological approaches is too widespread in scholarship. Mainstream historical Jesus scholars such as N. T. Wright or John Meier simply refer the reader to Malina or Malina-inspired work should the reader wish to learn more about the 'social world' of Jesus.[57] Furthermore, we might recall that in the results of a poll of over 70 bibliobloggers asking for their top five most influential scholars, Malina featured strongly.[58] Malina's work has even inspired the work of one of Malina's great enemies, John Dominic Crossan, of whom Malina claimed, 'what has been done with the social sciences is significant, much of it important enough to be plagiarized by John Dominic Crossan'.[59] Malina is clearly of importance for our analysis of understanding Jesus scholarship as in many ways he sits at the heart of the mainstream. And that ought to be worrying.

Notes

1. A. Marr, 'Interview with Noam Chomsky', *The Big Idea* (BBC2, 14 February, 1996), http://video.google.com/videoplay?docid=-4827358238697503#.
2. For discussion of the similar narratives concerning Israel and Palestine, ancient and modern, including a limited love for Israel and Judaism, see J. G. Crossley, *Jesus in an Age of Terror: Scholarly Projects for a New American Century* (London and Oakville: Equinox, 2008), pp. 143–94. Several examples of engagement with the politics of contemporary Israel can be found among historical Jesus scholars. For a more 'moderate' dispensationalist perspective see e.g. D. L. Bock, 'Some Christians See a "Road Map" to End Times', *Los Angeles Times* (18 June, 2003); cf. D. L. Bock and D. B. Wallace, *Dethroning Jesus: Exposing Popular Culture's Quest to Unseat the Biblical Christ* (Nashville: Thomas Nelson, 2007), pp. 186–92. For a fairly conventional mainstream perspective see e.g. B. Chilton, 'Moral Proportion and the Role of Churches in the Israel–Gaza War', Christians for a Fair Witness on the Middle East, http://christianfairwitness.com/writings/chilton-january2009.html; cf. idem, *A Feast of Meanings: Eucharistic Theologies from Jesus through Johannine Circles* (Leiden: Brill, 1994); idem, *Rabbi Jesus: An Intimate Biography* (New York: Doubleday, 2000). Chilton's views on the attack on Gaza reflect the dominant (pre-existing) narrative on the causes and omit too much contradictory evidence. For a collection and discussion of the deeper causes and a wider range of evidence see e.g. R. Fisk, 'Why Bombing Ashkelon Is the Most Tragic Irony', *Independent* (30 December, 2008); idem, 'Why Do They Hate the West So Much, We Will Ask', *Independent* (7 January, 2009); A. Shlaim, 'How Israel Brought Gaza to the Brink of Humanitarian Catastrophe', *Guardian* (7 January, 2009).
3. See further Crossley, *Jesus in an Age of Terror*, pp. 5, 161–71. As an aside, we may then counter by raising the question of why there may seem to be so many radical leftist theorists in the academy. But the fact that there are so many may already suggest that such figures may be among the easiest to absorb, as we

saw in Chomsky's views on the neutralizing of the radical left in universities (see Introduction). See N. Chomsky, *Understanding Power* (New York: New Press, 2002), p. 242. On the intellectual control and uses of 'fanaticism' see again A. Toscano, *Fanaticism: On Uses of an Idea* (London and New York: Verso, 2010).

4. R. Darnton, 'Workers Revolt: The Great Cat Massacre of the Rue Saint-Séverin', in idem, *The Great Cat Massacre and Other Episodes in French Cultural History* (London: Allen Lane, 1984), pp. 75–104 (77–78).
5. J. G. Crossley, 'Enoch Powell and the Gospel Tradition: A Search for a Homeland', in K. W. Whitelam and H. Moxnes (eds.), *Holy Land as Homeland? Models for Constructing the Historic Landscapes of Jesus* (Sheffield: Sheffield Phoenix Press, forthcoming).
6. Powell was Conservative Member of Parliament between 1950 and 1974, Minister of Health between 1960 and 1963, and an Ulster Unionist Member of Parliament between 1974 and 1987.
7. J. E. Powell, 'To the Annual General Meeting of the West Midlands Area Conservative Political Centre (Birmingham, 20 April, 1968)', in idem, *Reflections: Selected Writings and Speeches of Enoch Powell* (London: Bellew, 1992), pp. 161–69.
8. J. E. Powell, *No Easy Answers* (London: Sheldon Press, 1973); idem, *Wrestling with the Angel* (London: Sheldon Press, 1977).
9. J. E. Powell, 'Genesis of the Gospel', *JSNT* 42 (1991), pp. 5–16; idem, *The Evolution of the Gospel* (New Haven and London: Yale University Press, 1994).
10. S. Heffer, *Like the Roman: The Life of Enoch Powell* (London: Weidenfeld & Nicolson, 1998), p. 12.
11. Powell, 'Genesis of the Gospel', p. 5.
12. Powell, *Evolution*, pp. xxi, 207–208.
13. A. Brown, 'Gospel according to Powell: Christ Was Stoned to Death', *Independent* (16 August, 1994).
14. Heffer, *Like the Roman*, p. 943, bizarrely adds, 'though the oldest teachings on this question also point to stoning', without telling us what these mysterious 'oldest teachings' might even be!
15. Brown, 'Gospel according to Powell'.
16. For allegations of 'anti-Semitism' in contemporary historical Jesus scholarship see Crossley, *Jesus in an Age of Terror*, pp. 132–33, 174–76.
17. See e.g. Powell, 'To the Annual General Meeting', pp. 161–62, 165–67.
18. Heffer, *Like the Roman*, p. 60.
19. See further Crossley, 'Enoch Powell'.
20. For discussion with further bibliography see e.g. P. Head, 'The Nazi Quest for an Ayrian Jesus', *JSHJ* 2 (2004), pp. 55–89; S. Heschel, *The Aryan Jesus: Christian Theologians and the Bible in Nazi Germany* (Princeton: Princeton University Press, 2008).
21. G. Bornkamm, *Jesus of Nazareth* (London: Hodder & Stroughton, 1960), e.g. pp. 102, 223.
22. E.g. S. G. F. Brandon, *Jesus and the Zealots: A Study of the Political Factor in Primitive Christianity* (Manchester: Manchester University Press, 1967); idem, *The Trial of Jesus of Nazareth* (London: B. T. Batsford, 1968). Cf. O. Cullmann, *Jesus and the Revolutionaries* (New York: Harper Row, 1970);

M. Hengel, *Was Jesus a Revolutionist?* (Philadelphia: Fortress, 1971); E. Bammel and C. F. D. Moule (eds.), *Jesus and the Politics of His Day* (Cambridge: Cambridge University Press, 1984).

23. Cf. P. R. Davies, *Whose Bible Is It Anyway?* (London & New York: T&T Clark/ Continuum, wnd edn, 2004), pp. 142–55.
24. For discussion see Crossley, *Jesus in an Age of Terror*, pp. 57–142.
25. E.g. J. D. Crossan, *The Historical Jesus: The Life of a Mediterranean Jewish Peasant* (New York: HarperCollins; Edinburgh: T&T Clark, 1991); idem, *The Birth of Christianity. Discovering What Happened in the Years Immediately after the Execution of Jesus* (New York: HarperCollins; Edinburgh: T&T Clark, 1998). Cf. idem, *A Long Way from Tipperary* (San Francisco: HarperSanFrancisco, 2000).
26. See also S. Kelley, *Racializing Jesus: Race, Ideology and the Formation of Modern Biblical Scholarship* (London and New York: Routledge, 2002), pp. 182–210, for the intellectual influences on Crossan's work from nationalistic and racializing discourses through Heidegger and Bultmann and modern American biblical scholarship.
27. B. J. Malina, *The New Testament World: Insights from Cultural Anthropology* (London: SCM, 1981).
28. D. G. Horrell, 'Social-Scientific Interpretation of the New Testament: Retrospect and Prospect', in idem (ed.), *Social-Scientific Approaches to New Testament Interpretation* (Edinburgh: T&T Clark, 1999), pp. 3–27 (14).
29. E.g. R. S. Sugirtharajah, *Asian Biblical Hermeneutics and Postcolonialism: Contesting the Interpretations* (Sheffield: Sheffield Academic Press, 1998), pp. 105–106; E. S. Fiorenza, *Jesus and the Politics of Interpretation* (New York and London: Continuum, 2000), pp. 21–22, 82–114.
30. Crossley, *Jesus in an Age of Terror*, pp. 57–142.
31. Classically, E. W. Said, *Orientalism* (London: Penguin, 3rd edn, 2003), pp. 284–88.
32. Michael James's articles can be found at http://www.rense.com/Datapages/ mikejamesdat.htm and http://www.gnosticliberationfront.com/mike_james_ page_a_list_of_al.htm. Articles include 'Zionists Foment Race in Germany, Leave Clues', 'Jews Run Scared of Mike James, German State Attorney Cites Insanity: Learning to Live among the Sane and Comfortably Numb in the European Soviet Union of Zionist States', 'Our Alamo against the Jewish New World Order' and 'Revealed: British Premier Gordon Brown is a Pedophile'.
33. D. Jacobs-Malina, 'Letter' (6 January, 2005), *Asia Times Online*, http://www. atimes.com/atimes/letters_13.html.
34. Anonymous, 'International Response to the Bush Declaration on the Palestinian Right to Return', *Al Awda* (April, 2004), http://al-awda.org/bush-declaration.html.
35. http://www.al-arabeya.net/halots/?act=1&theclass=&serial=&cat=&page=6.
36. P. Manning, 'Grant Nadia Abu el-Haj Tenure Petition', *Petition Online*, http:// www.petitiononline.com/mod_perl/signed.cgi?Barnard2&1251.
37. J. H. Elliott, 'Jesus the Israelite Was Neither a "Jew" nor a "Christian": On Correcting Misleading Nomenclature', *JSHJ* 5 (2007), pp. 119–54. Because scholarship largely ignores its ideological genealogies, it should be repeated that virtually all of the recent discussions of the term 'Ἰουδαῖος and its

translation as 'Judean' or related terms has been dependent on the faulty *TDNT* article by K. G. Kuhn's for the linguistic detail, an article betraying its fascist context. See M. Casey, 'Some Anti-Semitic Assumptions in *The Theological Dictionary of the New Testament*', *NovT* 41 (1999), pp. 280–91.

38. B. J. Malina and R. L. Rohrbaugh, *Social-Science Commentary on the Gospel of John* (Minneapolis: Fortress Press, 1998), p. 44.
39. This makes the following statement by Malina and Rohrbaugh sound strange: 'when the terms *Judea* or *Judean* are used in the Gospel of John, they should be understood as referring to the persons living in a territory located in the southern and western part of the Roman province of Syria-Palestine... The Passover of the Judeans' (*Gospel of John*, p. 45). Cf. Malina and Rohrbaugh's description on p. 75 where 'Judean' is dropped in their own discussion of Passover: 'Israelite males were obliged by Mosaic command to go on pilgrimage to Jerusalem three times annually.'
40. M. Bockmuehl, 'God's Life as a Jew: Remembering the Son of God as Son of David', in B. R. Gaventa and R. B. Hays (eds.), *Seeking the Identity of Jesus: A Pilgrimage* (Grand Rapids and Cambridge: Eerdmans, 2008), pp. 60–78 (68).
41. M. Bockmuehl, 'Review of Malina, *New Testament World*, third edition', *BMCR* (19 April, 2002), available at http://ccat.sas.upenn.edu/bmcr/2002/2002-04-19.html.
42. B. J. Malina, 'Social-scientific Criticism', C. A. Evans (ed.), *Encyclopedia of the Historical Jesus* (London: Routledge, 2008), pp. 578–81.
43. Elliott, 'Jesus the Israelite', pp. 150–51, 153, 154.
44. Elliott, 'Jesus the Israelite', p. 151.
45. For further discussion of these issues, especially the political ramifications of the arguments of Esler and Elliott, including the critique by A. -J. Levine, see J. G. Crossley, 'Jesus the Jew since 1967', in H. Moxnes, W. Blanton and J. G. Crossley (eds.), *Jesus beyond Nationalism: Constructing the Historical Jesus in a Period of Cultural Complexity* (London and Oakville: Equinox, 2009), pp. 111–29.
46. See e.g. K. W. Whitelam, *The Invention of Ancient Israel: The Silencing of Palestinian History* (London and New York: Routledge, 1996); N. Abu el-Haj, *Facts on the Ground: Archaeological Practice and Territorial Self-Fashioning in Israeli Society* (Chicago and London: University of Chicago Press, 2001). For further discussion of the reception of these works see e.g. K. W. Whitelam, 'Representing Minimalism: The Rhetoric and Reality of Revisionism', in A. G. Hunter and P. R. Davies (eds.), *Sense and Sensitivity: Essays on Reading the Bible in Memory of Robert Carroll* (Sheffield: Sheffield Academic Press, 2002), pp. 194–223; Crossley, *Jesus in an Age of Terror*, pp. 161–71.
47. Malina and Rohrbaugh, *Gospel of John*, p. 44.
48. Crossley, *Jesus in an Age of Terror*, pp. 110–28.
49. R. Patai, *The Arab Mind* (New York: Hatherleigh Press, rev. edn, 2002). The version used by Malina is quoted in Malina, *Jesus and the Gospels*, p. 63 (italics in original).
50. See further Crossley, *Jesus in an Age of Terror*, pp. 119–28.
51. For discussion see e.g. S. Hersh, 'Annals of National Security: The Gray Zone – How a Secret Pentagon Program Came to Abu Ghraib', *The New*

Yorker (15 May, 2004); E. Qureshi, 'Misreading "the Arab Mind"', *Boston Globe* (30 May, 2004); Crossley, *Jesus in an Age of Terror*, pp. 119–28.

52. R. Patai, *Journeyman in Jerusalem: Memories and Letters, 1933–1947* (Salt Lake City: University of Utah Press, 1992).
53. R. M. Thomas, Jr, 'Raphael Patai, 85, a Scholar of Jewish and Arab Cultures', *New York Times* (25 July, 1996); D. Ben-Amos, 'Obituary: Raphael Patai (1910–1996)', *Journal of American Folklore* 110 (1997), pp. 314–16 (314).
54. R. Patai, *Encyclopedia of Zionism and Israel* (New York: Herzl Press, 1971); idem (ed.), *Essays in Zionist History and Thought* (New York: Herzl Press, 1971).
55. http://www.midstreamthf.com/books.html.
56. It is worth noting that critical re-evaluation of Malina's heritage is coming from within the Context Group. See e.g. Z. Crook, 'Honor, Shame, and Social Status Revisited', *JBL* 128 (2009), pp. 591–612.
57. E.g. J. P. Meier, *A Marginal Jew: Rethinking the Historical Jesus*. I. *The Roots of the Problem and the Person* (New York: Doubleday, 1991), pp. 10–11; idem, *A Marginal Jew: Rethinking the Historical Jesus*. III. *Companions and Competitors* (New York: Doubleday, 2001), p. 67; N. T. Wright, *Jesus and the Victory of God* (London: SPCK, 1996), pp. 52–53.
58. K. Brown, 'Biblioblog Top 10 Most Influential Authors and Books', *C. Orthodoxy* (20 June, 2009), http://corthodoxy.wordpress.com/2009/06/20/biblioblog-top-10-most-influential-authors-and-books/.
59. B. J. Malina, 'Social Scientific Methods in Historical Jesus Research', in W. Stegemann, B. J. Malina and G. Theissen (eds.), *The Social Setting of Jesus and the Gospels* (Minneapolis: Fortress Press, 2002), pp. 3–26 (4). See also L. Rosson, 'Crossan Dumps the Egalitarian Jesus', The Busybody (1 April, 2007), http://lorenrosson.blogspot.com/2007/04/crossan-dumps-egalitarian-jesus.html.

Chapter 9

Red Tory Christ

The rich man in his castle,
The poor man at his gate,
He made them, high or lowly,
And ordered their estate.
– 'All Things Bright and Beautiful', Cecil F. Alexander

ResPublica Premium Member – £12,000 per year...

- Invitations to the private ResPublica monthly members' policy dinners, with prominent political speakers and the opportunity to help frame the work of ResPublica
- Private briefing with the Director and Deputy Director of ResPublica
- Individual updates with the Director of ResPublica
- Exclusive invitation to the ResPublica annual reception with prominent political speaker

ResPublica Partner – £25,000 per year...

- Exclusive table at the ResPublica founders' annual private dinner with prominent political speaker

– ResPublica Individual Membership offers[1]

It was in 2007 when Ratzinger published his book on the historical Jesus,[2] a not insignificant date. While there were those who criticized the book for its poor quality,[3] this is only part of the story. In addition to a curious embrace by American evangelical scholars (see below), Ratzinger's book was enthusiastically received among a group of people close to John Milbank, the beating heart of the much-hyped world of Radical Orthodoxy now effectively centred at the University of Nottingham. This resulted in a 2008 conference and a 2010 publication, both of which lavished high praise on Ratzinger and his book. During this period and developing ideas from Radical Orthodoxy, Milbank's protégé, Phillip Blond, established a political think tank and his own brand of Red Toryism, both of which are extremely close to, and in high praise of, David Cameron who would, of course, become Prime Minister of the coalition government in 2010. As I hope will become clear throughout this chapter, this adoration of the Pope and the Prime Minister in recent years is closely linked and such links are manifest in the construction of a Jesus now associated with Milbank's Nottingham.[4]

The setting for this Jesus appears significant as it has come to a head during a crisis of neoliberalism: the banking crisis of 2008 and its aftermath. This very contemporary period has, apparently, ushered in an era of 'new politics' in the UK. In fact, what many of us think it has done is merely tweak the rhetoric of government and power and brought in new, less ferocious appearing figures to mask the most intense neoliberal agendas in recent British history. Furthermore, here we can also return to issues of intentionality, because Milbank, Blond and the Pope, and some of their most devoted followers, are well known for their hostility to contemporary liberalism and neoliberalism, yet have provided, partly through the Blond/Milbank inspired 'Big Society', an as yet unsuccessful masking of an aggressive neoliberal agenda (presumably unintentionally?), though some on the centre-left, such as John Harris, are showing signs of being impressed and questioning the idea, which I think is an accurate summary of the Big Society (and its theological counterpart), namely that such thinking is 'masking old tricks with new sophistry'.[5]

The New Liberals and the Structurally Liberal: Contextualizing the Red Tory Christ

The rhetoric of a 'new politics' in the UK effectively started to gain momentum around the 2010 General Election, won by the Conservative Party in coalition with the Liberal Democrats, and has provided some of the more spectacular examples of the liberal maintenance and masking of power in recent times. So far, the neoliberal philosophy of the Conservatives, first fully manifest in an 'emergency budget' involving drastic cuts to the public sector, has won the day, with leading Liberal Democrats still repeatedly claiming that they have kept a leash on the Conservatives. Support has also come from outside the membership of the Liberal Democrats. John Kampfner, the former editor of the left-wing *New Statesman*, writing in the now Liberal Democrat-supporting (and much maligned for doing so) *Guardian*, decided to switch his vote and support from Labour to the Liberal Democrats.[6] The main reasons included Labour's 'deceits on Iraq' and 'its embrace of the super-rich.' While there was 'palliative care for some of the disadvantaged,' they never challenged 'the fundamentals of a macroeconomic settlement that had rewarded the reckless.' Kampfner is not happy with the Conservative slashing of the public sector but he has found his decision 'bearable, with the prospect of better to come.' Whenever he feels uncomfortable with the decision, he recalls two words – 'Iraq' and 'banks' – and then feels better. This has been one of the more remarkable defences of supporting Conservatives by proxy given that the Conservatives as a whole managed to be even more vigorous defenders of the Iraq war and have long been the party of the super-rich, well before Blair and no doubt long after, and perhaps no surprise when over half the cabinet are millionaires. Kampfner adds that he would like to see the Liberal Democrats giving the administration 'a distinctively liberal hue, and to be seen to be doing it.' Is this not tantamount to admitting a liberal masking of those things he hates?

Cameron has his own fair share of 'useful idiots,' such as: Zac Goldsmith, the former editor of *The Ecologist* and a leading 'green' advisor to Cameron; Eric Pickles, the working-class 'man of the people' and Secretary of State for Communities and Local Government who went to Greenhead Grammar School and Leeds Polytechnic and *not* Eton and *not* Oxford; and Steve Hilton, the non-suit-wearing Conservatives' strategy director who 'voted Green' in the 2001 election. Hilton, widely believed to be behind Cameron's casual, 'progressive' and 'green' image rebranding, seems to have disgruntled some of the more traditionalist Conservatives by emailing regular 'strategy bulletins' which begin with the informal 'hi' and discuss 'cool' projects and other 'great examples of how harnessing the insights of behavioural economics and social psychology can help you to achieve your policy goals in a more effective and light-touch way.'[7] It is always helpful to have such figures around while embracing a system that seems sharply at odds with the very causes that the Goldsmiths and the Hiltons apparently espouse and with the very people Pickles is supposed to represent.[8]

Despite the funding cuts to universities, increased fees and the high neoliberal rhetoric used to defend such moves (see Conclusion), even influential academics and former academics, including left-leaning academics, have been sympathetic to the government-led agenda, particularly anything under the label 'Big Society.' Perhaps the most high profile examples remain Phillip Blond and John Milbank. Blond was previously lecturing in theology at the University of Cumbria before starting the think-tank ResPublica in 2009. While ResPublica claims non-party affiliation, its aims are in line with Blond's personal Red Tory project, part of the key thinking behind David Cameron's Big Society, and has earned Blond the title of Cameron's 'Philosopher King' (or 'Cameron's crank' by less misty-eyed critics).[9] Blond's Red Toryism reads like a return to that dangerous phrase for a politician, 'traditional values'. It extols things largely local: family, community, village life, voluntary associations, cooperatives, guilds, the local church, local markets, family and small businesses, high culture for all, tradable assets to supplement wages, small property ownership and the benevolent paternalism of our betters. The Red Tory agenda is, apparently, a cure for that unfortunate (and now largely dropped) pseudo-sociological term, Broken Britain.[10] Red Toryism is hostile to the advance of neoliberalism, economic and cultural liberalism, centralized state power, welfarism and secularism, all of which, Blond would argue, have been damaging for British culture.

Milbank, a ResPublica fellow, is of course most well known for being the dominant figure in the Radical Orthodoxy movement in theological circles. Milbank sees his personal political position as largely within 'that tradition of non-statist Christian Socialism, which views modern statism as involving the support of the very rich, a guarantee of their finances and an enabling additional support through "welfare" of their dispossessed workforce'. He sees his tradition as similar to Red Toryism and, indeed, sees both Red Toryism and 'my own brand of "Blue Socialism"' ('currently the majority') as respectable and compatible strands within Radical Orthodoxy.[11] Thus, in a letter to the *Guardian* in 2008, he wrote, 'we need now to invent a new sort of politics...a "traditionalist socialism" or a "red Toryism"'.[12] In 2010, shortly before the General Election, it seems Milbank was happy to stand shoulder-to-shoulder with Cameron's new philosopher-king as they co-wrote a piece in the *Guardian*, urging 'a new synthesis of the traditional left's emphasis on addressing economic inequity and the old right's concern with justified inequality'.[13] No surprise, then, that we get clear overlap with the concerns of Blond and Milbank: the role of the family, mutual banks, associations, trade guilds, individual ownership, hostility to excess wealth, high culture, a 'hierarchy of virtue', benevolent paternalism, principled elites, justified inequality and so on. Milbank has also long been known for his hostility to secularism, liberalism, capitalism, communism, much of Islam and, despite being an Anglican, (much of)

Protestantism. For Milbank, a Catholicizing turn would go some way to providing a cure for societal ills.[14]

Readers can draw their own conclusions about the role of virtuous elites and whether they would be happy in the warm paternal embrace of beloved betters like Milbank and Blond. What I first want to do here is show how the Red Tory project is very much involved in the development of neoliberalism, even if it fails to recognize this, and masks the neoliberal agenda of Cameron's Conservatives. Mentioning Blond and Milbank may seem strange as both have been fierce critics of neoliberalism and, more generally, liberalism, at least in its modern manifestations, and so it may be better to think of the pair and their sympathizers as 'structurally liberal'. Let me spell this out in more detail.

Blond may complain that neoliberalism and multinationals are destructive, but his solution seems to be one provoked by neoliberalism, and sometimes endorsed by strands of neoliberal thinking, including Thatcherism: nationalism. Blond's Red Toryism has a clear patriotic and nationalistic agenda. He calls on Conservatives to accept that the free market is ultimately 'unpatriotic' and has 'no loyalty to Britain, its people, its history or its future'. What the Conservatives need to do, Blond argues, is recover the notion of 'patriotic capital – a resource dedicated to a renewed Britain of real investment and widely distributed property'.[15] Culturally, Conservatives need to restore a common 'high civilization…that binds all Britons together in a vision of a culture worth participating and believing in' and 'a national virtue culture is required…a new binding common way of life of shared values and higher belief'.[16] Does this not play in to the hands of a nationalism and jingoism that Thatcher found so effective, and that the contemporary far right love? It could of course be argued that Blond is seeing his brand of nationalism as a reaction to neoliberalism. While he may think in these terms, Red Toryism's drive for both localism and nationalism are what Roland Boer and Alex Andrews call a 'symptom of global capitalism in its current form' and typical of capitalism's perpetual search for new markets.[17] In a world where everything is a commodity, Red Toryism fits in perfectly.

Blond may recall how he was 'appalled' by Thatcher's Conservatives and, while he 'hated Scargill', he 'still sympathised with the miners' and did not believe working-class communities should be abandoned if coal was deemed to be economically non-viable (it remains to be seen whether Blond's face is to be placed on miners' banners and memorabilia).[18] Yet, if Blond really felt so strongly, hitching his ride to the Conservative bandwagon, the very people responsible for the carefully planned destruction of the mining industry and mining communities, is a strange choice. The dramatic attack on the miners in the mid-1980s was the endgame of a pre-Thatcher battle between the Conservative Party and the miners, most immediately stretching back 15 years before, but a battle that had been fought over the past century: the Conservatives' hostility to miners, and vice versa, is deeply embedded in both the Conservative Party and mining communities. And there is a glaring issue here for anyone who experienced 1980s Britain and is now experiencing Cameron. As Gary Younge bitterly pointed out, 'As a young man Cameron looked out on the social carnage of pit closures and mass unemployment, looked at Margaret Thatcher's government and thought, these are my people.'[19]

Blond may think that the neoconservative project in Washington was a disaster for the Blair government. He is scathing of the Iraq war. The war was 'a clear foreign policy disaster' and exposed New Labour as 'shallow manipulators of truth and acolytes of whatever interest seemed the most powerful'. 'What is interesting', Blond adds, was the 'inability to determine a separate British interest from that of the neo-con view of the world then prevalent in Washington.'[20] Again, Blond may well believe such things, but to repeat, the Conservatives were overwhelmingly in support of the Iraq war and it would take a dramatic suspension of reality to think they would have opposed the Iraq war if they were in government at the time. We might add that key figures in the government and Cameron allies (e.g. Liam Fox, George Osborne, Ed Vaisey, William Hague and Michael Gove) are card-carrying neoconservatives or neoconservative sympathizers.[21] And it is equally clear that this brand of neoconservatism is in line with the Bush-Blair variety, whatever the rhetorical posturing of Cameron and his allies.[22] We might note, for instance, that Cameron was making loud neoconservative noises in his rise to the top. In a 2005 pro-Iraq invasion speech, Cameron made the then typical comparisons between the 'jihadists' and the Nazis, arguing that if there was withdrawal from Iraq or if Israel made 'massive concessions' it would somehow be analogous to the argument that 'by allowing Germany to remilitarise the Rhineland or take over the Sudetenland, we would satisfy Nazi ambitions'. In further 1930s comparisons, he talked of having the 'stomach for the fight' and claimed that 'willingness to cede ground and duck confrontation is interpreted as a fatal weakness'.[23] Any of this could have come from Bush or Blair, both of whom were more than comfortable using implausible historical analogies from the 1930s.

However, while we might see a degree of naivety on other issues and make the case that Blond is an idealist who is the unwitting pawn for some fairly ruthless politicians, in the case of neoconservative Washington and the Iraq war there is evidence that Blond was a little more aware of what he was doing. Writing in the *New York Times* in 2005 shortly after the 7 July London attacks, Blond and Adrian Pabst were using the kind of rhetoric found in 'the neo-con view of the world then prevalent in Washington.' Their language included phrases such as: 'the oft-quoted remark that Islam is a religion of peace is false'; 'there can be no accommodation with an ideology that seeks to fashion the whole world in its own image'; 'the essentially Islamic nature of this terror demands nothing less than a reformation in the name of an alternative Islam'; 'Islam is linked from the beginning with the practice of divinely sanctioned warfare and lethal injunctions against apostates and unbelievers'; and 'Islam experienced no period of wandering and exclusion; from its inception, Islam formed a unitary state bent on military conquest.'[24]

Blond and Pabst's argument also echoes the classic neoconservative line (found, for instance, in the arguments of Campus Watch favourite, Daniel Pipes) that 'recruits to the cause [al-Qaeda] are not the excluded uneducated poor, they are intellectuals with a radical critique of Western society and its impact on Islam.'[25] This move has to be made because Blond and Pabst want to show the faults of Islamic theology. While not wanting to ignore theological reasons (most notably the influence of Wahhabism), what this basic move conveniently does is to ignore some very real socio-economic factors, such as: the decline of secular nationalism in North Africa and the Middle East; the specific context of the key American ally, Saudi Arabia, the homeland of the majority of the September 11 killers; the destructive sanctions on Iraq; Palestine; the petro-crash; and US support for various dictators. All of these issues (and more) affect countless 'excluded uneducated poor' and feature in the rhetoric of those people we associate with al Qaeda.[26] The explosive issue of overpopulation and dramatic increases in slum dwelling in Muslim-dominated urban centres has provided a context for the emergence of the kind of political Islam we associate with al Qaeda and a receptive audience of literate and educated young males finding themselves unemployed.[27] Certainly we could also call such people 'intellectuals,' but Blond and Pabst simply ignore the crucial explanatory contexts.

Blond and Pabst vaguely mention that 'Western repression is everywhere fuelling the ranks of radical Islam,' but that is as far as they go on this issue. This point ought to have been made more vigorously instead of blaming virtually everything on Islamic theology. Islam, like Christianity, can be, and has been, peaceful, violent and somewhere in between, and the view that we can get back to a 'peaceful' or 'violent' essence of a religion like Islam or Christianity is simply outdated.[28] It is not simply a case of tracing theological strands to show why violence happens – if the history of interpretation has shown us anything, particularly when it comes to sacred texts, it is that people can make up anything required. So, more obviously, as the twentieth century has shown, if we really want to understand contemporary violence much depends on socio-economic contexts. Still, two British-based academics writing what a certain American audience may want to hear might just do the job of hiding any uncomfortable truths.

Blond may also think that modern manifestations of liberalism have been a failure. After all, he opens his key article on Red Toryism by denouncing the 'liberal left', which 'by any objective ascertainable measure this ascendancy has been a miserable and manifest failure... Liberalism is therefore really a philosophy of power...for liberals will and self-grounding and self-validating choice is all there is.'[29] However, and a sign that Blond may have become enamoured by power politics, he was quick to embrace the arch liberals of individual choice, the Liberal Democrats, headed by the Orange Book-supporting (i.e. the more overtly neoliberal end of the Liberal Democratic party) and free-market fan, Nick Clegg, in the Coalition government. On Twitter (11 May, 2010) Blond tweeted, 'This new government could combine the best of both parties and really create something truly good' and 'I still feel a lib/con coalition could do a great deal of good.'[30]

By now we ought to be observing that Blond's hostility to neoliberalism has been severely compromised. Indeed, a number of curiosities are raised if he thinks a cure can be found in Cameronism. If we are willing to suspend disbelief to the *nth* degree, let us assume for the moment that Cameron's neoliberalism is a thing of the not-so-distant past and that we are now going to see an assault on the destructive forms of contemporary capitalism: does Cameron not have a peculiar way of showing it? If Cameron were to refashion our economic system, the choice of George Osborne as Chancellor of the Exchequer seems a curious one. Cameron going out of his way to gain the support of the Murdoch Press, while his government were preparing cuts to the BBC,[31] would also count as another curious decision. Moreover, might not Cameron be a King Cnut for our own times, unable to change the tide of global capitalism even if he wanted to? Does Blond *really* believe Cameron will take on the neoliberal hegemony? Are we *really* to believe that Blond will function as successful counter to the hardcore Thatcherites dominating the Cameron government? It does seem as if Blond's Red Tory project is spectacularly unrealistic if it expects that a Conservative government will follow the Red Tory agenda through, including the challenge to global capitalism.

To get some idea of the extent Britain has now adopted neoliberal solutions we might turn to American perceptions where British neoliberalism has even shocked the US establishment. The president himself did not approve of the extreme cutting proposed by countries such as the UK and does not seem to have been aware that the UK might implement Red Tory measures to compensate. From the heart of the American media, the *New York Times* were publishing articles expressing concern. Cameron's government were unambiguously described as going too far. One reporter, John F. Burns, claimed that Cameron's pre-government Conservatives offered a 'compassionate but persistently fuzzy image', but after ten weeks in office even rivals Thatcher and her attacks on unions and 'government bloat' while 'privatizing national industries and vigorously pursuing free-market policies'. Burns even suggested that Cameron's coalition government will go further than Thatcher in 'a wider effort to break the mo[u]ld of big government in Britain that...has largely prevailed since World War II'. While a generally polite article, Burns still refers to Cameron's economic course as involving 'almost savage austerity' in contrast to Obama. A *New York Times* leader column was more disturbed by the route taken by Cameron when it spoke of 'a dark shadow' that is 'the needlessly draconian emergency budget', and while 'some cutbacks' were necessary, if only 'to reassure Europe's panicky bond markets', this budget is 'misguided'.[32] All this from ideological soul mates in the centrist-liberal camp!

The Conservative government, with all the neoliberal and neoconservative tendencies of its New Labour predecessor, have become the government for which Blond and Milbank are effectively propagandists. It is difficult to avoid the conclusion that Milbank and Blond are either naive in thinking that they will make this now traditionally (thanks to Thatcher) neoliberal party change its neoliberal ways, that they have succumbed to the allure of power and will do anything to defend their decisions, or that they simply feel there is no turning back. Whichever way, they too provide a comforting facade for such a neoliberal government which will happily nod in the direction of the Milbank/Blond-inspired Big Society and all its concern for extended families, neighbourly love, mutuality and so on, while neoliberal policies remain unharmed. When Cameron and Osborne make drastic cuts, including welfare cuts deemed 'clearly regressive' (especially for low-income working families) by the Institute for Fiscal Studies,[33] are we only to believe that it is mere coincidence that this chimes with a hard Thatcherite agenda? Should we not worry because neighbours, associations and communities will be along to help while the recipients of the cuts wait for, or cash in, their tradable assets? Interestingly enough, in the early days of Blond's project he was aware of the issue that the Red Tories could mask neoliberal policies: 'The claim by David Cameron to tackle disadvantage through the revival of civil society looks to many on the left like ideological cover for a revived neoliberal agenda. But is it?'[34] The answer to Blond has to be a resounding 'yes'.

There is something else to this peculiar movement which now needs to be discussed in more detail, not only because it is crucial for the rest of this book but because it also explains another agenda being smuggled in. This something else involves the involvement of Radical Orthodoxy, now focused at the Milbank-dominated Centre for Theology and Philosophy at the University of Nottingham. Here we have another curiosity: this sectarian Christian background is rarely mentioned in any of the political output in the mainstream media, thus presenting the image of 'an impeccably secular conservative tendency' while allowing theology to slip under the radar and assume its place in a political system nervous of religion without anyone the wiser.[35] Yet Radical Orthodoxy has deep concerns for a divinely imposed hierarchical cosmos, a theological nostalgia to match the political nostalgia, anti-(much of) Islam and anti-secularism. And we should not forget Milbank's most prominent ideas surrounding the need of theology to resist the domination of secular modes of thought and promote a distinctive Christian explanation of reality.[36]

It is not difficult to see how all this is readily transferable into both religio-cultural dominance and the benevolent paternalism of Red Toryism. Speaking (somehow) for Muslims, Blond and Pabst wrote in another *New York Times* article, and without reference to statistical evidence to back up their dramatic claim, 'What Muslims most object to is not a difference of belief but its absence from European consciousness. Thus the recovery of Christianity in Europe is not a sectarian project but rather the only basis for the political integration of Muslims and peaceful religious coexistence.'[37] The authors may not have mentioned that they were disciples of Radical Orthodoxy or that Milbank is known for his dislike for much of the great rival, Islam, where he simply replays an outdated Orientalist discourse, while looking for the eventual Christianization of Islam and, presumably, the neutering of any non-Christian religious alternatives to secularism.[38] But when we recall the similarities with Red Toryism, then this paternalism can only be seen as that distinctive brand of cultural Christian supremacy, a kind of cultural Euro-caliphate in the making.

A Red Tory, Radically Orthodox Jesus

> Milbank's argument closely mirrors the old Orientalist justifications of economic exploitation which touted the 'benefit' of 'civilization' and 'civilizing values.' In Milbank's free-market ideology, it is the 'Third World national development projects' which instead represent the worst excesses of colonial 'exploitation.' Colonialism itself is washed clean by the orthodox baptismal waters of Milbank's historical revisionism.
>
> – Deane Galbraith[39]

Put one way, it is difficult not to admire Milbank's ambition. Not content with presumably believing he can purge neoliberalism from a neoliberal political party, he also believes he can find centre-ground with the papacy on the issue of women and sexuality. Put another way, it is difficult not to be puzzled with Milbank's choice of friends: the Conservatives have long been hated for their time in office in the 1980s and 1990s while the Pope has been at the centre of various controversies from the paedophilia scandals to attitudes towards condoms and Aids. But siding with the powerful is the common thread from Red Tories to the adoration for the Pope. We might add that a similar version of this specific brand of contemporary Christian supremacy and the drive for power, with imperialistic language, is clearly reflected in the work of N. T. Wright, particularly on the resurrection of Jesus and Pauline theology.[40] For now, we can see how the historical Jesus fares in the hands of the Centre for Theology and Philosophy at Nottingham. In 2008, as mentioned above, the Centre hosted a well-attended and well-organized conference (with a very enthusiastic and extremely vocal Blond among the audience) on the Pope's recent book on the historical Jesus.[41] Coming as a shock to this perhaps naive writer brought up on Sanders, Vermes, Casey and Crossan, the conference was overwhelmingly favourable to the Pope's book on the historical Jesus, which by the standards of historical Jesus scholarship would otherwise ordinarily be classed, rightly or wrongly, as work from the 'fundamentalist' fringe and would be dismissed for using massively outdated scholarship.[42]

Indeed, at the conference and in some contributions to the volume which emerged from the conference (edited by Pabst and Angus Paddison), there is something of the emperor's new clothes about the devotion to what is, by historical-critical standards at least and as many have pointed out, a terrible book. According to the editors, 'Pope Benedict's intervention makes a substantial contribution to contemporary thinking on Jesus.'[43] For Roland Deines, 'It deals purposefully, vigorously and polemically with methodological questions regarding Jesus and earliest Christianity.'[44] But Milbank's foreword takes pride of place: 'Remarkably, for a contemporary systematic theologian, the Pope has always had a professional concern with biblical exegesis...the Pope has already outwitted his deriders... The Pope's case gets even stronger.'[45]

The logic of Milbank's position (and implicit in other contributions) means that some important historical critical scholarship has to be inadequate. Milbank is quite explicit and claims that 'Pope Benedict makes a very good point, if controversial case for saying that scepticism at these points has meant that many statements ascribed to Jesus have been refused authenticity by critics on otherwise feeble grounds' and that the

> lack of Christian faith has issues in an implausible denial of much continuity between Jesus' own teachings and later Christian belief. But as he contends, any objective literary reading of the New Testament (of which nearly all 'biblical critics' seem constitutionally incapable) shows the exact opposite – a tremendous, if complex and accelerating, *continuum*.[46]

Several related points can be raised here. Milbank provides no evidence concerning 'feeble grounds' or in what ways 'nearly all "biblical critics"' constitutionally show the opposite of the continuum between Jesus and the divine Christ. In fact, in an age where conservative scholars have been in the ascendency, the continuity 'between Jesus' own teachings and later Christian belief' is actually mainstream scholarship, even if some of us are not convinced on the issue of Christology. Indeed, Olivier-Thomas Venard, whose exegesis Milbank regards as 'brilliant and refreshingly accurate',[47] provides a common assessment of present scholarship: 'An early high Christology unifying diverse traditions about Jesus appears ever more plausible to historians of early Christianity.'[48] This view is echoed elsewhere in the volume.[49]

However, we might add that the reasons for scepticism concerning the links between the historical Jesus and the deification of Christ are not 'feeble'. A standard argument might point out that the earliest Gospel, Mark, has Sabbath disputes over certain details over what can or cannot be done on the Sabbath (Mk 2:23–3:6) while John's Sabbath dispute in John 5 has Jesus doing things completely absent from Mark (and the Synoptics), such as encouraging the breaking of a biblical Sabbath commandment (Jer. 17:21–22), and also has the claims that 'the Jews' threw stones at Jesus because he was 'also calling God his own Father, thereby making himself equal to God' (Jn 5:18). John's Gospel has other statements such as 'the Father and I are one' (Jn 10:30) and again this results in a reaction we do not typically get to christological issues in the Synoptics: 'the Jews' attempt to stone Jesus because 'though only a human being, [you] are making yourself God' (Jn 10:33). Right or wrong, it is hardly an unreasonable claim to suggest that this dramatic Christology, as Milbank's now retired Nottingham colleague Maurice Casey has argued in detail, is the product of developing Christianity and not of the historical Jesus or even the Synoptics.[50] Otherwise, why leave out such dramatically elevated stories in the earlier traditions? This is not, however, the place to discuss whether this is an accurate assessment, but the uncontroversial point is that the development of Christology is obviously something which needs careful study and not some arm-waving dismissal of virtually everything. It has to be stated bluntly, Milbank's attack on critical biblical scholarship is reminiscent of the attacks on 'liberal' scholarship found among certain conservative evangelical Christians in America, such as Hal Lindsey's attacks in *The Late Great Planet Earth*.[51]

This connection with American 'fundamentalism' is important for understanding the agendas of Milbank, Blond and associates because it becomes clear that there is a kind of Christian superiority, or even a Radical Orthodox cultural totalitarianism, being subtly and not-so-subtly constructed over against an Other which is designated (inaccurately) as non-Christian or secular or (in the case of Milbank, Blond and Pabst) Islamic. In a more gentle approach than Milbank's, and not necessarily Radical Orthodox, we see such assumptions implied, to some extent, in the contribution by Angus Paddison. Paddison works from

> the conviction that the practices involved in following Jesus are inseparable from scriptural reading. As such, disciples enjoy an interpretative privilege because they participate in the world which Scripture wills to make known... It is not that a hermeneutic of

> discipleship regards itself as antithetical to the interests of the modern university. What it does do is calmly point out the hermeneutical priority and advantage of Scripture's 'implied exegete'...[52]

Given that we noted explicit use of the language of imperialism in chapter 7, it is worth playing with some extreme categories to show one of the problems if Paddison's logic is pushed too far: do Stalinists enjoy an interpretative privilege in understanding Stalin? Do fascists have a hermeneutical priority and advantage in understanding Hitler, even if they would not necessarily point this out calmly?

However, the full assault on historical criticism and anything else deemed a secular Other is found in Milbank's foreword. So, for instance, those biblical scholars who are sceptical towards the historicity of statements attributed to Jesus and perpetuate an apparently 'implausible denial of much continuity between Jesus' own teachings and later Christian belief' have 'the same lack of Christian faith',[53] a quite stunning statement which not only goes further than the Pope but would have to include committed Christians from Bultmann to Allison, assuming for one moment that we were going to take seriously Milbank's claim that 'nearly all' biblical critics downplay the continuity between Jesus and the deification of Christ. The overwhelming majority of historical critics in New Testament studies have been Christian and, as has been pointed out, the results (including the numerous historical Jesuses) unsurprisingly come across as Christian![54]

What this should already be telling us is that what we are dealing with, intentionally or not, is an equation of Radical Orthodoxy, and its sympathizers, with Christianity. Indeed, the Christian cultural imperialism, implicit and explicit in the agendas we have already associated with Milbank, Blond and Pabst when presenting themselves as political thinkers in the media, comes through again by further subtle digs at Islam just to make sure religious rivals are part of the problem rather than a potential solution. Milbank points out – in the book on Ratzinger's Jesus, recall – that while Muhammad was not deemed God, Islam 'has often needed to attribute all teachings back to him in the hadith as the directly declared will of Allah'. What this seemingly innocent point means for Milbank 'is the danger of mainstream Sunni Islamic positivism and voluntarism...which arguably, perhaps, helped, by concealed influence, to corrupt later Western medieval biblical exegesis, participatory ontology, eschatology and political theory'.[55] So, once this unfortunate influence is removed, what we are now left with is, presumably, the Catholicizing Christianity of Milbank, just as we get the return of Christendom with Blond and Pabst as the overarching cultural rule which will look after the Muslims under its benign wing. If we were feeling a little mischievous, we might point out that Judaism and Islam receive the perhaps not proportionally dissimilar amount of token space in the book as the space Pabst and Blond would give to Muslims in a Christianized Europe.[56] Moreover, the contributions of Adele Reinhartz (on Judaism) and Mona Siddiqui (on Islam) are the only ones lumped together in Pabst and Paddison's introduction, which notes 'their perspectives...as Jewish and Islamic scholars'.[57]

Clearly, then, there is also a remarkable amount in common with high-profile strands of the American Christian Right: critical biblical scholars are just wrong; critical Christian biblical scholars are not really Christians or are under the sway of devilish secularism; the historical Jesus was always God; God must be, as in Intelligent Design, shown to be active in history; Islam is a great negative and there must be vigilance concerning its influence on Christians – think of certain receptions of Obama! Indeed, an issue noted with legitimate surprise by certain contributors to the Paddison and Pabst volume is that Ratzinger's book was well received by, or in agreement with, traditional enemies from conservative evangelical America.[58] While this overlapping of Catholic thought and the Catholicizing wing of Anglicanism on the one hand, and the Bible Belt on the other, may seem unlikely, we should perhaps not be so surprised. After all, the Catholic Mel Gibson was remarkably successful in marketing his Catholic *Passion of the Christ* to American evangelicals, presumably in part due to a reaction against the perception of a liberal secularism. The enemy of my enemy is my friend indeed.

We also can partly account for this seemingly unlikely overlap as a symptom of contemporary capitalism. As we saw in chapters 2 and 7 in more detail, from the 1970s onward, stagnation, deregulation, increasing working hours, rising indebtedness, the decline of trade unions and the general social dislocations and atomization of society associated with neoliberalism were crucial in the rise of the evangelical Right in America as a serious political force who could, as we saw, be highly active in engaging in issues (evolution, homosexuality etc.) which deflect attention from the socio-economic problems faced. Not dissimilarly, the hostility towards neoliberalism in the agendas of Milbank, Blond and Pabst is clearly combined with a yearning for a stable past, a prominent reaction to widespread socio-economic insecurity in our postmodern times[59] and a desire for the restoration of various traditional bases of community action and protection while deflecting attention away from the neoliberalism of their political masters, the Conservative Party. The yearning for the past is also neatly paralleled in the romanticizing and nostalgic turn to the pre-critical Jesus of the Pope who, according to Pabst and Paddison, 'Refreshingly…does not adhere to modern conventions or postmodern fashions. Rather he renews the patristic and medieval synthesis of reason and revelation'.[60]

The Pope and his Jesus presumably give us something solid to hold onto in these turbulent times. But this grand nostalgic vision only deflects our attention away from socio-economic realities in a similar manner to the ways in which we have seen, and will see, with the religious Right in America as many vote against their class interests in favour of religion and Intelligent Design. For example, when Ratzinger analyses the extended Temptation story (Mt. 4:1–11; Lk. 4:1–13), he notes that Jesus is not indifferent to the abolition of hunger but 'he places these things in the proper context and the proper order' because bread alone is not enough and everything that proceeds from the mouth of the Lord is what counts (Deut. 8:3).[61] For Ratzinger, when God is put second or set aside temporarily, 'it is supposedly more important things that come to nothing'. What proves this is not only 'the negative outcome of the Marxist experiment' but also the well-meaning aid offered by the West to developing countries that has left God out of the picture. This has contributed to the collapse of societies and brought about the 'third world'.[62] This seems an outrageously bad analysis of poverty, not least because, historically, people have starved when God was also in the picture. Needless to say, such analysis masks the neoliberal strings attached to the 'well-meaning' aid offered by the West and the deep economic structures which keep people in poverty. To claim that leaving God out of the picture causes such poverty seems somewhat perverse, as does the uncritical support for a book which hammers this point home so emphatically. As with his Radical Orthodox supporters, there is the impression that the imposition of a system of virtuous religious elites is what is required to remedy the situation in Africa at least:

> Instead of giving them God, the God who has come close to us in Christ, which would have integrated and brought to completion all that is precious and great in their own traditions, we have given them cynicism of a world without God in which all that counts is power and profit, a world that destroys moral standards so that corruption and unscrupulous will to power are taken for granted…[63]

But, presumably, an underlying reason for all the masking and deflecting, as it was with the political output of Milbank, Blond and Pabst, is to get a certain kind of religious superiority put in place, and Ratzinger's book does this explicitly. The Pope and his Jesus also echo the ideologically convenient masking of socio-economic issues we found in Blond and Pabst's inadequate analysis of Islam and violence and in the vision of a world re-enchanted with religion (of a certain kind). Indeed, this is done by tapping into the mainstream scholarly tradition of Jesus the Great Man which I discussed in chapter 4. Milbank summarizes the Pope's Jesus in relation to what came next as follows:

> So the Pope concludes that, without the hypothesis of Jesus' messianic and God-consciousness (true or deluded), the irruption of the Church into history becomes harder to explain. Furthermore, he implies, the nature of the influence exerted by Jesus and the historical effects to which he gave rise render the notion that he was deluded perhaps... somewhat implausible...if Jesus was deluded, there would somehow be an incongruous mismatch between such a capacity for self-deceit and the sheer grandeur and enormity of his self-presentation.[64]

The idea that a whole complex of socio-economic issues may have given rise to the Jesus movement and ultimately to a new religious movement is simply not entertained. There is no suggestion, say, that the building projects in Tiberias and Sepphoris while Jesus was growing up might have some powerful explanatory force. There is no suggestion that broader macro-sociological developments involving empire and communications could have contributed to the spread of the new Christian message and been part of long-term developments in monotheism in the ancient world.

We could go on, but the point is that there are a whole host of reasons for historical change, including the rise of Christianity, which when airbrushed out of history allow the possibility of limited questions such as 'how else can you explain Christianity if Jesus was not God or not really bodily resurrected?' or the like. To airbrush crucial socio-economic developments out of history in such a way has its negative counterpart in the childish idea that wars happen because people like Hitler and Saddam are bad or that people are deprived because they have not got on their bikes and found a job. In other words, it plays right into the hands of the sort of individualism we now associate with the free market; there is no society indeed! So what we now conveniently get is another individual Jesus to add to our list: this is Jesus the world-changing individual on steroids and he would have to be played by someone even bigger than that postmodern icon, Arnie.

Concluding Remarks

The more 'atheist Jesuses' make Jesus palatable for a culture which has, like the American evangelical Right, emerged as a symptom of contemporary forms of capitalism (see chapter 8). We can now add another notable case with the Red Tory Christ, whether we are thinking of the 'religious' or the 'political' aspects of all the accompanying contributors to this 'movement', and even though it is ostensibly challenging neoliberal dominance. While there has been much soul-searching on the issue of eschatology, for instance, contemporary political views are less thought about, not least due to scholarship, like any other practice, being deeply embedded in its cultural context to the point where many political traits in scholarship are too embedded and often too well hidden to be questioned. But what we have in the case of Milbank, Blond and their hijacking of Ratzinger is a dramatic case of explicit (and perhaps confused) attempted Christianization of politics and a very contemporary politicization of Jesus.

Notes

1. http://www.respublica.org.uk/respublica-individual-membership.
2. J. Ratzinger, *Jesus of Nazareth: From the Baptism in the Jordan to the Transfiguration* (London: Bloomsbury, 2007), simultaneously published in German as *Jesus von Nazareth* (Freiburg im Breisgau: Herder, Milan, 2007).
3. G. Vermes, 'Review of Ratzinger, *Jesus of Nazareth*', *Times* (19 May, 2007); G. Lüdemann, *Eyes That See Not: The Pope Looks at Jesus* (Santa Rosa: Polebridge Press, 2008); M. Casey, *Jesus of Nazareth: An Independent Historian's Account of His Life and Teachings* (London and New York: T&T Clark, 2010), pp. 28–30.
4. Indeed, the links between Milbank, the Pope and Red Tories has been discussed on the ResPublica website: http://www.respublica.org.uk/blog/2010/09/benedict-red-tories-and-blue-labour.
5. J. Harris, 'From John Lewis to Workers' Co-ops: These Tories Love Wrongfooting the Left', *Guardian* (18 April, 2011). Milbank, though closely tied in with Blond, identifies more with 'Blue Socialism' (see below). Similarly, the Labour peer, Maurice Glasman, has been a vocal advocate of 'Blue Labour'. See e.g. M. Little, 'Confronting the City', *Red Pepper* (November, 2009), http://www.redpepper.org.uk/Confronting-the-city/.
6. J. Kampfner, 'Yes, I Feel Queasy. But I Don't Regret Backing the Lib Dems', *Guardian* (1 August, 2010).
7. B. Carlin, 'Setback for Cameron as Senior Conservatives Revolt Against Shaven-headed "10-year-old" Image Supremo', *Daily Mail* (3 January, 2010).
8. See Harvey's assessment on neoliberalism and environmental issues in D. Harvey, *A Brief History of Neoliberalism* (Oxford: OUP, 2005), pp. 172–75.

9. P. Blond, 'David Cameron's "Philosopher King" Explains How his Party Will Help Those Betrayed by Labour', *Daily Mail* (13 October, 2009); J. Raban, 'Cameron's Crank', *London Review of Books* 32.8 (22 April, 2010).
10. Note the subtitle to Blond's flagship book, *Red Tory: How Left and Right Have Broken Britain and How We Can Fix It* (London: Faber and Faber, 2010).
11. Milbank, 'Politics of Paradox'.
12. J. Milbank, 'Letter: Red Toryism Is the Best Hope of a New Progressive Politics', *Guardian* (22 May, 2008).
13. P. Blond and J. Milbank, 'No Equality in Opportunity', *Guardian* (27 January, 2010). See also the interview with Milbank published in May 2010: N. Schneider, 'Orthodox Paradox: An Interview with John Milbank', The Immanent Frame (17 May, 2010), http://blogs.ssrc.org/tif/2010/03/17/orthodox-paradox-an-interview-with-john-milbank/.
14. Cf. N. Coombs, 'The Red Tories' True Colours', *Guardian* (4 November, 2009).
15. P. Blond, 'Red Tory', in J. Cruddas and J. Rutherford (eds.), *Is the Future Conservative?* (London: Lawrence & Wishart, 2008), pp. 79–90 (89).
16. Blond, 'Red Tory', p. 90.
17. R. Boer and A. Andrews, 'Thin Economics; Thick Moralising: Red Toryism and the Politics of Nostalgia', *Bulletin for the Study of Religion* 40 (2011), pp. 16–24 (23). Boer and Andrews also note the far right and fascist tendencies in Blond's Red Toryism. On these tendencies see also Raban, 'Cameron's Crank'; Seymour, *Cameron*, pp. 76–77.
18. Blond, *Red Tory*, p. 25.
19. G. Younge, 'I Hate Tories. And Yes, It's Tribal', *Guardian* (4 May, 2010). Cameron's view of the miners' strike was that it was tragic but emphasizes the 'rights' of management, business, investment and people going about their lives, i.e. the submission of the workers to their betters. See Seymour, *Cameron*, p. 9.
20. Blond, *Red Tory*, pp. 128–29.
21. See e.g. R. Seymour, *The Meaning of David Cameron* (Winchester and Washington: Zero Books, 2010), pp. 78–82. If any further reminding were required see M. Gove, 'I Can't Fight My Feelings Any More: I Love Tony', *Times* (25 February, 2003).
22. Nathan Coombs also points to the intellectual links Red Toryism and Radical Orthodoxy have with the Platonic 'noble lie' and that figurehead of neoconservatism, Leo Stauss. See N. Coombs, 'The Political Theology of Red Toryism', PSA Annual Conference, Edinburgh, 31 March–1 April, 2010, pp. 1–15 (12–23), http://www.psa.ac.uk/journals/pdf/5/2010/1296_1499.pdf.
23. B. Russell, 'Cameron: Don't Repeat Errors of 1930s with "Jihadists"', *Independent* (24 August, 2005). See also D. Cameron, 'Time to Be Counted', *Guardian* (17 March, 2003) and Seymour, *Cameron*, pp. 80–81.
24. P. Blond and A. Pabst, 'The Roots of Islamic Terrorism', *New York Times* (28 July, 2005).
25. Cf. D. Pipes, 'God and Mammon: Does Poverty Cause Militant Islam?', *The National Interest* 66 (Winter 2001–02), also available at http://www.danielpipes.org/article/104. For decisive criticisms of this sort of analysis see G. Achcar, *The Clash of Barbarisms: September 11 and the New World Disorder* (London: Saqi, 2006), p. 171, n. 65.

26. For a full discussion see J. G. Crossley, *Jesus in an Age of Terror: Scholarly Projects for a New American Century* (London and Oakville: Equinox, 2008), pp. 58–99.
27. M. Watts, 'Revolutionary Islam', in D. Gregory and A. Pred (eds.), *Violent Geographies: Fear, Terror, and Political Violence* (New York and London: Routledge, 2007), pp. 175–203; cf. M. Davis, *Planet of Slums* (London and New York: Verso, 2006).
28. For the problems surrounding the construction of 'religion' in relation to violence and peace, secularism, liberalism and the state, see the discussions in, for instance, R. T. McCutcheon, *Religion and the Domestication of Dissent: or, How to Live in a Less Than Perfect Nation* (London and Oakville: Equinox, 2005); T. Fitzgerald, *Discourse on Civility and Barbarity: A Critical History of Religion and Related Categories* (Oxford: Oxford University Press, 2007); W. T. Cavanaugh, *The Myth of Religious Violence: Secular Ideology and the Roots of Modern Conflict* (Oxford: Oxford University Press, 2009); C. Martin, *Masking Hegemony: A Genealogy of Liberalism, Religion and the Private Sphere* (London and Oakville: Equinox, 2010).
29. Blond, 'Red Tory', p. 79.
30. http://twitter.com/phillip_blond.
31. M. Sweney, 'Culture Secretary Jeremy Hunt Tells BBC to Prepare for Deeper Cuts', *Guardian* (28 October, 2010).
32. Anonymous, 'Editorial: Britain's Budget Pain', *New York Times* (8 July, 2010), http://www.nytimes.com/2010/07/09/opinion/09fri1.html.
33. Press Release, 'New IFS Research Challenges Chancellor's "Progressive Budget" Claim', Institute for Fiscal Studies (25 August, 2010), http://www.ifs.org.uk/pr/progressive_budget.pdf. The press release adds, 'Those who lose the least are households of working age without children in the upper half of the income distribution.' This cannot be comfortable reading for those advocating the importance of family life.
34. P. Blond, 'The True Tory Progressives', *Guardian* (30 May, 2008).
35. Coombs, 'Political Theology of Red Toryism', pp. 1, 10–13.
36. Most famously, J. Milbank, *Theology and Social Theory* (Oxford: Blackwell, 1990).
37. P. Blond and A. Pabst, 'Integrating Islam into the West', *New York Times* (4 November, 2008).
38. Compare the following wild generalizations from Milbank which could have come straight from the anti-Islamic and nationalistic English Defence League: 'instead of founding something like a church, Muhammad bequeathed a perpetual crisis: what new single authority is to replace the one prophetic authority that has revealed the word of the one God? This is why Islam has tended constantly to generate both tyrannies and dangerous charismatic rebellions. It is also why it lacks concepts of social space between the individual person and sovereign central authority: the idea of the corporation or free association which in the West has only been enabled by a sense of the formation of the body of Christ... Islam does not in reality possess many resources with which to challenge this [Western decadence and consumerism] and has itself become more decadent than the West... there is simply no tradition of Islamic democracy...the majority Islamic

religious view that political law and the political state are full aspects of a religious order is not compatible with Christian religious views. There can be no "dialogue" about this...this constitutive aspect of Islam does in fact need to be defeated... Suddenly the idea that we do indeed have to defend 'Christendom' seems not entirely ridiculous to all those in the West who think clearly and vigorously...the arrival of Islam in Europe is a danger... It is a threat in population terms... We cannot give way to this – for example in terms of what happens in Islamic schools, public swimming baths, etc... Europe and the Americas are Christian worlds... In the very long term I suspect that we will see a gradual Christianization of Islam' (in L. Felipe Pondé, 'An Interview with John Milbank and Conor Cunningham', in C. Cunningham and P. M. Chandler [eds.], *Belief and Metaphysics* [London: SCM, 2007], pp. 501–27 [505–508]). See also J. Milbank, 'Christianity, the Enlightenment and Islam', *ABC Religion and Ethics* (24 August, 2010), http://www.abc.net.au/religion/articles/2010/08/24/2991778.htm?topic1=home&topic2= , which, equally lacking in any evidence, has the notable line, 'the lamentably premature collapse of the Western colonial empires'. For a successful demolition of Milbank's article see D. Galbraith, 'John Milbank's Atavistic Orthodoxy', *Religion Bulletin* (6 September, 2010), http://religionbulletin.wordpress.com/2010/09/06/john-milbanks-atavistic-orthodoxy/.

39. Galbraith, 'John Milbank's Atavistic Orthodoxy'.
40. J. G. Crossley, 'Manufacturing Resurrection: Locating Contemporary Scholarly Arguments', *Neot.* (forthcoming).
41. Ratzinger, *Jesus of Nazareth*.
42. R. Deines, 'Can the "Real" Jesus be Indentified with the Historical Jesus? A Review of the Pope's Challenge to Biblical Scholarship and the Ongoing Debate', in A. Pabst and A. Paddison (eds.), *The Pope and Jesus of Nazareth: Christ, Scripture and the Church* (London: SCM in association with The Centre of Theology and Philosophy, University of Nottingham, 2010), pp. 199–232 (212–13), may be right when he claims that 'Clearly, Pope Benedict is not a fundamentalist'. But this does not avoid the issue that, as a work of historical Jesus scholarship, Ratzinger's book has a great deal in common with a certain type of American conservative evangelical view on the historical Jesus. Indeed, the extremely conservative evangelical Craig Blomberg loved Ratzinger's book and recommended it to fellow evangelicals! C. Blomberg, 'Review of Ratzinger, *Jesus of Nazareth*', *Denver Journal* 10 (August, 2007), http://www.denverseminary.edu/article/jesus-of-nazareth-from-the-baptism-in-the-jordan-to-the-transfiguration/: 'Almost all of the book could have been written by informed evangelical New Testament scholars and almost all of the major positions taken agree exactly with what those scholars increasingly agree is the heart of what a certain teaching or deed of Jesus means... Evangelical readers can derive considerable encouragement from the pope's positions.'
43. A. Pabst and A. Paddison, 'Introduction', in Pabst and Paddison (eds.), *The Pope*, pp. 1–9 (1).
44. Deines, 'Historical Jesus', p. 204.
45. J. Milbank, 'Foreword: Jesus of Nazareth in the Context of Benedict XVI's Theology', in Pabst and Paddison (eds.), *The Pope*, pp. xxiii–xxix (xxvi, xxvii, xxvii).

46. Milbank, 'Foreword', p. xxvii. It is notable that even in Pabst and Paddison's sympathetic volume a conservative (and also sympathetic) scholar such as Richard Hays does not accept that Ratzinger is convincing on method and the historical Jesus. See R. B. Hays, 'Ratzinger's Johannine Jesus: A Challenge to Enlightenment Historiography', in Pabst and Paddison (eds.), *The Pope*, pp. 109–18. See also the comments of M. Bockmuehl, 'Saints' Lives as Exegesis', in Pabst and Paddison (eds.), *The Pope*, pp. 119–33 (120–23).
47. Milbank, 'Foreword', p. xxvii.
48. O.-T. Venard, 'The Prologue of John and Matthew and the Heart of Matthew (John 1.18 and Matthew 12.46–13.58): Does the Jesus of the Synoptic Gospels Really Say Nothing Different from the Prologue of John?', in Pabst and Paddison (eds.), *The Pope*, pp. 134–58 (136).
49. Deines, 'Historical Jesus', p. 206: 'For this position he could have drawn on a number of reputable scholarly positions.'
50. Casey, *Jewish Prophet*. Historical critical problems with Ratzinger's not particularly critical exegesis are raised elsewhere in the Pabst and Paddison volume. Cf. Hays, 'Historiography', p. 115; Bockmuehl, 'Saints' Lives', pp. 122–23.
51. E.g. H. Lindsey, *The Late Great Planet Earth* (Grand Rapids: Zondervan, 1970), e.g. p. 91.
52. A. Paddison, 'Following Jesus with Pope Benedict', in Pabst and Paddison (eds.), *The Pope*, pp. 176–95 (176–77).
53. Milbank, 'Foreword', p. xxvii.
54. Casey, *Jewish Prophet*, pp. 162–78; P. R. Davies, *Whose Bible Is It Anyway?* (Sheffield: Sheffield Academic Press, 1995); J. Berlinerblau, *The Secular Bible: Why Nonbelievers Must Take Religion Seriously* (Cambridge: Cambridge University Press, 2005); M. Casey, 'Who's Afraid of Jesus Christ? Some Comments on Attempts to Write a Life of Jesus', in J. G. Crossley and C. Karner (eds.), *Writing History, Constructing Religion* (Aldershot: Ashgate, 2005), pp. 129–46 (129–30); J. G. Crossley, *Why Christianity Happened: A Sociohistorical Account of Christian Origins* (Louisville: Westminster John Knox, 2006), pp. 1–34; H. Avalos, *The End of Biblical Studies* (Amherst, NY: Prometheus Books, 2007).
55. Milbank, 'Foreword', p. xxviii.
56. A. Reinhartz, 'The Gospel according to Benedict: Jesus of Nazareth and Jews and Judaism', in Pabst and Paddison (eds.), *The Pope*, pp. 233–46; M. Siddiqui, '"Searching for the Face of the Lord" – Hope or Heresy?', in Pabst and Paddison (eds.), *The Pope*, pp. 247–61.
57. Pabst and Paddison, 'Introduction', p. 7.
58. Hays, 'Historiography', p. 113; Bockmuehl, 'Saints' Lives', p. 121.
59. E.g. D. Harvey, *The Condition of Postmodernity* (Oxford: Blackwell, 1989), pp. 83–85; P. Anderson, *The Origins of Postmodernity* (London and New York: Verso, 1998), pp. 104–105. Compare, of course, Arnal, *Symbolic Jesus*, and his thesis on the construction of Jewish identity in Jesus scholarship.
60. Pabst and Paddison, 'Introduction', p. 1.
61. Ratzinger, *Jesus*, pp. 31–33.
62. Ratzinger, *Jesus*, p. 33.
63. Ratzinger, *Jesus*, pp. 198–99.
64. Milbank, 'Foreword', p. xxviii.

Chapter 10

Conclusion: They Know It and They Don't

> We are not aware of this, nevertheless we do it...
>
> – Karl Marx[1]

> ...they know very well what they are doing, but still they are doing it...
>
> – Slavoj Žižek[2]

One purpose of a book like this is to provide a context for future specific case studies on an aspect of Jesus and New Testament scholarship relating to neoliberalism and its cultural wings. We have certainly seen how issues surrounding neoliberalism have had a profound impact on historical Jesus studies over the past forty years. The whole industry has been swept along, like so much in contemporary culture, by neoliberal trends, from the intensification of marketing different Jesuses and Jesus the Great Man to a historical Jesus (or a historical Jesus who did not exist) being fought over in the so-called 'culture wars.' All too often these Jesuses buy into dominant neoliberal trends and contribute to the masking of social realities. Even when some of the scholarship and thinking on Jesus and the Gospels thinks it is opposing dominant political and cultural trends, it can still manage to produce a context utterly complementary to the politics the scholar personally utterly opposes (see chapter 4). By way of analogy with the influence of dominant political trends on previous eras of New Testament studies, none of this ought to be a surprise, but as there remains a relative ignorance in mainstream historical Jesus studies of such historical analysis of its own intellectual history, then this point cannot be made too strongly. Perhaps most pertinently for contemporary mainstream historical Jesus scholarship, we have now seen even further evidence that the scholarly constructions of 'Jesus the Jew' are regularly patronizing constructions maintaining cultural superiority over the Jewish other while also telling us just how 'Jewish' Jesus was. Not only is this trend influenced by political issues surrounding the state of Israel and shifting understandings of Judaism (as I argued in *Jesus in an Age of*

Terror), but it is clearly part of contemporary multicultural thinking on Otherness in 'late' capitalism.

The prominent debates of this past decade, including the failure of the Jesus Project, partly due to a lack of funding, are not only a convenient place to finish because it brings us right up to the present (chapter 6) but it also ends at the global economic crisis of 2008 and its aftermath. Quite what this recession will bring culturally and intellectually remains to be seen of course, but already we are seeing signs of notable political moves which will impact higher education. In the UK, for instance, the Conservative-Liberal Democrat Coalition has not only seized the moment to impose an even more intensified neoliberal agenda, but there is clear evidence that there is a political move (aided by the previous Labour government) to put neoliberalism at the heart of universities, as is already a reality in at least key parts of the American system.

In November 2009, the Independent Review of Higher Education Funding and Student Finance (for English universities) was launched and its results were published in October 2010. It was headed by Lord John Browne, former Group Chief Executive of BP, and its recommendations included removal of the cap on fees and allowing universities theoretically to charge whatever was necessary for undergraduate courses. While the recommendations of the Browne Review were accepted with qualifications (e.g. a cap on fees), the language of the market and education as a commodity is not only clear enough,[3] but also to the point where such language is put forward as being common sense. For instance, the interestingly named 'Core Facts' section included phrases such as the following: 'allowing universities to put quality first and charge accordingly' and 'careers advice in all schools of the kind currently being given in the private sector'.[4] The Browne Review, which obviously had to indicate that this rise in fees will be a wonderful thing, was perfectly open in its use of the language we might associate with neoliberalism: 'The money will follow the student' (p. 6); 'genuine competition for students' (p. 10); 'the increase in employed university graduates accounted for 6% of growth in the private sector... Employing graduates creates innovation, enabling firms to identify and make more effective use of knowledge, ideas and technologies' (p. 16); 'demand led competition' (p. 36); 'institutions will face increased competition. They will compete for students' (p. 51); and, just to show that neoliberalism cannot ultimately avoid state intervention or a bit of Keynesianism, 'targeted investment in priority subjects' (p. 50).[5] In light of the Browne Review, and the Comprehensive Spending Review (i.e. massive cuts to public spending), Universities and Science Minister, David Willetts, added other aspects of neoliberalism with which we should now be familiar. For instance, he praised universities for how they have done 'a lot better in the past few years' in securing funding from businesses.[6] It will be interesting to see the ways in which the popularity of Chomsky, Marx, Foucault, Harvey or, indeed, liberation theologians and plenty of other critics of this frame of reference, is to be accommodated in this ideological model of education.

In every meeting I have attended and every conversation I have with people in universities, and this includes university management, people really do not like the educational values underlying the Browne Review and the Comprehensive Spending Review, are deeply cynical about what the Coalition are doing and openly express their hostility, though I have heard some claim, remarkably, that by going along with it all while defiantly professing our own grand educational ideals against the Coalition we are somehow subverting the system (though this does remind me of subversion in the sense of Eagelton's comments on 'Putting the anus back into *Coriolanus*'). Yet still we all plan for the inevitable, do what is expected of us and are given what looks like no choice. Such is the power of certain forms of ideology coupled with cynicism. If this approach to economics and education (again, already a reality in key parts of the American system) continues in this manner it would suggest that the age of neoliberalism in which we place historical Jesus study *may* well remain an important context for the foreseeable future.

Ending our narrative around the 'secular' controversies surrounding the Jesus Project is also convenient because it brings us to the controversial and widely publicized article by Ronald Hendel published in *Biblical Archaeology Review* concerning the apparent 'battle royal between faith and reason' and with particular reference to the Society of Biblical Literature.[7] SBL even responded to Hendel and invited further reflection by its members.[8] Hendel is part of a growing criticism in biblical studies concerned with the rise of vocal (and even proselytizing) evangelicals and 'fundamentalists' at SBL and calls for a clearer commitment to critical biblical scholarship. While there are those of us with no particular desire to advocate an evangelical position or any position of faith (or none), the constructing of such a stark opponent ends up being important in creating a specific academic identity and perpetuating certain cultural trends.[9]

As we have seen, one function of the constructed extremes, as it is in contemporary politics, is to maintain the credibility of the centre. If we accept the argument that academia is deeply embedded in societal power structures, then such argumentation takes on another dimension: one function of loving to hate the extreme(s) is, as we have seen, to discredit certain challenges to power. In political terms, a cultural function of the far right is not only to make the power of the liberal consensus look respectable but also to discredit challenges to liberal stances on class structure, poverty, foreign policy and so on. To take a relevant but slightly different route, if there is one non-religious figure presently constructed as an extremist it is Hector Avalos. Whatever we may think of his arguments on the 'end of biblical studies', there is at least a challenging core which gets brushed over or deflected in all the uproar and controversy: in one of his critiques of biblical scholarship and the SBL (on the now defunct SBL Forum, as it happens) he raised the issues of class and poverty, claiming in part of his argument that he 'saw scholars nearly trample homeless people while rushing to yet another appointment or session, perhaps one on the supposed prophetic call to help the poor.'[10]

In Hendel's article, we read, 'While the cultured despisers of reason may rejoice – including some postmodernists, feminists and eco-theologians – I find it dispiriting.' There are indeed deep problems with the rise of postmodernity,[11] coupled as it is with a ferocious form of hyper free-market capitalism, and its accompanying irrationalism. However, it is notable that 'some' feminists and eco-theologians have been tied in with this critique. I am not sure what sorts of feminists and eco-theologians Hendel may have in mind, but the critique remains sufficiently general potentially to taint two approaches with oppositional potential, including one which is involved in tackling perhaps the most important issue of our time, climate change. Of course, I may be pushing Hendel's argument and beliefs too far, but without a notable qualification there is not only the obvious distancing but also, rightly or wrongly, a discrediting of views constructed as extreme.

This sort of reasoning obviously makes a certain kind of scholarship normative and, if we were to push strands of the logic, perhaps immune from the political problems famously associated with 'fundamentalism'. In his response to Hendel in the SBL discussion, John van Seters cites (against other uses of the same text) H. D. Betz's 1997 SBL presidential address and the importance of a space where 'critical inquiry can take place' and is to be 'kept free from external interference by religious institutions, political policies, ideologiacl [sic] warfare, and commercial exploitation', adding that this is, in fact, 'the danger in which the SBL now very much finds itself'.[12] Yet, there is a problem *if* this line is pushed too hard, or even taken to one logical conclusion, namely that the ideal centre can apparently avoid these issues, given the right circumstances. However, what might reasonably be called the rational centre in the history of scholarship has long been affected by, and perpetuated, political trends, whether we like it or not, and whether scholars knew it or not. The Nazi Jesus was carried out by learned German professors, developing cultural trends of superiority before them and continued in important (non-fascist) scholarship after which it, in turn, as Shaun Kelley has shown, found its way into liberal (including politically liberal) and mainstream North American Jesus scholarship.[13] Mainstream scholarship has given us the superficially positive 'Jesus the Jew', a figure who is a largely patronizing construct perpetuating superiority over against Judaism. The placing of Jesus in 'the Mediterranean' is supposed to support Jesus' otherness, has sometimes morphed into the (contemporary) 'Arab world' (with all the usual stereotypes) in some high-profile social scientific criticism and yet remains standard work for those referencing the 'context' of Jesus. Further examples have been given throughout this book and the point ought to be clear.

The debate over whether SBL and biblical scholarship can incorporate issues of faith will no doubt continue and the numbers on both sides are sufficiently high that we may not get a 'winner' in the immediate future. But what I would stress is that whichever of these models is taken, it is not going to be likely that the political battles we see in contemporary culture will be so easily avoided. Indeed, if the idea of a more pure and uncorrupted centre were to win through, then we have good reason to believe that political warfare will be perpetuated by more subtle means. And where 'fundamentalist' and evangelical historical Jesus scholars may find the rational liberal centre important in maintaining their credibility, the liberal rational centre may too find that 'fundamentalist' and evangelical historical Jesus scholars are important in maintaining their cultural value and intellectual credibility.[14] Maybe we are really dealing with a love that dare not speak its name...?

But any arguments concerning the perpetuation of neoliberalism, and its numerous cultural offshoots, should not necessarily equal inevitability. One general historical point may prove to be particularly crucial: again, the 2008 recession. The longer-term effects of 2008 are only just starting to become apparent and we may not be able to establish a full political, economic, social, intellectual and cultural impact for many years yet. At the risk of pushing a historical analogy too far, the impact of economic crises in the early 1970s, as we saw, helped bring about political, economic, social, intellectual and cultural changes and the major recession of 2008 may contribute similarly significant changes.

We are already starting to see some serious reactions across different continents, as well as countering tendencies among those suggesting the cure for a crisis in neoliberalism is more neoliberalism. So, for instance, the Thatcheresque rhetoric of 'there's no alternative' coming from neoliberal advocates (even if they may not like the label) such as David Cameron, George Osborne and Nick Clegg may well have worked its ways throughout Britain, even among those set to lose jobs, because of the apparent need for 'austerity measures.' Yet there is, unsurprisingly perhaps, plenty of resistance. Even before the government cuts really begin to have a more widespread impact on employment in the UK, 26 March 2011 saw 500,000 people gather in London under the heading 'March for the Alternative.' Already gaining some profile is the direct action group, UK Uncut, targeting corporate tax avoidance and banks through peaceful occupations of high-street shops and banks. British students have apparently been transformed from a perceived state of apathy to angry demonstrators against changes in educations, especially against the imminent £9,000 per year fee/tax/debt for most future university students and the cutting of the Educational Maintenance Allowance for 16–19 year-olds. Such trends are visible internationally. In Wisconsin, and tied in with the 'austerity' fallout from 2008, the attack led by Republican Governor Scott Walker on the collective bargaining of public sector unions has led to high-profile extended protests. In North Africa and the Middle East, what seems to be a complex combination of socio-economic factors has led to some remarkable uprisings against Western-backed dictators. And we could continue with examples of reactions from Greece to Latin America.

While the specific connections between unrest in, say, Cairo and London can be overdone, the international connections between private and state power, and their various client rulers, along with the impact on populations, are clearer when we accept a broader and interconnected global economic picture. Western powers were previously supporters of Mubarak and Gaddafi and, at the time of writing, the Saudis remain apparently integral to geo-political strategies. But key actors in response are also making the connections. From the heart of the Egyptian uprising, Kamal Abbas and the Centre for Trade Unions and Workers Services sent a message of solidarity to the workers of Wisconsin, claiming 'As our just struggle for freedom, democracy and justice succeeded, your struggle will succeed.'[15] As Noam Chomsky notes, 'The two are closely intertwined. Labor movements have been in the forefront of protecting democracy and human rights and expanding their domains, a primary reason why they are the bane of systems of power, both state and private.'[16] Of course, all of the above are reactions to specific cases, but in basic and general terms we can say that the neoliberal consensus, at least in Anglo-American terms, is facing challenges.

But despite these upheavals and reactions, this does not mean the neoliberal order is going to crumble and, to hark back to the Introduction, dominant powers and discourses have the capacity to absorb and reassert. At the time of writing, Cameron's neoliberal agenda continues, Western powers have managed yet again to make claims for humanitarian concern by switching sides away from once-favoured dictators in a matter of just weeks and thus remain intimately involved, and Walker has hardly rolled over in Wisconsin. But with such challenges emerging, there is no inevitability about the march of neoliberalism, at least in its current configurations, in the upcoming decades. There is still much to play for.

Notes

1. K. Marx, *Capital: A Critical Analysis of Capital Production: Volume 1* (London: Lawrence and Wishart, 1974), pp. 78-79.
2. S. Žižek, *The Sublime Object of Ideology* (London and New York: Verso, 1989), p. 29.
3. S. Collini, 'Browne's Gamble', *London Review of Books* 32 (4 November, 2010), pp. 23–25.
4. http://hereview.independent.gov.uk/hereview/.
5. J. Browne et al., *Securing a Sustainable Future for Higher Education: An Independent Review of Higher Education and Funding and Student Finance* (12 October, 2010), http://www.bis.gov.uk/assets/biscore/corporate/docs/s/10-1208-securing-sustainable-higher-education-browne-report.pdf.
6. The full footage is available at http://news.bbc.co.uk/democracylive/hi/house_of_commons/newsid_9124000/9124299.stm.
7. R. Hendel, 'Farewell to SBL: Faith and Reason in Biblical Studies', *BAR* 36 (July/August, 2010), http://www.bib-arch.org/bar/article.asp?PubID=BSBA&Volume=36&Issue=4&ArticleID=9.
8. http://www.sbl-site.org/membership/farewell.aspx.
9. The following appeared in slightly different form as J. G. Crossley, 'Does the Centre Need an Extreme?', *Bible and Interpretation* (May 2010), http://www.bibleinterp.com/opeds/centre357929.shtml.
10. H. Avalos, 'The Ideology of the Society of Biblical Literature and the Demise of an Academic Profession', SBL Forum April, 2006, http://www.sbl-site.org/

publications/article.aspx?articleId=520. This includes links to the responses to Avalos.

11. Given my explicit criticisms of things postmodern in Crossley, 'Centre', I have to admit to being a little confused by what Hendel means in his suggestion that my article uses 'postmodern strategies'. See R. Hendel, 'Knowledge and Power in Biblical Scholarship', *Bible and Interpretation* (June, 2010), http://www.bibleinterp.com/articles/know357930.shtml.
12. http://www.sbl-site.org/membership/farewell.aspx.
13. S. Kelley, *Racializing Jesus: Race, Ideology and the Formation of Modern Biblical Scholarship* (London and New York: Routledge, 2002).
14. Again, on the overtly politicized variants of arguments concerning the construction of extremes and fanaticism see A. Toscano, *Fanaticism: On Uses of an Idea* (London and New York: Verso, 2010).
15. K. Abbas, '"We Stand with You as You Stood with Us": Statement to Workers of Wisconsin by Kamal Abbas of Egypt's Centre for Trade Unions and Workers Services' (20 February, 2011), http://www.michaelmoore.com/words/must-read/statement-kamal-abbas.
16. N. Chomsky, 'The Cairo–Madison Connection', *ZSpace* (11 March, 2011), http://www.zcommunications.org/the-cairo-madison-connection-by-noam-chomsky.

Bibliography

Abbas, K., '"We Stand with You as You Stood with Us": Statement to Workers of Wisconsin by Kamal Abbas of Egypt's Centre for Trade Unions and Workers Services' (20 February, 2011), http://www.michaelmoore.com/words/must-read/statement-kamal-abbas.

Abu el-Haj, N., *Facts on the Ground: Archaeological Practice and Territorial Self-Fashioning in Israeli Society* (Chicago and London: University of Chicago Press, 2001).

Achcar, G., *The Clash of Barbarisms: September 11 and the New World Disorder* (London: Saqi, 2006).

Adams, E., *The Stars Will Fall from Heaven: Cosmic Catastrophe and the World's End in the New Testament and Its World* (London: T&T Clark/Continuum, 2007).

Adorno, T. W., *The Stars Down to Earth and Other Essays* (London: Routledge, 2001).

Allison, D. C., 'Eschatology', in J. B. Green, S. McKnight and I. H. Marshall (eds.), *Dictionary of Jesus and the Gospels* (Downers Grove and Leicester: IVP, 1992), pp. 206–209.

— *Resurrecting Jesus: The Earliest Christian Tradition and its Interpreters* (London and New York: Continuum, 2005).

— *The Historical Christ and the Theological Jesus* (Grand Rapids: Eerdmans, 2009).

— *Constructing Jesus: Memory, Imagination, and History* (Grand Rapids: Baker, 2010).

Amis, M., 'The Voice of the Lonely Crowd', *Guardian* (1 June, 2002).

— 'The Age of Horrorism', *Observer* (10 September, 2006).

Anderson, P., *The Origins of Postmodernity* (London and New York: Verso, 1998).

Anderson, P. N., *The Fourth Gospel and the Quest for Jesus: Modern Foundations Reconsidered* (London: T&T Clark, 2006).

— 'Why This Study Is Needed, and Why It Is Needed Now', in Anderson, Just and Thatcher (eds.), *John, Jesus, and History*, I, pp. 13–73.

— 'Das "John-, Jesus-, and History"-Projekt. Neue Beobachtungen zu Jesus und eine Bi-optische Hypothese', *ZNT* 23 (2009), pp. 12–26.

— 'The John, Jesus, and History Project – New Glimpses of Jesus and a Bi-Optic Hypothesis', *Bible and Interpretation* (February, 2010), http://www.bibleinterp.com/articles/john1357917.shtml.

— 'A Fourth Quest for Jesus... So What, and How So?', *Bible and Interpretation* (July, 2010), http://www.bibleinterp.com/opeds/fourth357921.shtml#sdfootnote4sym.

Anderson, P. N., F. Just, and T. Thatcher (eds.), *John, Jesus, and History*. I. *Critical Appraisals of Critical Views* (Atlanta: SBL, 2007).

— (eds.), *John, Jesus, and History. II. Aspects of Historicity in the Fourth Gospel* (Atlanta: SBL, 2009).
Anonymous, 'Author Interview: N. T. Wright', InterVarsity Press, http://www.ivpress.com/spotlight/2200.php.
Anonymous, 'Editorial: Britain's Budget Pain', *New York Times* (8 July, 2010), http://www.nytimes.com/2010/07/09/opinion/09fri1.html.
Anonymous, 'International Response to the Bush Declaration on the Palestinian Right to Return', *Al Awda* (April, 2004), http://al-awda.org/bush-declaration.html.
Anonymous, 'Complete List of Biblioblogs', *Biblioblog Top 50* (Undated) http://biblioblogtop50.wordpress.com/biblioblogs/.
Arnal, W., *The Symbolic Jesus: Historical Scholarship, Judaism and the Construction of Contemporary Identity* (London and Oakville: Equinox, 2005).
— 'A Parting of the Ways? Scholarly Identities and a Peculiar Species of Ancient Mediterranean Religion', in Z. A. Crook and P. A. Harland (eds.), *Identity and Interaction in the Ancient Mediterranean: Jews, Christians and Others: Essays in Honour of Stephen G. Wilson* (Sheffield: Sheffield Phoenix Press, 2007), pp. 253–75.
Avalos, H., 'The Ideology of the Society of Biblical Literature and the Demise of an Academic Profession', *SBL Forum* (April, 2006), http://sbl-site.org/Article.aspx?ArticleID=520.
— *The End of Biblical Studies* (Amherst, NY: Prometheus Books, 2007).
Bach, A., 'Bush's Bible: A Wild Beast Loosed upon the World', *Postscripts* 2 (2006), pp. 109–25.
Badiou, A., *Saint Paul: The Foundation of Universalism* (Stanford: Stanford University Press, 2003).
— *The Meaning of Sarkozy* (London and New York: Verso, 2008).
Bailey, S., 'Satan Is Pat Robertson's Theological Mentor', Scotteriology (14 January, 2010), http://scotteriology.wordpress.com/2010/01/14/satan-is-pat-robertsons-theological-mentor/.
Bakunin, M., *Selected Works* (New York: Alfred A. Knopf, 1972).
Bammel, E., and C. F. D. Moule (eds.), *Jesus and the Politics of His Day* (Cambridge: Cambridge University Press, 1984).
Barnett, P., *Finding the Historical Christ: After Jesus Volume Three* (Grand Rapids: Eerdmans, 2009).
Barton, S. C., 'Historical Criticism and Social-Scientific Perspectives in New Testament Study', in J. B. Green (ed.), *Hearing the New Testament: Strategies for Interpretation* (Grand Rapids: Eerdmans, 1995), pp. 61–89.
Bauckham, R., *Gospel Women: Studies of the Named Women in the Gospels* (Edinburgh: T&T Clark, 2002).
— *Jesus and the Eyewitnesses: The Gospels as Eyewitness Testimony* (Grand Rapids: Eerdmans, 2006).
— *The Testimony of the Beloved Disciple: Narrative, History and Theology in the Gospel of John* (Grand Rapids: Baker, 2007).
Beattie, T., *The New Atheists: The Twilight of Reason and the War on Religion* (London: Darton Longman and Todd, 2007).
Berlinerblau, J., *The Secular Bible: Why Nonbelievers Must Take Religion Seriously* (Cambridge: Cambridge University Press, 2005).

— *Thumpin' It: The Use and Abuse of the Bible in Today's Presidential Politics* (Louisville: Westminster John Knox, 2008).

Ben-Amos, D., 'Obituary: Raphael Patai (1910–1996)', *Journal of American Folklore* 110 (1997), pp. 314–16.

Bermejo Rubio, F., 'The Fiction of the "Three Quests": An Argument for Dismantling a Dubious Historiographical Paradigm', *JSHJ* 7 (2009), pp. 211–53.

Bird, M. F., 'The Peril of Modernizing Jesus and the Crisis of Not Contemporizing the Christ', *Evangelical Quarterly* 78 (2006), pp. 291–312.

— 'On Writing (1): Finding Time to Write', *Euangelion* (1 February, 2007), http://euangelizomai.blogspot.com/2007/02/on-writing-1-finding-time-to-write.html.

Bird M. F., and J. G. Crossley, *How Did Christianity Begin? A Believer and Non-believer Examine the Evidence* (London: SPCK, 2008).

Blanton, W., *Displacing Christian Origins: Philosophy, Secularity, and the New Testament* (Chicago: University of Chicago Press, 2007).

— 'Neither Religious nor Secular: On Saving the Critic in Biblical-Criticism', in Boer (ed.), *Secularism and Biblical Studies*, pp. 141–61.

Blomberg, C., 'Review of Ratzinger, *Jesus of Nazareth*', *Denver Journal* 10 (August, 2007), http://www.denverseminary.edu/article/jesus-of-nazareth-from-the-baptism-in-the-jordan-to-the-transfiguration/.

Blond, P., 'Red Tory', in J. Cruddas and J. Rutherford (eds.), *Is the Future Conservative?* (London: Lawrence & Wishart, 2008), pp. 79–90.

— 'The True Tory Progressives', *Guardian* (30 May, 2008).

— 'David Cameron's "Philosopher King" Explains How His Party Will Help Those Betrayed by Labour', *Daily Mail* (13 October 2009).

— *Red Tory: How Left and Right Have Broken Britain and How We Can Fix It* (London: Faber and Faber, 2010).

Blond, P., and A. Pabst, 'The Roots of Islamic Terrorism', *New York Times* (28 July, 2005).

— 'Integrating Islam into the West', *New York Times* (4 November, 2008).

Blond, P., and J. Milbank, 'No Equality in Opportunity', *Guardian* (27 January, 2010).

Bock, D. L., 'Some Christians See a "Road Map" to End Times', *Los Angeles Times* (18 June, 2003).

Bock, D. L., and D. B. Wallace, *Dethroning Jesus: Exposing Popular Culture's Quest to Unseat the Biblical Christ* (Nashville: Thomas Nelson, 2007).

Bockmuehl, M., *Jewish Law in Gentile Churches: Halakhah and the Beginning of Christian Public Ethics* (Edinburgh: T&T Clark, 2000).

— 'Review of Malina, *New Testament World*, third edition', *BMCR* (19 April, 2002), available at http://ccat.sas.upenn.edu/bmcr/2002/2002-04-19.html.

— 'God's Life as a Jew: Remembering the Son of God as Son of David', in B. R. Gaventa and R. B. Hays (eds.), *Seeking the Identity of Jesus: A Pilgrimage* (Grand Rapids/Cambridge: Eerdmans, 2008), pp. 60–78.

— 'Saints' Lives as Exegesis', in Pabst and Paddison (eds.), *The Pope*, pp. 119–33.

Boer, R., 'An Intrinsic Eagleton?', *JCRT* 9.1 (2008), pp. 1–17.

— 'Tag: Haiti', Stalin's Moustache (January 2010), http://stalinsmoustache.wordpress.com/tag/haiti/.

— 'SBL Censorship: "Sausage-fests" Are Unacceptable', Stalin's Moustache (23 October, 2010), http://stalinsmoustache.wordpress.com/2010/10/23/sbl-censorship-sausage-fests-are-unacceptable/.

— 'Why Does the SBL Not Like Sausages or Sausage-fests? Or, How to Deal with Censorship', Stalin's Moustache (23 October, 2010), http://stalinsmoustache.wordpress.com/2010/10/23/why-does-the-sbl-not-like-sausages-or-sausage-fests-or-how-to-deal-with-censorship/.
Boer, R. (ed.), *Secularism and Biblical Studies* (London and Oakville: Equinox, 2010).
Boer, R., and A. Andrews, 'Thin Economics; Thick Moralising: Red Toryism and the Politics of Nostalgia', *Bulletin for the Study of Religion* 40 (2011), pp. 16–24.
Bornkamm, G., *Jesus of Nazareth* (London: Hodder & Stroughton, 1960).
Brandon, S. G. F., *Jesus and the Zealots: A Study of the Political Factor in Primitive Christianity* (Manchester: Manchester University Press, 1967).
— *The Trial of Jesus of Nazareth* (London: B. T. Batsford, 1968).
Braudel, F., *The Mediterranean and the Mediterranean World in the Age of Philip II* (3 vols.; London: Collins, 1972–73).
Brooker, C., *Newswipe*, episode 3, first aired 2 February, 2010 (BBC/Zeppotron), available at http://www.youtube.com/watch?v=0cNsxTfyVEo.
Brooks, D., 'The Underlying Tragedy', *New York Times* (14 January, 2010).
Brown, A., 'Gospel according to Powell: Christ Was Stoned to Death', *Independent* (16 August, 1994).
Brown, K., 'Biblioblog Top 10 Most Influential Authors and Books', C. Orthodoxy (20 June, 2009), http://corthodoxy.wordpress.com/2009/06/20/biblioblog-top-10-most-influential-authors-and-books/.
Brown, W., *Regulating Aversion: Tolerance in the Age of Identity and Empire* (Princeton: Princeton University Press, 2006).
Browne, J., et al., *Securing a Sustainable Future for Higher Education: An Independent Review of Higher Education and Funding and Student Finance* (12 October, 2010), http://www.bis.gov.uk/assets/biscore/corporate/docs/s/10-1208-securing-sustainable-higher-education-browne-report.pdf.
Burke, P., 'History of Events and the Revival of the Narrative', in P. Burke (ed.), *New Perspectives on History Writing* (London: Polity, 2nd edn, 2001), pp. 283–300.
Burkeman, O., 'Mulled Whine', *Guardian* (12 December, 2006).
Cameron, D., 'Time to Be Counted', *Guardian* (17 March, 2003).
Carlin, B., 'Setback for Cameron as Senior Conservatives Revolt against Shaven-headed "10-year-old" Image Supremo', *Daily Mail* (3 January, 2010).
Carlson, S. C., 'Sans-Biblioblogue?', Hypotyposeis (25 November, 2005), http://www.hypotyposeis.org/weblog/2005/11/sans-biblioblogue.html.
— 'Ethical Considerations relating to Pseudonymous Biblioblogging', Hypotyposeis (14 February, 2009), http://www.hypotyposeis.org/weblog/2009/02/ethical-considerations-relating-to.html.
Carlyle, T., *On Heroes and Hero-Worship and the Heroic in History* (Berkeley: University of California, 1993).
Carr, E. H., *What Is History?* (London: Penguin, 2nd edn, 1987).
Carrier, R. C., 'Amherst Conference', Richard Carrier Blogs (January 10, 2009), http://richardcarrier.blogspot.com/2009/01/amherst-conference.html.
— 'Bayes's Theorem for Beginners: Formal Logic and Its Relevance to Historical Method', in Hoffmann (ed.), *Sources of the Jesus Tradition*, pp. 81–107.
Casey, M., *From Jewish Prophet to Gentile God: The Origins of New Testament Christology* (Louisville: Westminster John Knox, 1991).

— 'Where Wright is Wrong: A Critical Review of N.T. Wright's *Jesus and the Victory of God*', *JSNT* 69 (1998), pp. 95–103.

— 'Some Anti-Semitic Assumptions in *The Theological Dictionary of the New Testament*', *NovT* 41 (1999), pp. 280–91.

— 'Who's Afraid of Jesus Christ? Some Comments on Attempts to Write a Life of Jesus', in J. G. Crossley and C. Karner (eds.), *Writing History, Constructing Religion* (Aldershot: Ashgate, 2005), pp. 129–46.

— *Jesus of Nazareth: An Independent Historian's Account of His Life and Teachings* (London and New York: T&T Clark, 2010).

Caulkin, G., 'Darren Bent in Foul-mouthed Twitter Controversy', *Times* (31 July, 2009).

Cavanaugh, W. T., *The Myth of Religious Violence: Secular Ideology and the Roots of Modern Conflict* (Oxford: Oxford University Press, 2009).

Chilton, B. D., *A Feast of Meanings: Eucharistic Theologies from Jesus through Johannine Circles* (Leiden: Brill, 1994).

— *Rabbi Jesus: An Intimate Biography* (New York: Doubleday, 2000).

— 'Moral Proportion and the Role of Churches in the Israel–Gaza War', Christians for a Fair Witness on the Middle East (January, 2009), http://christianfairwitness.com/writings/chilton-january2009.html.

— 'Plus ça change... "The Jesus Seminar" and "The Jesus Project"', *Bible and Interpretation* (January, 2009), http://www.bibleinterp.com/articles/chilton1.shtml.

Chomsky, N., *Media Control: The Spectacular Achievements of Propaganda* (New York: Seven Stories Press, 2nd edn, 2002).

— *Understanding Power* (New York: New Press, 2002).

— '2004 Elections', *ZNet* (29 November, 2004), http://www.zcommunications.org/2004-elections-by-noam-chomsky.

— *What We Say Goes: Conversations on U.S. Power in a Changing World* (New York: Metropolitan, 2007).

— 'Noam Chomsky on 1968', *New Statesman* (8 May, 2008), http://www.newstatesman.com/politics/2008/05/iraq-war-chomsky-1968-vietnam.

— 'Haiti Post-Earthquake', *ZCommunications* (11 March, 2010), http://www.zcommunications.org/haiti-post-earthquake-by-noam-chomsky.

— 'The Cairo-Madison Connection', *Z Space* (11 March, 2011), http://www.zcommunications.org/the-cairo-madison-connection-by-noam-chomsky.

Chomsky, N., and G. Achcar, *Perilous Power: The Middle East and U.S. Foreign Policy* (Boulder and London: Paradigm Publishers, 2007).

Collini, S., 'Browne's Gamble', *London Review of Books* 32 (4 November, 2010), pp. 23–25.

Coombs, N., 'The Red Tories' True Colours', *Guardian* (4 November, 2009).

— 'The Political Theology of Red Toryism', PSA Annual Conference, Edinburgh, 31 March–1 April, 2010, pp. 1–15, http://www.psa.ac.uk/journals/pdf/5/2010/1296_1499.pdf.

Crook, Z. A., 'Honor, Shame, and Social Status Revisited', *JBL* 128 (2009), pp. 591–612.

Crook, Z. A., and P. A. Harland (eds.), *Identity and Interaction in the Ancient Mediterranean: Jews, Christians and Others: Essays in Honour of Stephen G. Wilson* (Sheffield: Sheffield Phoenix Press, 2007).

Crossan, J. D., *The Historical Jesus: The Life of a Mediterranean Jewish Peasant* (San Francisco: HarperCollins; Edinburgh: T&T Clark, 1991) .
— *Jesus: A Revolutionary Biography* (San Francisco: HarperCollins, 1994).
— *The Birth of Christianity. Discovering What Happened in the Years Immediately after the Execution of Jesus* (New York: HarperCollins; Edinburgh: T&T Clark, 1998).
— *A Long Way from Tipperary* (San Francisco: HarperSanFrancisco, 2000).
Crossan, J. D., and J. L. Reed, *Excavating Jesus: Beneath the Stones, behind the Texts* (New York: HarperCollins; London: SPCK, 2001).
Crossley, J. G., 'Politics, Secularism and New Testament Studies', Earliest Christian History (19 May, 2006), http://earliestchristianhistory.blogspot.com/2006/05/politics-secularism-new-testament.html.
— *Why Christianity Happened: A Sociohistorical Account of Christian Origins 26–50CE* (Louisville: Westminster John Knox, 2006).
— *Jesus in an Age of Terror: Scholarly Projects for a New American Century* (London and Oakville: Equinox, 2008).
— 'Once Again on the Historical Jesus, Who Is Deciding Jewish Identity?', Earliest Christian History (21 December, 2008), http://earliestchristianhistory.blogspot.com/2008/12/once-again-on-historical-jesus-who-is.html.
— 'Starting Points and the Attack on Gaza', Earliest Christian History (9 January, 2009), http://earliestchristianhistory.blogspot.com/2009/01/starting-points-and-attack-on-gaza.html.
— 'Fishing-gate', Earliest Christian History (3 February, 2009), http://earliestchristianhistory.blogspot.com/2009/02/fishing-gate.html.
— 'John Hobbins, Jesus in an Age of Terror and Imperialism', Earliest Christian History (23 March, 2009), http://earliestchristianhistory.blogspot.com/2009/03/john-hobbins-jesus-in-age-of-terror-and.html.
— 'Writing about the Historical Jesus: Historical Explanation and "the Big Why Questions", or Antiquarian Empiricism and Victorian Tomes?', *Journal for the Study of the Historical Jesus* 7 (2009), pp. 63–90.
— 'Jesus the Jew since 1967', in H. Moxnes, W. Blanton and J. G. Crossley (eds.), *Jesus beyond Nationalism: Constructing the Historical Jesus in a Period of Cultural Complexity* (London and Oakville: Equinox, 2009), pp. 111–29.
— 'Does the Centre Need an Extreme?', *Bible and Interpretation* (May 2010), http://www.bibleinterp.com/opeds/centre357929.shtml.
— 'N. T. Wrong and the Bibliobloggers', *Bible and Critical Theory* 6.1 (2010), pp. 1–15.
— 'Biblioblogging, "Religion", and the Manufacturing of Catastrophe', *Bulletin for the Study of Religion* 39 (2010), pp. 23–29.
— *Reading the New Testament: Contemporary Approaches* (London and New York: Routledge, 2010).
— 'Jesus and the Law: Taking E. P. Sanders to Some Logical Conclusions', in R. L. Webb and M. S. Goodacre (eds.), *Jesus as Restoration Prophet: Engaging the Work of E.P. Sanders* (London and New York: Continuum/T&T Clark, forthcoming).
— 'Can John's Gospel Really Be Used to Reconstruct a Life of Jesus? An Assessment of Recent Trends and a Defence of a Traditional View', in T. L. Thompson and T. S. Verenna (eds.), *'Is This Not the Carpenter?' The Question of the Historicity of the Figure of Jesus* (Sheffield and Oakville: Equinox, 2011, forthcoming).

— 'Enoch Powell and the Gospel Tradition: A Search for a Homeland', in K. W. Whitelam and H. Moxnes (eds.), *Holy Land as Homeland? Models for Constructing the Historic Landscapes of Jesus* (Sheffield: Sheffield Phoenix Press, forthcoming).

— 'Manufacturing Resurrection: Locating Some Contemporary Scholarly Arguments', *Neot.* 45 (2011), pp. 50–76.

Crossley, J. G., and C. Karner (eds.), *Writing History, Constructing Religion* (Aldershot: Ashgate, 2005).

Csillag, T., 'For Scholars, a Combustible Question: Was Christ Real?', *Toronto Star* (27 December, 2008), http://www.thestar.com/News/Ideas/article/55754.

Caulkin, G., 'Darren Bent in Foul-mouthed Twitter Controversy', *Times* (31 July, 2009).

Cullmann, O., *Jesus and the Revolutionaries* (New York: Harper Row, 1970).

Darnton, R., *The Great Cat Massacre and Other Episodes in French Cultural History* (London: Allen Lane, 1984).

Davies, P. R., *Whose Bible Is It Anyway?* (Sheffield: Sheffield Academic Press, 2nd edn, 2004).

Davis, M., *Planet of Slums* (London and New York: Verso, 2006).

Dawkins, R., 'Religion's Misguided Missiles', *Guardian* (15 September, 2001).

DeConick, A., 'My Decision about the Jesus Project', The Forbidden Gospels Blog (5 February, 2009), http://forbiddengospels.blogspot.com/2009/02/my-decision-about-jesus-project.html.

— 'Tragedy in Haiti', The Forbidden Gospels Blog (January, 2010), http://forbiddengospels.blogspot.com/2010/01/tragedy-in-haiti.html.

Deines, R., 'Can the "Real" Jesus be Indentified with the Historical Jesus? A Review of the Pope's Challenge to Biblical Scholarship and the Ongoing Debate', in Pabst and Paddison (eds.), *The Pope*, pp. 199–232.

Denton, D. L., *Historiography and Hermeneutics in Jesus Studies: An Examination of the Work of John Dominic Crossan and Ben F. Meyer* (London and New York: T&T Clark/Continuum, 2004).

Dillon, M., and J. Reid, *The Liberal Way of War: Killing to Make Life Live* (New York and London: Routledge, 2009) .

Eagleton, T., 'Awakening from Modernity', *Times Literary Supplement* (20 February, 1987).

— *Ideology: An Introduction* (London and New York, Verso, 1991; updated version, 2007).

— *The Illusions of Postmodernism* (Oxford: Blackwell, 1996).

— 'Lunging, Flailing, Mispunching', *London Review of Books* 28.20 (October, 2006).

— *Terry Eagleton Presents Jesus Christ: The Gospels* (London: Verso, 2007).

— 'Was Jesus Christ a Revolutionary?', *New Internationalist* 411 (1 May, 2008).

— *Reason, Faith, and Revolution: Reflections on the God Debate* (New Haven and London: Yale University Press, 2009).

Ehrman, B. D., *Jesus: Apocalyptic Prophet of the New Millennium* (Oxford: Oxford University Press, 1999).

— *Misquoting Jesus: The Story behind Who Changed the Bible and Why* (New York: HarperOne, 2005).

— *Jesus, Interrupted: Revealing the Hidden Contradictions in the Bible (and Why We Don't Know about Them)* (New York: HarperOne, 2009).

Elkind, P., 'The Trouble with Steve Jobs', CNN Money (5 March, 2008) http://money.cnn.com/2008/03/02/news/companies/elkind_jobs.fortune/index.htm.
Elliott, J. H., 'Jesus the Israelite Was Neither a "Jew" nor a "Christian": On Correcting Misleading Nomenclature', *JSHJ* 5 (2007), pp. 119–54.
Engels, F., 'On the History of Earliest Christianity (1894)', in K. Marx and F. Engels, *Collected Works Volume 27, Engels: 1890–95* (London: Lawrence & Wishart, 1990), pp. 447–69.
Evans, C. A., *Fabricating Jesus: How Modern Scholars Distort the Gospels* (Nottingham: IVP, 2007).
Evans, R. J., *In Defence of History* (London: Granta, 2nd edn, 2000).
Felipe Pondé, L., 'An Interview with John Milbank and Conor Cunningham', in C. Cunningham and P. M. Chandler (eds.), *Belief and Metaphysics* (London: SCM, 2007), pp. 501–27.
Fiorenza, E. S., *In Memory of Her: A Feminist Theological Reconstruction of Christian Origins* (London: SCM, 2nd edn, 1994).
Fiorenza, E. S., *Jesus and the Politics of Interpretation* (New York and London: Continuum, 2000).
Fisk, R., 'Why Bombing Ashkelon Is the Most Tragic Irony', *Independent* (30 December, 2008).
— 'Why Do They Hate the West So Much, We Will Ask', *Independent* (7 January, 2009).
Fitzgerald, T., *Discourse on Civility and Barbarity: A Critical History of Religion and Related Categories* (Oxford: Oxford University Press, 2007).
Fox, M. V., 'Bible Scholarship and Faith-Based Study: My View', *SBL Forum*, http://sbl-site.org/Article.aspx?ArticleID=490.
Freedland, J., 'The Innocent Smoothies of Politics Are Still the Party of the Rich', *Guardian* (9 March, 2010).
Funk, R. W., 'The Watershed of the American Biblical Tradition: The Chicago School, First Phase, 1892–1920', *JBL* 95 (1976), pp. 4–22.
— *Honest to Jesus: Jesus for a New Millennium* (San Francisco: HarperSanFrancisco, 1996).
Funk, R. W., R. W. Hoover and the Jesus Seminar, *The Five Gospels: The Search for the Authentic Words of Jesus* (New York: Schribner, 1993).
Galbraith, D., 'John Milbank's Atavistic Orthodoxy', *Religion Bulletin* (6 September 2010), http://religionbulletin.wordpress.com/2010/09/06/john-milbanks-atavistic-orthodoxy/.
— 'Did Jesus Rise from the Dead? Casey on Jesus (5) – Did Jesus Consider Himself to Be "The Son of Man"?', *Remnant of Giants* (21 April, 2011), http://remnantofgiants.wordpress.com/2011/04/21/caseys-jesus-5-son-of-man/.
— 'Did Jesus Rise from the Dead? Casey on Jesus (7) – Visionary Experiences of Jesus' Resurrection', *Remnant of Giants* (23 April, 2011), http://remnantofgiants.wordpress.com/2011/04/23/caseys-jesus-7-visions-of-jesus-resurrection/.
Georgi, D., 'The Interest in Life of Jesus Theology as a Paradigm to the Social History of Biblical Criticism', *HTR* 85 (1992), pp. 51–83.
Godfrey, N., 'Chomsky, Crossley and the betrayal of an independent approach to historical Jesus studies', *Vridar* (21 April, 2010), http://vridar.wordpress.com/2010/04/21/chomsky-crossley-and-the-betrayal-of-an-independent-approach-to-historical-jesus-studies/.

Goodacre, M., 'Biblioblogging Top 50 for January and Other Wrongs', NT Blog (3 February, 2009), http://ntweblog.blogspot.com/2009/02/biblioblogging-top-50-for-january-and.html.

— 'N T Wrong: Transmission Cut?', NT Blog (17 February, 2009), http://ntweblog.blogspot.com/2009/02/n-t-wrong-transmission-cut.html.

Gove, M., 'I Can't Fight My Feelings Any More: I Love Tony', *Times* (25 February, 2003).

Gregory, D., *The Colonial Present: Afghanistan, Palestine, Iraq* (Oxford: Blackwell, 2004).

Green, J., 'Scholars to Debate if Jesus Existed', *Ottawa Citizen* (10 January, 2007 [sic?]), http://www2.canada.com/ottawacitizen/news/story.html?id=f659e6b0-913b-4032-9264-52f1831d345f&k=92094.

— 'Why Can't We Ask If Jesus Existed?', *Ottawa Citizen* (6 December, 2008), http://communities.canada.com/ottawacitizen/blogs/meaning/archive/2008/12/06/why-can-t-we-ask-if-jesus-existed.aspx.

Grice, A., 'Sir Gus O'Donnell: "People Make Better Policy Advisers if They Have Been on the Front Line"', *Independent* (19 December, 2005).

Haggerty, K. D., and R. V. Ericson (eds.), *The New Politics of Surveillance and Visibility* (Toronto and London: University of Toronto Press, 2006).

Hallward, P., 'Our Role in Haiti's Plight', *Guardian* (13 January, 2010).

Hardt, M. and A. Negri, *Empire* (Cambridge, MA and London: Harvard University Press, 2000).

— *Associations, Synagogues, and Congregations: Claiming a Place in Ancient Mediterranean Society* (Minneapolis: Fortress, 2003).

— 'Spheres of Contention, Claims of Pre-eminence: Rivalries among Associations in Sardis and Smyrna', in R. S. Ascough (ed.), *Religious Rivalries and the Struggle for Success in Sardis and Smyrna* (Waterloo: Wilfrid Laurier University Press, 2005), pp. 53–63, 259–62 .

— *The Dynamics of Identity in the World of the Early Christians* (London and New York: T&T Clark/Continuum, 2009).

Harris, S., *The End of Faith: Religion, Terror, and the Future of Reason* (London: Simon & Schuster, 2004).

Harvey, D., *The Condition of Postmodernity* (Oxford: Blackwell, 1989).

— *The New Imperialism* (Oxford: Oxford University Press, 2003).

— *A Brief History of Neoliberalism* (Oxford: Oxford University Press, 2005).

— *The Enigma of Capital and the Crises of Capitalism* (London: Profile Books, 2010).

Hays, R. B., 'Ratzinger's Johannine Jesus: A Challenge to Enlightenment Historiography', in Pabst and Paddison (eds.), *The Pope*, pp. 109–18.

Head, P., 'The Nazi Quest for an Ayrian Jesus', *JSHJ* 2 (2004), pp. 55–89.

Hendel, R., 'Knowledge and Power in Biblical Scholarship', *Bible and Interpretation* (June, 2010), http://www.bibleinterp.com/articles/know357930.shtml.

Hendel, R., 'Farewell to SBL: Faith and Reason in Biblical Studies', *BAR* 36 (July/August, 2010), http://www.bib-arch.org/bar/article.asp?PubID=BSBA&Volume=36&Issue=4&ArticleID=9.

Heffer, S., *Like the Roman: The Life of Enoch Powell* (London: Weidenfeld & Nicolson, 1998).

Hengel, M., *Was Jesus a Revolutionist?* (Philadelphia: Fortress, 1971).

— *The Charismatic Leader and His Followers* (Edinburgh: T&T Clark, 1981).

Herman, E., 'Christopher Hitchens and the Uses of Demagoguery', *ZMag* (September 22, 2002), http://www.zmag.org/znet/viewArticle/11646.
Herman, E. S., and N. Chomsky, *Manufacturing Consent: The Political Economy of the Mass Media* (London: Vintage, 1988).
Hersh, S., 'Annals of National Security: The Gray Zone – How a Secret Pentagon Program Came to Abu Ghraib', *The New Yorker* (15 May, 2004).
Herzog, W. R., *Prophet and Teacher: An Introduction to the Historical Jesus* (Louisville: Westminster John Knox, 2005).
Heschel, S., *The Aryan Jesus: Christian Theologians and the Bible in Nazi Germany* (Princeton: Princeton University Press, 2008).
Hitchens, C., 'That Bleeding Heart Wolfowitz', *Slate* (22 March, 2005), http://www.slate.com/id/2115170/.
Hobbins, J. F., 'Good and Bad Imperialism', Ancient Hebrew Poetry (23 March, 2009), http://ancienthebrewpoetry.typepad.com/ancient_hebrew_poetry/2009/03/good-and-bad-imperialism.html.
— 'What's Wrong with N. T. Wrong's Anti-Imperialism', Ancient Hebrew Poetry (24 March, 2009), http://ancienthebrewpoetry.typepad.com/ancient_hebrew_poetry/2009/03/whats-wrong-with-n-t-wrongs-antiimperialism.html.
— 'A First Reading in Marxism for Students of the Bible', Ancient Hebrew Poetry (27 March, 2009), http://ancienthebrewpoetry.typepad.com/ancient_hebrew_poetry/2009/03/a-first-reading-in-marxism-for-students-of-the-bible-.html.
— 'The Unnatural Natural Disaster: What We Need to Learn from Haiti', Ancient Hebrew Poetry (January, 2010), http://ancienthebrewpoetry.typepad.com/ancient_hebrew_poetry/2010/01/the-unnatural-natural-disaster-what-we-need-to-learn-from-haiti.html.
Hobsbawm, E. J., *On History* (London: Abacus, 1997).
— *Uncommon People: Resistance, Rebellion and Jazz* (London: Abacus, 1998).
— *The New Century* (London: Abacus, 2000).
— *Revolutionaries* (New York: New Press, 2001).
— *Interesting Times: A Twentieth Century Life* (London: Abacus, 2002).
Hoffmann, R. J., 'A Discourse on Method: The Jesus Project', *Bible and Interpretation* (January, 2009), http://www.bibleinterp.com/hoffman1/hoffman1.shtml.
— 'Threnody: Rethinking the Thinking behind The Jesus Project', *Bible and Interpretation* (October, 2009), http://www.bibleinterp.com/opeds/hoffman1044.shtml.
— 'Of Rocks, Hard Places and Jesus Fatigue', in Hoffmann (ed.), *Sources of the Jesus Tradition*, pp. 9–16.
Hoffmann R. J. (ed.), *Sources of the Jesus Tradition: Separating History from Myth* (New York: Prometheus, 2010).
Hoffmann, R. J., et al., 'Gerd Lüdemann: A Declaration of Solidarity' *Bible and Interpretation* (24 February, 2009), http://www.bibleinterp.com/articles/ludeman_case/solidarity.shtml.
Horrell, D. G., 'Social-Scientific Interpretation of the New Testament: Retrospect and Prospect', in D. G. Horrell (ed.), *Social-Scientific Approaches to New Testament Interpretation* (Edinburgh: T&T Clark, 1999), pp. 3–27.
Huller, S., 'This Site is Now a Top 50 Biblioblog (Even if the Bastards at Biblioblog Top 50 Site Refuses to Acknowledge it)', Stephan Huller's Observations (31 May,

2011), http://biblioblogLibrary.com/archives/stephan-hullers-observations-biblioblog-top-50.html.
Jacobs-Malina, D., 'Letter' (6 January, 2005), *Asia Times Online*, http://www.atimes.com/atimes/letters_13.html.
Jameson, F., 'Postmodernism, or, The Cultural Logic of Late Capitalism', *New Left Review* (July–August, 1984), pp. 53–92.
— *Postmodernism, or, The Cultural Logic of Late Capitalism* (London and New York: Verso, 1991).
Joseph, C., 'Haiti: The Land of Bitter Tears!', Christ, My Righteousness (January 2010), http://christmyrighteousness9587.wordpress.com/2010/01/14/haiti-will-survive/.
Kampfner, J., 'Yes, I Feel Queasy. But I Don't Regret Backing the Lib Dems', *Guardian* (1 August, 2010).
Käsemann, E., *New Testament Questions of Today* (London: SCM, 1969).
Kautsky, K., *Foundations of Christianity: A Study in Christian Origins* (London: Orbach & Chambers, 1925).
Kelley, S., *Racializing Jesus: Race, Ideology and the Formation of Modern Biblical Scholarship* (London and New York: Routledge, 2002).
— 'Race, Aesthetics, and Gospel Scholarship: Embracing and Subverting the Aesthetic Ideology', in L. Nasrallah and E. S. Fiorenza (eds.), *Prejudice and Christian Beginnings: Investigating Race, Gender, and Ethnicity in Early Christian Studies* (Fortress: Minneapolis, 2009), pp. 191–209.
Ker, D., 'It's One Thing to Slaughter a Pig on the Sacred Altar', Lingamish (2 February, 2009), http://lingamish.com/2009/02/its-one-thing-to-slaughter-a-pig-on-the-sacred-altar/.
— 'So, What's Going on Here?', Lingamish (15 February, 2009), http://lingamish.com/2009/02/so-whats-going-on-here/.
Klein, N., 'Put away the Cuddly Toys. Now It's Time to Get Tough', *Guardian* (3 March, 2003).
— 'Baghdad Year Zero: Pillaging Iraq in Pursuit of a Neocon Utopia', *Harper's* (September, 2004), pp. 43–53.
— *The Shock Doctrine: The Rise of Disaster Capitalism* (London: Allen Lane, 2007).
Kloppenborg, J. S., 'As One Unknown, without a Name? Co-opting the Apocalyptic Jesus', in Kloppenborg with Marshall (eds.), *Apocalypticism, Anti-Semitism and the Historical Jesus*, pp. 19–21.
Kloppenborg, J. S., with J. W. Marshall (eds.), *Apocalypticism, Anti-Semitism and the Historical Jesus: Subtexts in Criticism* (London and New York: T&T Clark/Continuum, 2005).
Kowaliński, P., 'The Genesis of Christianity in the Views of Contemporary Marxist Specialists of Religion', *Antonianum* 47 (1972), pp. 541–75.
Krejci, M., 'An Atheist's Dilemma: Should We Bend the Bible for Justice?', *SBL Forum* (2008), http://sbl-site.org/Article.aspx?ArticleID=779.
LaHaye, T., *Rapture (under Attack)* (Sisters, OR: Multnomah Press, 1998).
Le Donne, A., *The Historiographical Jesus: Memory, Typology, and the Son of David* (Waco: Baylor, 2009).
Leichman, A. J., 'New Quest for Historical Jesus Draws Skeptics, Scholars', *Christian Post* (December 10, 2008).

Levine, A.-J., *The Misunderstood Jew: The Church and the Scandal of the Jewish Jesus* (San Francisco: HarperCollins, 2006).
Lindsey, H., *The Late Great Planet Earth* (Grand Rapids: Zondervan, 1970).
Linville, J., 'What Disaster Will God Send to Punish T.V. Land for Pat Robertson?', Dr Jim's Thinking Shop and Tea Room (13 January, 2010), http://drjimsthinkingshop.com/2010/01/13/what-disaster-will-god-send-to-punish-t-v-land-for-pat-robertson/.
Little, M., 'Confronting the City', *Red Pepper* (November, 2009), http://www.redpepper.org.uk/Confronting-the-city/.
Littlejohn, R., 'Why I Wouldn't Go on Question Time with the Unsavoury Nick Griffin', *Daily Mail* (20 October, 2009).
Loftus, J. W., 'Reason 1,937 Why I Want Nothing to Do with Christianity: Pat Robertson on Haiti's Disaster', Debunking Christianity (January 2010), http://debunkingchristianity.blogspot.com/2010/01/reason-1937-why-i-want-nothing-to-do.html.
Lukásc, G., *History and Class Consciousness: Studies in Marxist Dialectics* (London: Merlin Press, 1971).
— *The Resurrection of Jesus: History, Experience, Theology* (London: SCM Press, 1994).
Lüdemann, G., 'The Intolerant Gospel', *Free Inquiry* (February/March, 2006), http://www.secularhumanism.org/index.php?section=library&page=luedemann_26_2.
— 'What Really Happened? The Rise of Primitive Christianity, 30–70 C.E.', *Free Inquiry* (April/May, 2007), pp. 24–31.
— *Eyes That See Not: The Pope Looks at Jesus* (Santa Rosa: Polebridge Press, 2008).
Lyon, D., *Surveillance after September 11* (Cambridge: Polity, 2003).
— *Theorizing Surveillance: The Panopticon and Beyond* (Cullompton: Willan, 2006).
— *Surveillance Studies: An Overview* (Cambridge: Polity, 2007).
Lyons, J., 'A More Sensible Regime!', Archives of Reception of the Bible (9 February, 2007), http://receptionofthebible.blogspot.com/2007/02/more-sensible-regime.html.
— 'What Kind of Blogger Are You?', Archive of Reception of the Bible (29 October, 2008), http://receptionofthebible.blogspot.com/2008/10/what-kind-of-blogger-are-you.html.
— 'OFFICIAL NOTICE FROM THE OFFICE OF BISHOP N. T. WRONG', Archives of Reception of the Bible (13 November, 2008), http://receptionofthebible.blogspot.com/2008/11/official-notice-from-office-of-bishop.html.
Lyotard, J. -F., *The Postmodern Condition: A Report on Knowledge* (Manchester: Manchester University Press, 1984).
McCullough, P. G., 'Wrong Has Fun with Labels', kata ta biblia (31 October, 2008), http://patmccullough.com/2008/10/31/nt-wrong-has-fun-with-labels/.
McCutcheon, R. T., *Manufacturing Religion: The Discourse on Sui Generis Religion and the Politics of Nostalgia* (Oxford: Oxford University Press, 1997).
— *Religion and the Domestication of Dissent: or, How to Live in a Less Than Perfect Nation* (London and Oakville: Equinox, 2005).
McGaughy, L. C., 'Robert W. Funk – A Profile', *Fourth R* 19.2 (March–April 2006), pp. 4–6.
McGrath, J. F., 'Who Is the Wisest? Jesus, Solomon or Pat Robertson? (Biblioblogging and the Haitian Earthquake)', Exploring Our Matrix (January 2010), http://

exploringourmatrix.blogspot.com/2010/01/who-is-wisest-jesus-solomon-or-pat.html.

McMillan, S., 'Facebook Furore as Palace Youngster Reveals His Plan to Millions', *Guardian* (8 July, 2008).

MacDonald, D. R., 'An Alternative Q and the Quest of the Earthly Jesus', in Hoffmann (ed.), *Sources of the Jesus Tradition*, pp. 17–44.

Mack, B. L., *A Myth of Innocence: Mark and Christian Origins* (Philadelphia: Fortress, 1988).

Malina, B. J., *The New Testament World: Insights from Cultural Anthropology* (London: SCM, 1981).

— *The Social World of Jesus and the Gospels* (London: Routledge, 1996).

— 'Social Scientific Methods in Historical Jesus Research', in W. Stegemann, B. J. Malina and G. Theissen (eds.), *The Social Setting of Jesus and the Gospels* (Minneapolis: Fortress Press, 2002), pp. 3–26.

— 'Social-scientific Criticism', C. A. Evans (ed.), *Encyclopedia of the Historical Jesus* (London: Routledge, 2008), pp. 578–81.

Malina. B. J., and R. L. Rohrbaugh, *Social-Science Commentary on the Gospel of John* (Minneapolis: Fortress Press, 1998).

Mandel, E., *Late Capitalism* (London: Verso, 1975).

Manning, P., 'Grant Nadia Abu el-Haj Tenure Petition', *Petition Online*, http://www.petitiononline.com/mod_perl/signed.cgi?Barnard2&1251.

Marr, A. 'Interview with Noam Chomsky', *The Big Idea* (BBC2, 14 February, 1996), http://video.google.com/videoplay?docid=-4827358238697503#.

Marsh, C., 'Quests of the Historical Jesus in New Historicist Perspective', *BibInt* 5 (1997), pp. 403–37.

Martin, C., *Masking Hegemony: A Genealogy of Liberalism, Religion and the Private Sphere* (London and Oakville: Equinox, 2010).

Marx, K., *The Eighteenth Brumaire of Louis Bonaparte* (New York: International Publishers, 1963).

— *Capital: A Critical Analysis of Capital Production: Volume 1* (London: Lawrence and Wishart, 1974).

Masalha, N., *The Bible and Zionism: Invented Traditions, Archaeology and Post-colonialism in Israel-Palestine* (London: Zed, 2007).

Meier, J. P., *A Marginal Jew: Rethinking the Historical Jesus.* I. *The Roots of the Problem and the Person* (New York: Doubleday, 1991).

— *A Marginal Jew: Rethinking the Historical Jesus.* III. *Companions and Competitors* (New York: Doubleday, 2001).

— 'Did the Historical Jesus Prohibit All Oaths? Part 1', *JSHJ* 5 (2007), pp. 175–204.

— 'Did the Historical Jesus Prohibit All Oaths? Part 2', *JSHJ* 6 (2008), pp. 3–24 .

Milbank, J., *Theology and Social Theory* (Oxford: Blackwell, 1990).

— 'Letter: Red Toryism is the Best Hope of a New Progressive Politics', *Guardian* (22 May, 2008).

— 'The Politics of Paradox', *Telos* (13 March, 2009), http://www.telospress.com/main/index.php?main_page=news_article&article_id=302#at.

— 'Foreword: Jesus of Nazareth in the Context of Benedict XVI's Theology', in Pabst and Paddison (eds.), *The Pope*, pp. xxiii–xxix.

— 'Christianity, the Enlightenment and Islam', *ABC Religion and Ethics* (24 August, 2010), http://www.abc.net.au/religion/articles/2010/08/24/2991778.htm?topic1=home&topic2=.
Miller, R. J., *The Jesus Seminar and Its Critics* (Santa Rosa: Polebridge, 1999).
Mirowski, P., and D. Plehwe (eds.), *The Road from Mont Pelerin: The Making of the Neoliberal Thought Collective* (Cambridge, MA: Harvard University Press 2009).
Moxnes, H., 'The Historical Jesus: From Master Narrative to Cultural Context', *BTB* 28 (1999), pp. 135–49.
— *Putting Jesus in His Place: A Radical Vision of Household and Kingdom* (Louisville: Westminster John Knox, 2003).
Moxnes, H., W. Blanton, and J. G. Crossley (eds.), *Jesus beyond Nationalism: Constructing the Historical Jesus in a Period of Cultural Complexity* (London and Oakville: Equinox, 2009).
Murray, C., *Murder in Samarkand: A British Ambassador's Controversial Defiance of Tyranny in the War on Terror* (Edinburgh and London: Mainstream Publishing, 2006).
Myles, R.J., 'Dandy Discipleship: A Queering of Mark's Male Disciples', *Journal of Men, Masculinities, and Spirituality* 4 (2010), pp. 66-81.
Neusner, J., 'Visiting the Vatican', *Bible and Interpretation* (February 2010), http://www.bibleinterp.com/articles/pope357908.shtml.
Obama, B., 'Remarks by the President on a New Beginning', The White House: Office of the Press Secretary (2009), http://www.whitehouse.gov/the-press-office/remarks-president-cairo-university-6-04-09.
O'Collins, G., 'The Resurrection: The State of the Question', in S. T. Davis, D. Kendall and G. O'Collins (eds.), *The Resurrection: An Interdisciplinary Symposium on the Resurrection of Jesus* (Oxford: Oxford University Press, 1997), pp. 5–28.
Pabst, A., and A. Paddison, 'Introduction', in Pabst and Paddison (eds.), *The Pope*, pp. 1–9.
Pabst, A., and A. Paddison (eds.), *The Pope and Jesus of Nazareth: Christ, Scripture and the Church* (London: SCM in association with The Centre of Theology and Philosophy, University of Nottingham, 2010).
Paddison, A., 'Following Jesus with Pope Benedict', in Pabst and Paddison (eds.), *The Pope*, pp. 176–95.
Patai, R., *Encyclopedia of Zionism and Israel* (New York: Herzl Press, 1971).
— *Journeyman in Jerusalem: Memories and Letters, 1933–1947* (Salt Lake City: University of Utah Press, 1992).
— *The Arab Mind* (New York: Hatherleigh Press, rev. edn, 2002).
Patai, R. (ed.), *Essays in Zionist History and Thought* (New York: Herzl Press, 1971).
Penner, T., '*Die Judenfrage* and the Construction of Ancient Judaism: Toward a Foregrounding of the Backgrounds Approach to Early Christianity', in P. Gray and G. O'Day (eds.), *Scripture and Traditions: Essays on Early Judaism and Christianity* (Leiden: Brill, 2008), pp. 429–55.
— '"Home Is Where the Heart Is" – A Concluding Methodological Prescript', unpublished paper delivered to the 'Holy Land as Homeland?' seminar, University of Oslo, 6–8 March, 2009.
Perry, M., *Marxism and History* (London: Palgrave, 2002).
Pimlott, B., 'Brushstrokes', in M. Bostridge (ed.), *Lives for Sale: Biographers' Tales* (London and New York: Continuum, 2004), pp. 165–70.

Pipes, D., 'God and Mammon: Does Poverty Cause Militant Islam?', *The National Interest* 66 (Winter, 2001–02), also available at http://www.danielpipes.org/article/104.
Plehwe, D., B. J. A. Walpen and G. Neunhoffer (eds.), *Neoliberal Hegemony: A Global Critique* (London: Routledge, 2007).
Porter, S., *The Criteria for Authenticity in Historical Jesus Research* (Sheffield: Sheffield Academic Press, 2000).
Powell, J. E., *A Lexicon to Herodotus* (Cambridge: Cambridge University Press, 1938).
— *The History of Herodotus* (Cambridge: Cambridge University Press, 1939).
— *Herodotus: A Translation* (Oxford: Clarendon, 1949).
— *No Easy Answers* (London: Sheldon Press, 1973).
— *Wrestling with the Angel* (London: Sheldon Press, 1977).
— 'Genesis of the Gospel', *JSNT* 42 (1991), pp. 5–16.
— *Reflections: Selected Writings and Speeches of Enoch Powell* (London: Bellew, 1992), pp. 161–69.
— *The Evolution of the Gospel* (New Haven and London: Yale University Press, 1994).
Powell, M. A., *The Jesus Debate: Modern Historians Investigate the Life of Christ* (Oxford: Lion, 1998).
Press Release, 'New IFS Research Challenges Chancellor's "Progressive Budget" Claim', Institute for Fiscal Studies (25 August 2010), http://www.ifs.org.uk/pr/progressive_budget.pdf.
Price, R. M., *The Incredible Shrinking Son of Man: How Reliable Is the Gospel Tradition?* (Amherst, NY: Prometheus Books, 2003).
— 'The Abhorrent Void: The Rapid Attribution of Fictive Sayings and Stories to a Mythic Jesus', in Hoffmann (ed.), *Sources of the Jesus Tradition*, pp. 109–17.
— 'The Quest of the Mythical Jesus', http://www.centerforinquiry.net/jesusproject/articles/the_quest_of_the_mythical_jesus (no date).
— 'The Jesus Mirage', http://www.centerforinquiry.net/jesusproject/articles/the_jesus_mirage (no date).
Prothero, S., *American Jesus: How the Son of God Became a National Icon* (New York: Farrar, Straus and Giroux, 2003).
Qureshi, E., 'Misreading "the Arab Mind"', *Boston Globe* (30 May, 2004).
Raban, J., 'Cameron's Crank', *London Review of Books* 32.8 (22 April, 2010).
Ratzinger, J., *Jesus of Nazareth: From the Baptism in the Jordan to the Transfiguration* (London: Bloomsbury, 2007).
Reinhartz, A., 'The Gospel according to Benedict: Jesus of Nazareth and Jews and Judaism', in Pabst and Paddison (eds.), *The Pope*, pp. 233–46.
Reis, D., 'Surveillant Discipline: Panoptic Vision in Early Christian Self-Definition,' *The Bible and Critical Theory* 4 (2008), pp. 23.1–23.21.
Rodriguez, R., *Structuring Early Christian Memory: Jesus in Tradition, Performance, and Text* (London and New York: T&T Clark/Continuum, 2010).
Rosenberg, P., 'A Whole World of Heroes', in H. Bloom (ed.), *Thomas Carlyle* (New York: Chelsea House, 1986), pp. 95–108.
Russell, B., 'Cameron: Don't Repeat Errors of 1930s with "Jihadists"', *Independent* (24 August, 2005).
Rosson, L., 'Crossan Dumps the Egalitarian Jesus', The Busybody (April 1, 2007), http://lorenrosson.blogspot.com/2007/04/crossan-dumps-egalitarian-jesus.html.

Said, E. W., *Orientalism* (London: Penguin, 3rd edn, 2003).
Sanders, E. P., *Jesus and Judaism* (London: SCM, 1985).
— *The Historical Figure of Jesus* (London: Penguin, 1993).
Sanders, E. P., and M. Davies, *Studying the Synoptic Gospels* (London: SCM; Philadelphia: Trinity, 1989).
Schneider, N., 'Orthodox paradox: an interview with John Milbank', The Immanent Frame (17 May, 2010), http://blogs.ssrc.org/tif/2010/03/17/orthodox-paradox-an-interview-with-john-milbank/.
Seymour, R., *The Liberal Defence of Murder* (London and New York: Verso, 2008).
— *The Meaning of David Cameron* (Winchester and Washington: Zero Books, 2010).
Shea, D., 'Pat Robertson: "Haiti 'Cursed' by 'Pact to the Devil' (VIDEO)', *Huffington Post* (13 January, 2010). http://www.huffingtonpost.com/2010/01/13/pat-robertson-haiti-curse_n_422099.html.
Sherwood, Y., 'Bush's Bible as a Liberal Bible (Strange though that Might Seem)', *Postscripts* 2 (2006), pp. 47–58.
Shlaim, A., 'How Israel Brought Gaza to the Brink of Humanitarian Catastrophe', *Guardian* (7 January, 2009).
Siddiqui, M., '"Searching for the Face of the Lord" – Hope or Heresy?', in Pabst and Paddison (eds.), *The Pope*, pp. 247–61.
Sieghart, M. -A., 'Radio 4 Profile: Sir Gus O'Donnell, Cabinet Secretary', *BBC News* (2 March, 2010), http://news.bbc.co.uk/1/hi/uk_politics/8543950.stm.
Smith, J. Z., *Drudgery Divine: On the Comparison of Early Christianities and the Religions of Late Antiquity* (Chicago: University of Chicago Press, 1990).
Steel, M., *Vive la Revolution* (London: Scribner, 2003).
Sugirtharajah, R. S., *Asian Biblical Hermeneutics and Postcolonialism: Contesting the Interpretations* (Sheffield: Sheffield Academic Press, 1998).
Sweney, M., 'Culture Secretary Jeremy Hunt Tells BBC to Prepare for Deeper Cuts', *Guardian* (28 October, 2010).
Terri, 'Ugh', Wheat among Tares (January, 2010), http://wheatamongtares.blogspot.com/2010/01/ugh.html.
Thatcher, M., 'Aids, Education and the Year 2000!', *Woman's Own* (31 October, 1987), pp. 8–10.
Theissen, G., and A. Merz, *The Historical Jesus: A Comprehensive Guide* (London: SCM, 1998).
Thomas Jr, R. M., 'Raphael Patai, 85, a Scholar of Jewish and Arab Cultures', *New York Times* (25 July, 1996).
Thompson, E. P., *The Poverty of Theory and Other Essays* (London: Merlin Press, 1978).
Thompson, T. L., *The Messiah Myth: The Near Eastern Roots of Jesus and David* (New York: Basic Books, 2005).
Thompson, T. L., and T. S. Verenna (eds.), *'Is This Not the Carpenter?' The Question of the Historicity of the Figure of Jesus* (Sheffield and Oakville: Equinox, 2011, forthcoming).
Tokasz, J., 'Scholars to Explore Existence of Jesus', *Buffalo News* (30 November, 2008), http://www.buffalonews.com/cityregion/northernsuburbs/story/508858.html.
Toscano, A., *Fanaticism: On Uses of an Idea* (London and New York: Verso, 2010).
Uffman, C., 'Where Was God in the Earthquake?', Metanoia (January, 2010), http://www.craiguffman.com/2010/01/where-was-god-in-the-earthquake.html.

Vander Stichele, C. and T. Penner, *Contextualizing Gender in Early Christian Discourse: Thinking beyond Thecla* (London and New York: Continuum/T&T Clark, 2009).

Venard, O.-T., 'The Prologue of John and Matthew and the Heart of Matthew (John 1.18 and Matthew 12.46–13.58): Does the Jesus of the Synoptic Gospels Really Say Nothing Different from the Prologue of John?', in Pabst and Paddison (eds.), *The Pope*, pp. 134–58.

Vermes, G., *The Religion of Jesus the Jew* (London: SCM, 1993).

— 'Review of Ratzinger, *Jesus of Nazareth*', *Times* (19 May, 2007).

Watts, J., 'Pat Robertson: Haiti "Cursed" after "Pact to the Devil" (Video)', The Church of Jesus Christ (January 2010), http://thechurchofjesuschrist.us/2010/01/pat-robertson-haiti-cursed-after-pact-to-the-devil.

Watts, M., 'Revolutionary Islam', in D. Gregory and A. Pred (eds.), *Violent Geographies: Fear, Terror, and Political Violence* (New York and London: Routledge, 2007), pp. 175–203.

— 'Jim West Interviews Bishop N. T. Wrong', Biblioblogs (February, 2009), http://www.biblioblogs.com/featured-blogs/2009-02/.

West, J., 'John, Jesus and History', Zwinglius Redivivus (1 November, 2009), http://zwingliusredivivus.wordpress.com/2011/01/09/john-jesus-and-history/.

Whitelam, K. W., *The Invention of Ancient Israel: the Silencing of Palestinian History* (London and New York: Routledge, 1996).

— 'Representing Minimalism: The Rhetoric and Reality of Revisionism', in A. G. Hunter and P. R. Davies (eds.), *Sense and Sensitivity: Essays on Reading the Bible in Memory of Robert Carroll* (Sheffield: Sheffield Academic Press, 2002), pp. 194–223.

Wiggins, S. A., 'Theodicy versus Idiocy', Sects and Violence in the Ancient World, http://sawiggins.wordpress.com/2010/01/14/theodicy-versus-idiocy/.

Williams, R. 'A Hundred Years of Culture and Anarchy', *The Spokesman* 8 (December, 1970), reprinted in R. Williams, *Culture and Materialism* (London and New York: Verso, 1980), pp. 3–8.

Witherington III, B., *Women in the Ministry of Jesus: A Study of Jesus' Attitudes to Women and Their Roles as Reflected in His Early Life* (Cambridge: Cambridge University Press, 1984).

— *New Testament History: A Narrative Account* (Carlisle: Paternoster; Grand Rapids: Baker, 2001).

— 'What's in a Name? Rethinking the Historical Figure of the Beloved Disciple in the Fourth Gospel', in Anderson, Just, and Thatcher (eds.), *John, Jesus, and History*, II, pp. 209–12.

— 'Haiti – Where Was God?', Bible and Culture (January 2010), http://blog.beliefnet.com/bibleandculture/2010/01/haiti---a-case-study-for-theodicy.html.

Wright, N. T., *Jesus and the Victory of God* (London: SPCK, 1996).

— *The Original Jesus: The Life and Vision of a Revolutionary* (Oxford: Lion, 1996).

— *The Resurrection of the Son of God* (London: SPCK, 2003).

Wright, N. T., and M. J. Borg, *The Meaning of Jesus: Two Visions* (London: SPCK, 2008).

Wrong, N.T., 'History of Christian-American Zionism', N. T. Wrong Blog (21 June, 2008), http://ntwrong.wordpress.com/2008/06/21/american-christian-zionism/.

— 'Burke Lecture 2008: The Challenge of Islamophobia', N. T. Wrong Blog (4 July, 2008), http://ntwrong.wordpress.com/2008/07/04/burke-lecture-2008-islamophobia/.
— 'Hector Avalos Blogs', N. T. Wrong Blog (5 August, 2008), http://ntwrong.wordpress.com/2008/08/05/hector-avalos-blogs/.
— 'Israeli David and Arab Goliath', N. T. Wrong Blog (13 August, 2008), http://ntwrong.wordpress.com/2008/08/13/israeli-david-and-arab-goliath/.
— 'At the Airport for SBL', N. T. Wrong Blog (16 November, 2008), http://ntwrong.wordpress.com/2008/11/16/at-the-airport-for-sbl/.
— 'Capitalism, Middle East Invasions, Resource Exploitation, Advertised as 'Civilized Christianity' versus 'Terrible Islam' – 1922', N. T. Wrong Blog (18 October, 2008), http://ntwrong.wordpress.com/2008/10/18/1922-cartoon/.
— 'List of Bibliobloggers – Conservative or Liberal?', N. T. Wrong Blog (29 October, 2008), http://ntwrong.wordpress.com/2008/10/29/list-of-bibliobloggers/.
— 'On Conservative and Liberal Biblioblogs', N. T. Wrong Blog (30 October, 2008), http://ntwrong.wordpress.com/2008/10/30/on-conservative-and-liberal-biblioblogs/.
— 'Yigael Yadin, the Bible, Archaeology, and Orientalism – When Captions Precede their Photos', N. T. Wrong (10 November, 2008), http://ntwrong.wordpress.com/2008/11/10/yigael-yadin-the-bible-archaeology-and-orientalism/.
— 'Israel: "Profundity" of Ideas as Justification for Colonialism; Bodily Desire as Justification for Dispossession', N. T. Wrong Blog (24 November, 2008), http://ntwrong.wordpress.com/2008/11/24/israel-balfour/#comments.
— 'Anti-Israel Christmas Carols Prove Effective in Provoking Israeli Arseholes', N. T. Wrong Blog (11 December 2008), http://ntwrong.wordpress.com/2008/12/11/anti-israel-christmas-carols/.
— 'Eilat Mazar Uses Fundamentalist Christian Cult to Link Archaeological Finds to "King David"', N. T. Wrong Blog (2 January, 2009), http://ntwrong.wordpress.com/2009/01/02/eilat-w-mazar-biblical-archaeology/.
Younge, G., 'I Hate Tories. And Yes, It's Tribal', *Guardian* (4 May, 2010).
Zindler, F. R., 'Prolegomenon to a Science of Christian Origins', in Hoffmann (ed.), *Sources of the Jesus Tradition*, pp. 140–56.
Žižek, S., *The Sublime Object of Ideology* (London and New York: Verso, 1989).
— 'Why We All Love to Hate Heider', *New Left Review* 2 (March–April, 2000), pp. 37–45.
— *Welcome to the Desert of the Real! Five Essays on September 11 and Related Dates* (London and New York: Verso, 2002).
— *The Puppet and the Dwarf: The Perverse Core of Christianity* (Cambridge, MA: MIT Press, 2003).
— *First as Tragedy, Then as Farce* (London and New York: Verso, 2009).

Index of Ancient Sources

Index of Authors

Index of Subjects